Evelyn Beatrice Longman

Evelyn Beatrice Longman

The Woman Who Sculpted Golden Boy, Thomas Edison, and Other Monuments

Patricia Hoerth Batchelder

ROWMAN & LITTLEFIELD
Lanham • Boulder • New York • London

Rowman & Littlefield
Bloomsbury Publishing Inc., 1385 Broadway, New York, NY 10018, USA
Bloomsbury Publishing Plc., 50 Bedford Square, London wC1B 3DP, UK
Bloomsbury Publishing Ireland, 29 Earlsfort Terrace, Dublin 2, D02 AY28, Ireland
www.rowman.com

86-90 Paul Street, London EC2A 4NE

British Library Cataloguing in Publication Information Available

Library of Congress Cataloging-in-Publication Data
Names: Hoerth Batchelder, Patricia, author.
Title: Evelyn Beatrice Longman : the woman who sculpted Golden Boy, Thomas Edison, and other monuments / Patricia Hoerth Batchelder.
Description: Lanham : Rowman & Littlefield, [2025] | Includes bibliographical references and index.
Identifiers: LCCN 2024059541 (print) | LCCN 2024059542 (ebook) | ISBN 9798881804244 (cloth) | ISBN 9798881804268 (ebook)
Subjects: LCSH: Longman, Evelyn Beatrice, 1874-1954. | Women sculptors--United States--Biography. | LCGFT: Biographies.
Classification: LCC NB237.L6 H64 2025 (print) | LCC NB237.L6 (ebook) | DDC 730.92 [B]--dc23/eng/20241230
LC record available at https://lccn.loc.gov/2024059541
LC ebook record available at https://lccn.loc.gov/2024059542

For product safety related questions contact productsafety@bloomsbury.com.

♾™ The paper used in this publication meets the minimum requirements of American National Standard for Information Sciences—Permanence of Paper for Printed Library Materials, ANSI/NISO Z39.48-1992.

For Hope, Susan, Carol, Edward, and—especially—Batch,
who introduced me to Evelyn Beatrice Longman,
and became as keen a supporter for this author
as his grandfather was for his grandmother

Contents

Acknowledgments

It hadn't dawned on me that I'd meet so many helpful people doing research for this book, nor that I'd make new friends. But eager archivists and librarians rolled out carts piled with file-filled boxes, microfilm, scrapbooks, and photo albums and made space for me to pore over them. They generously made copies and scanned photographs. Undaunted, they sought more documents, answers to more questions—even during the pandemic, when their offices were closed. This book simply would not exist without their unfailing assistance:

Jennifer Hadley, at Olin Library, Wesleyan University; Wayne Hammond and Anne Peale, at Chapin Library, Williams College; Thayer Tolles and her staff at the Metropolitan Museum of Art; Harrison Wick, archivist at Indiana University of Pennsylvania, and Donna Cashdollar at the IUP museum; Kathy Parrish and Gayle Fullerton at the Naval Research Lab; Marilyn Rabetz, Loomis art teacher who curated the 1993 Longman exhibition at Loomis Chaffee; historian Charlie Spickerman, Middleburg, NY; David Avitabile, reporter, the *Mountain Eagle* and *Schoharie News*; Julie Aronson, Cincinnati Art Museum; Sheldon Hochheiser, archivist, AT&T; Donzella Maupin, archivist, Hampton University; Alison Parman, Wadsworth Atheneum Museum of Art; Hannah Mellino, Olivet College; Meredith Mann, New York Public Library; Bart Ryckbosh, archivist, Art Institute of Chicago; Will Doty and Sammi Merritt, University of Illinois archives; Jeremiah McCarthy, Diana Thompson and Ian Cofre, National Academy of Design; Kay Coats, Iowa State Historical Museum; Neda Amouzadeh and Jennifer Page, National Museum of Women in the Arts; Melissa Bourgoin, Smithsonian Reference Services; Jennifer Bryan, U.S. Naval Academy; Todd Gardner, National Portrait Gallery; Gwen Pier, National Sculpture Society.

Bonnie French, a Longman descendant who has done exhaustive research into the family, shared her findings and helped untangle the branches of the Bollen/Adnam/Longman family trees; Windsor resident Elizabeth Burke also shared her research into Longman's life.

Art historian Margaret Samu completed deep research on three monumental Longman sculptures for her thesis at Wellesley College. She gave me a tour of Longman works at The Met, sat for an interview, and answered questions by email over the following months. I relied heavily on her research and expertise.

Two women worked with me from the first visits to Chesterwood and Loomis Chaffee in September 2017, through repeated visits and emails, and I suspect will continue to do so: archivist and history professor Karen Parsons at Loomis Chaffee and Dana Pilson, curatorial researcher at Chesterwood. It's an absolute joy doing this work with them. They each have also done great work of their own: Dana, publishing an article explaining how French and Longman influenced each other; and Karen, guiding her high school students to the primary source material of Longman and Batchelder for their educational projects. Dana very graciously also read the manuscript with an eye to the world of art of which I was unfamiliar, and Karen gathered almost all the photographs for this story. I am profoundly grateful to them both.

Two writers of other biographical works whom I met once I began working on Longman's biography have been generous and supportive as well. Eve Kahn, as she wrote about model Hettie Anderson, who posed for Longman, shared important Longman documents she came across and has been a cheerleader ever since (having written the biography of Connecticut painter Mary Rogers Williams). Laurie Gwen Shapiro, who came to Oklahoma City for research on her biography of Amelia Earhart, has been extremely generous with a plethora of information about the publishing scene that I, a newspaper reporter, needed to know.

New York City art dealer Joel Rosenkranz is an angel quietly standing in the corner, making doors open. He has sold Longman's works, owns some, worked with the Rabetzes on the Longman exhibit and booklet, and, amazingly, introduced me to his sister, who became my agent. Rita Rosenkranz is a dream of an agent, the kind who sells the book and becomes a friend—the kind of friend who took a deep dive into my native Oklahoma, and keeps coming back!

I'm grateful for friends who were willing to read the manuscript: Susan Ross, early on, when I needed to know whether the story was as interesting to others as it is to me; independent editor Alice Peck, when I needed a professional appraisal; Bailey Stephenson, when I needed to know about structure and narrative arc; Sara Braden, when I needed another set of eyes looking at readability.

My beloveds in the CommonWealth Urban Farm community—especially Lia—have been very respectful of my mornings, which are dedicated to writing; any necessary interruption was followed by profuse apology. Dear friends Jane Taylor and Jane Wheeler, Linda Temple and Linda Koenig, Diane Parker and Soup Night pals, and Norman Quaker friends continue to listen and cheer and strengthen me through this long process.

My busy family—sister, nephews, nieces, grands—are all in with creative projects, and maintain the perfect balance between asking how the book is going, and not asking. My son Will has been incredible because he's saying to me what I said so many times to him when he was growing up: "You can do it"—not as a cheerleader, but stating the fact, with sincere confidence, just as I have known it to be true of him. Ruth Stevens, a Batchelder family friend, gave us a room in her midtown Manhattan apartment when I went to the city on fact-finding missions and to conferences of Biographers International.

The Batchelder siblings answered questions, shared stories, and are the most eager to read their grandparents' tale. It is to them I dedicate this book, and especially to Batch, who not only introduced me to his grandmothers but who has been the best listener when I needed to read the manuscript aloud—hardly ever making suggestions, reliably shedding tears, and then doing domestic chores so I could get to it.

Of course, it is to Evelyn Beatrice Longman, and Horton Batchelder, and to Skip, whom I owe the greatest gratitude. They wrote the story first.

Introduction

It was a new challenge for me as a journalist to get to know someone I couldn't interview—or at least, interview their peers. Of course I knew this was the case when I started learning about Evelyn Beatrice Longman. No diary or journal either, but there were scrapbooks, photo albums, letters, newspaper articles—and there was her sculpture, which, she had insisted, would speak for itself.

Her story seemed fascinating, compelling, and, as is true of the stories of so many important women, it never had been fully told.

Nathaniel Horton ("Batch") Batchelder III and I met at a protest on a busy Oklahoma City intersection in 2001. We crossed paths at such events over the next decade, but in 2013 we began having lunch in preparation for companion talks at a peace symposium. At one point I asked him about his family, and he told me about his grandfather, who, he said, was a little bit famous, as the first headmaster at Loomis Chaffee School, a preparatory school in Windsor, Connecticut. But when I Googled Nathaniel Horton Batchelder, I got Evelyn Beatrice Longman.

I was surprised that Longman came up instead of Batchelder, but images of her sculpture captured my attention. She had created beautiful figures! Then I discovered the connection: She had been married to Nathaniel Horton Batchelder.

When I next met Batch for lunch, I teased him that when I Googled his grandfather, his grandmother came up. He said, yes, "she was a great sculptor, but she wasn't my grandmother." That was a perplexing statement. Batch explained that Evelyn was the only grandmother he had ever known (though just barely, as he was nine when she died, and she had been ill since he could remember). But, he insisted, she wasn't his "real grandmother." That would be Gwendolen Sedgwick Batchelder, his grandfather's first wife and the mother of his father. As a veteran newspaper journalist, I had a hunch about good stories, and this one looked promising.

Even before *we* married, Batch and I began traveling to visit Longman sculptures, and I spent days among files and scrapbooks, especially in the archives at Loomis Chaffee School, learning her history. This story unfolded with many little episodes, layers, questions—enough, I thought, for a book. But would I have what it took to meet the challenges of such a long-term project? Batch was all in, thrilled at getting to know his grandmother better bit by bit. And bit by bit, the story grew more and more compelling—enough to keep me going; so compelling that I wanted others to know it as well.

As many good stories often do, Longman's begins with an impoverished childhood. Then her mother's death when Evelyn was five, separation from her siblings, and working full-time in a Chicago warehouse at the age of fourteen. Incredibly, she early-on realized that she wanted to create monumental public sculptures, and so, she was presented with the daunting riddle of how to get from uneducated Chicago warehouse worker to New York City sculptor. As a woman, this would mean cracking a marble, or bronze, ceiling.

Talented, irresistibly charming, fiercely determined, unafraid of risks, she overcame poverty, sexism, impaired stamina, and made it to the top of Mount Parnassus, as her teacher and beloved friend, sculptor Daniel Chester French said she would. Perhaps you, adventurous reader, are one of the millions who saw her *Golden Boy* atop New York City, or on the cover of your telephone book.

Together with French and architect Henry Bacon, the three created something else with which we all are familiar: the Lincoln Memorial and much of its artwork. Keeping to that small circle of friends and colleagues, Longman kept her life private to focus on her work—until she was forty-three years old and met a widower, that first headmaster of Loomis Chaffee School. Thus began the second almost-half of Evelyn's life, when she married, moved to a boys' prep school in suburban Connecticut, and became the mother of a three-year-old—shocking her friends, who wondered what would happen to her career.

Longman's tenacity never wavered. She impacted Horton Batchelder, as well as the Loomis School community, and she kept making art her way in spite of a cultural shift away from figurative and monumental sculpture and toward abstract expressionism. Her greatest challenges came nearer the end of her life, and these were due to her own insistence. Yet, as we say, as one would expect of the tenacious Longman, she persisted: she created more busts, bas-reliefs, and monumental sculpture than she did in the first part of her life living in New York City.

Evelyn Beatrice Longman Batchelder was a charming force who, as French said, "smiled until the world smiled back."

Not only is hers a fascinating, compelling story, it raises questions for us—as intensely lived lives sometimes do: Why is it that some sink from poverty and others excel out of it? How is it that some know early-on that they're capable of greatness, and is that necessary to do great things? How are we to know that what we do now may be wrong as time goes by? Who defines beauty? How in this world do we live our truth? How are we to know when it's time to surrender our plans; when it's time to hang in there? How is it that one can remain fiercely focused and suddenly make a decision that could threaten everything?

Meet Mary Evelyn Beatrice Longman . . .

Chapter 1

I Could Do That

I know I could do that if I had the chance.

—Mary Evelyn Beatrice Longman

It is the earliest extant photo of Evelyn Beatrice Longman. 1883. Second grade, Sheldon School, Chicago. Second row, second from right. In dark, heavy, pleated dress with high collar. Straight, dark hair parted in the middle, pulled back and fastened behind her neck. No little-girl bangs. Lips slightly open, eyes steady, looking straight into the camera. In her lap rest long, tapered fingers.

This nine-year-old already has been tossed about from Chicago to relatives in Ontario and back again in a chaotic existence since her mother died four years earlier. While her classmates look grim, each seemingly squinting into the camera, Longman's gaze is clear, direct, and exudes intelligence, curiosity, expectation, fearlessness—evidence of a girl who, long before she was ten, negotiated life's challenges with tenacity, resolve, and creativity.

Six years later, at the end of elementary school, without money to get to a mandatory graduation event, she wasn't allowed to advance. As so many children did, she went to work instead of finishing school. And after four years doing office work for three dollars a week at Wilson Brothers, a men's furnishings warehouse in downtown Chicago, the eighteen-year-old and her older sister Louise joined throngs attending the Chicago World's Fair of 1893. It was there, in the legendary "White City," that Longman proclaimed—unequivocally, though it seemed ludicrous—the dream of her life.

The sisters were among the masses headed to Jackson Park, where more than two hundred buildings of the World's Columbian Exposition occupied some

Figure 1.1 The earliest known photograph of Mary Evelyn Beatrice Longman: in 1883, second grade, Sheldon School, Chicago. Second row, second from right. Source/Credit: Photograph by Kuhn Bros. From the collection of the Loomis Chaffee Archives. Loomis Chaffee School, Windsor, Connecticut USA.

six hundred acres bordering Lake Michigan. Aboard the southbound Illinois Central Railroad's express train, even from afar, Longman and her sister could have caught glimpses of the glinting golden dome that adorned the Administration Building. At the train terminal exit, the fair entrance fee was fifty cents, then the crowd of visitors poured through the lofty grand entrance at the base of the gilded dome, surrounded by more painted murals and statuary than anyone could possibly comprehend. (Sculptor Karl Bitter, for one, had created twenty-eight allegorical groups on the growth of civilization.)

Outside on the festival plaza, two large U.S. flags snapped in the breeze, elaborate bandstands and ornate obelisks on either side. Stretched out before the swarm of visitors was a grand basin of water—representing the four-hundred-year anniversary of Columbus's trip to America, which the fair celebrated. Along the basin, the gleaming White City—the architectural "masterpiece" of the fair: massive classical buildings painted white and adorned front and back, top and bottom, with scads of sculpture.

Designed to invite visitors to somehow shake the city grime and the day's troubles from their memory and enter an other-world, it represented an extravagant, ideal universe of order and, as the consistency of the *Beaux Arts* architecture was meant to encourage, unity. On the entrance side of bridges, with animal sculptures mounted on corners on either side of the basin, was the epic *Columbian Fountain*. Designed by Frederick William MacMonnies, the huge Barge of State was 150 feet in diameter, surmounted with multiple figures, the largest a monumental *Columbia*. The fountain's water dropped in a waterfall twelve feet down steps into the basin.

At the far end of the reservoir, called the Court of Honor, was a colossal golden figure, *Republic*, representing the United States. Designed by sculptor Daniel Chester French, it stood sixty-five feet high atop a thirty-five-foot base. In keeping with the fair's ideals, French's *Republic* held a globe with an eagle on top and a staff with a laurel-wreathed cross on top that said "Liberty," symbols representing "American confidence and pride . . . strength and immortality . . . freedom."[1]

The fair was born into a confusing time. The rapid growth of industry had led to the creation of monopolies in iron, steel, lumber, petroleum, and railroads. This produced great fortunes for owners, called captains of industry or, often, "robber barons," due to ruthless business practices. Mark Twain named the era the Gilded Age, describing the thin veneer of industrialists' extraordinary wealth compared to the extreme poverty of many Americans. Labor and management were in conflict, sometimes violently.

Chicago's very name reflected continuing divisions in the country: Initially settled by a man escaping enslavement, Chicago was named for a wild onion that Native Americans, obviously in the Americas long before Columbus, called *Chegakou*.[2] Native Americans were not recognized as U.S. citizens.

African Americans' success during Reconstruction had ended when Jim Crow laws were established beginning in 1877; separation, persecution, and killings of blacks continued with lynching and massacre.

Immigration soared. People in rural areas, faced with the vagaries of weather and insects, resulting crop loss, and hunger, also began migrating to cities.

Chicago, with its wooden houses and sidewalks, often experienced conflagrations, including the Great Chicago Fire of 1871, which killed three hundred people and destroyed eighteen thousand buildings. As Chicagoans rushed to rebuild following the Great Fire, people flocked to the city; some weeks, two thousand more people entered than left. In one decade, the population grew by six hundred thousand. In 1900, inhabitants would number 1.7 million. While businesses rebuilt and, with its first skyscraper, Chicago began to move up, the need for housing did not keep pace with the swell, and the city became a place of both wealth and squalor. As immigrants, rural residents, and others flocked to Chicago for work in the stockyards, steel mills, and other industries, the cheaply constructed, crowded tenements where the poor lived created health problems for their occupants.

The fair, then, was designed to celebrate American "civilization"; bring order out of chaos; renew the promise that American innovation, civic spirit, teamwork, and unity were still vital in the land; assert U.S. industrial prowess and reassure the country's populace "during an era dominated by tensions over immigration, urbanization, race, class, and Euro-American westward expansion."[3]

Nine thousand sculptures and paintings filled the seventy-four galleries in the Palace of Fine Arts.

The more than twenty million fairgoers could view sixty-five thousand exhibits, including Whitney's cotton gin, the world's largest conveyer belt, the forty-three steam engines, and 127 generators at the fair's power plant. Electricity was a big hit at the fair, which was lit at night—a new and exciting experience for visitors.

The latest electrical inventions on display included incubators for poultry eggs, chairs for executions, an electric sidewalk, an early fax machine that sent pictures over telegraph lines; irons, sewing machines, laundry machines; Otis elevators and Thomas Edison's Kinetoscope, which produced the first moving pictures. A seventy-foot tower of light bulbs amazed, as many visitors were yet to see their first light bulb, though Edison had invented it fourteen years before.[4]

Entire villages in the fair's midway, designed to offer lessons in ethnography and human development, presented visitors with glimpses of "primitive" cultures, in contrast with "civilization," as presented in the White City. Most visitors were more enticed by entertainment, including the first Ferris wheel, and shopping for newly introduced items: carbonated soda, Wrigley's fruit gum, Pabst Blue Ribbon beer, Aunt Jemima pancake mix, Cream of Wheat, Cracker Jacks. Indeed, one of the goals of fair organizers had been to encourage confidence in American business and their products, fostering a consumer society.[5]

Despite their requests, Native people, African Americans, and women were not included on the National Commission planning the Fair. With pressure from women, Congress authorized the all-white, all-male National

Commission to create a Board of Lady Managers, which organizers considered a complementary gesture. The 115 Lady Managers petitioned Congress that women's exhibits not be separate but integrated throughout the fair. Fair directors decided otherwise, and a Women's Building—designed by a female architect, Sophia G. Hayden, of Boston—was built. Like all the great halls, the women's building was unfinished on the inside; instead, exhibits were set up amid skeletal interiors. The exhibits revealed the cultural dichotomies of women's roles: the traditional view of women—childrearing, teaching, cooking, healing—was dominant in spite of some exhibits that showed women's accomplishments in industry, science, art, literature, and other professions.

The Bureau of Indian Affairs and the Ethnological Bureau exhibits in the Government Building focused on Indian customs and life in North and South America, in which they contrasted "the red man as a savage wrapped in a blanket, and his child in the dress of civilization, endeavoring to master benignant mysteries."[6] In an effort to convey what he thought was the fair's attempt to show that non-whites were primitive and not "civilized," Richard Henry Pratt, who founded the Carlisle Indian School in Pennsylvania, which removed Indian children from their families and expunged every ounce of Native American that his teachers could, entered his own exhibit to show the Native American to be "a fully capable American citizen."[7]

Fair organizers dismissed African American leaders' requests to be engaged in the planning process, though they had hoped to show the progress African Americans and their communities had made since emancipation. Blacks were refused positions to help with construction, administration, and operations, except in menial ways. All-white committees also denied any exhibit space to African Americans, except for Hampton Institute's display in the U.S. Department of Education's exhibit.

Journalist Ida B. Wells published thousands of copies of a pamphlet, which she distributed at the fair. In it, U.S. abolitionist and statesman Frederick Douglass, a fair commissioner for the Republic of Haiti, stated that for the "colored people of America, morally speaking, the World's Fair in Chicago . . . is . . . a whited sepulcher." Douglass accused fair organizers' ethnic exhibits on the midway as presenting the "Negro as a repulsive savage."[8]

The White City had been aptly named.

The European-inspired architecture of the White City had its critics. Architects Frank Lloyd Wright and Louis Sullivan called the architecture a "sham," which set American architectural design back forty years.

When the fair was over, the temporary buildings were destroyed as planned, and some, including *Republic*, were brought down by another Chicago fire. With its cornucopia of industrial production, the fair succeeded in defining the moment for the wealthy, and providing a distraction, if not reassurance, for the poor. Ironically, another economic depression developed as the result of a bank failure on May 1, opening day of the World's Fair.

Surely unaware how she, a poor young woman, could navigate into this other world—of beauty, wealth, and privilege—which she now, irrevocably, had seen, Evelyn Beatrice Longman was about to experience her defining moment.

The classicism of the White City looked beautiful to her. The abundance of sculpture, not only adorning the buildings, but also in the Fine Arts Palace, included some created by women.[9] But it was the work of Daniel Chester French that captivated her. In addition to his *Republic*, French had created two other major works that were displayed at the fair, including *Quadriga*, a gilded chariot with four horses, representing the "spirit of discovery." Working with his onetime student Edward Clark Potter, who modeled animals, they also designed four, twelve-foot-tall White City–white statues on either side of the two entrances to the Agriculture Building. On the south-canal entrance were *Farmer*, a man in a hat, holding a shovel and the reins of a large horse, and *Teamster*, an African American man, one arm leaning against another of Potter's large horses.

At the Agriculture Building's lakeside entrance, near French's *Republic*, stood two more monumental French and Potter works: *Indian Corn* and *Wheat*. Ceres, Greek goddess of the harvest, stood beside a massive bull, holding a fistful of maize. Opposite was an "Indian maiden" leaning against

Figure 1.2 Daniel Chester French's Corn Maiden, 1893 World's Columbian Exposition, Chicago. Source/Credit: Chesterwood Archives; Chapin Library, Williams College, Gift of the National Trust for Historic Preservation / Chesterwood, a National Trust Historic Site, Stockbridge, Massachusetts.

another bull, cornstalk in hand. She was draped in a simpler garment, with a head wrap fastened over her long braid.

That prophetic day, the eighteen-year-old, uneducated female warehouse worker stood before Daniel Chester French's twelve-foot *Indian Corn* and shocked her sister with these words: "I could do that. I know I could do that if I had the chance."[10]

NOTES

1. Harold Holzer, *Monument Man: The Life & Art of Daniel Chester French* (Hudson, NY: Princeton Architectural Press, 2019), 144–45.
2. Reid Badger, *The Great American Fair: The World's Columbian Exposition and American Culture* (Chicago: Nelson Hall, 1979), 31.
3. Thayer Tolles, "American Sculpture at the World's Columbian Exposition, Chicago, 1893." https://www.metmuseum.org/toah/hd/cwfs/hd_cwfs.htm, accessed February 15, 2023.
4. *American Experience*, "Chicago City of the Century. World's Columbian Exhibition 1893," aired on PBS, January 13, 2003. https://www.pbs.org/wgbh/americanexperience/features/chicago-worlds-columbian-exposition-1893/.
5. Julie Kirsten Rose, "The World's Columbian Exposition: Idea, Experience, Aftermath," Bachelor's thesis, English Department, University of Virginia, August 1996. http://dx.doi.org/10.18130/V33609.
6. Badger, 105.
7. Ibid.
8. Ibid., 106.
9. Tolles. "When faced with a deadline that he felt he couldn't meet, sculptor Lorado Taft, who taught at the Art Institute of Chicago, asked Daniel Burnham, the fair's director of works, for permission to bring on some of his female sculpting students to assist him. Burnham reportedly replied that he could hire white rabbits if he wanted—whatever would help him get the job done. And so the ten female sculpting students, some of whom exhibited their works at the fair, were known as the 'white rabbits'—but it could just as well have been because they looked like white rabbits, covered in plaster dust climbing up and down ladders as they worked."
10. Louise Longman, unpublished memoir, Evelyn Beatrice Longman Collection, Loomis Chaffee Archives, Loomis Chaffee School, Windsor, Connecticut, USA.

Chapter 2

Born into a Dream

To thine own self be true.

—William Shakespeare, and Evelyn Beatrice Longman

Who knows what Louise Longman was thinking following her sister's discomfiting comment. She was either amused—that Evelyn would say something so ludicrous—or rattled: knowing her sister's fierce tenacity, Evelyn's brazen statement should be taken seriously. In any case, Louise relayed the story to Ontario aunts and uncles, and within days, two showed up in Chicago to nip this idea in the bud. They wanted Evelyn to know that the art world was not one they felt suitable for their niece. And they roundly scolded her for her presumption.[1]

They probably knew their moral outrage would not dissuade this young woman. As they had experienced from early-on, even as a child Longman had been meeting the challenges of her life her way. Perhaps it was knowing this that compelled them to take her comment seriously, realizing it would require an in-person appearance even to have a chance at deterring her. But if her history was an indication, Longman's determination would not be overcome by aunts or adversity. For her mother's family, perhaps Evelyn Beatrice Longman was too much like her father.

Edwin Henry Longman grew up in Yeovil, England, a market village in southern England's limestone scarplands, a crazy quilt palette of green with manor houses and hedge-rowed lanes between hamlets, which sounds romantic enough, but not so grand for those in the lower middle class. A musician and artist at heart, Henry's job as a bank cashier may not have given expression to his artistic side; nor, as the town's sole, glove-making industry was disappearing, did the area's dwindling economic base hold the promise that he might become the country gentleman he evidently longed to be. He was not to the manor born.

Moreover, he and his wife, Mary Ann Bollen, had suffered the loss of two young children. The prospect of a new life in Canada, where other families from southern England had already moved, must have enflamed the embers of Henry's hope for a less-plebeian life. They emigrated in 1857 and settled with their remaining two children in London, Ontario, where Henry offered music lessons. A third child, Eva Clara, was born there a year later.

Unknown is how Longman met Clara Delitia Valentina Adnam, his second wife. When Clara was thirteen, her parents and siblings also had emigrated from southwest England to Ontario and settled as farmers in the Bothwell area. Perhaps Longman was a traveling music teacher (Bothwell is fifty miles from London). In any case, on Valentine's Day 1863, in Chicago, Clara Delitia Valentina Adnam delivered a child, Clara Delitia Valentina, "Vally." Three months later, on May 21, the day after her nineteenth birthday, Adnam married forty-year-old Longman in Racine, Wisconsin. A location so distant from Bothwell may have had something to do with the fact that unwed, pregnant Clara came from a conservative family, and, in any case, Henry already had a wife and three children, evidently residing in Chicago. One wonders how much of this her family, or even Clara, knew.

Both of Henry's families now lived in Chicago. Perhaps he should be given the benefit of the doubt: divorce at that time in Ontario required an act of Parliament, and, seemingly, he tried to take care of both families. He failed miserably—not that it would have been easy. As so many impoverished people in Chicago did at the time, the two families moved often, and, at least in 1870, his two wives and both families moved in together.

On Sunday morning, October 8, 1871, Henry, the organist at St. Mary's Catholic Church, played Sunday mass. In a booming city with more and more wooden buildings, wood-paved streets, and wooden sidewalks, there were frequent fires, increased warnings of extreme danger. That evening, amid a drought and strong southwest winds, a spark somewhere south of downtown lit the city afire.

Within a few hours, a conflagration raged across central Chicago, demolishing thousands of buildings, including the roof of the pumping station, making firefighting impossible. The flames rampaged through the city until rain arrived Tuesday morning. St. Mary's Church burned to the ground. The "garden city of the west," now barren of trees, bushes, or flowers, reeked of damp, acrid smoke. A forest of gray tendrils rose along the four miles of obliteration.

For three days, the family didn't see Henry. Without his church job and no doubt with music lessons suddenly far from a priority for burned-out families, the means to live the life Henry had hoped for in the New World would appear to have escaped him. But then, inexplicably, in September 1873, Clara and Henry bought fifty-seven acres of land, sight unseen, in Adams County, Winchester Township, in southern Ohio, for $3,500 "in hand." Clara's hand, actually, as Cook County records show the property was purchased in her name.[2]

Two years after the Great Chicago Fire, months in which they sometimes lived in a barn, Henry, Clara, and their four children (Vally, Louise, Claude, and Edwin) would have walked through the haunting vestiges of Chicago's Great Central Depot. Inferno-proof limestone walls and massive triple arches over the tracks still stood like Roman ruins. Train, boat, and stagecoach delivered the family to their new place in the Ohio countryside: a ramshackle barn and a log cabin, the front door standing open. Cows roamed the house.

The young ones had space to play outdoors, Henry taught a few music lessons, sold a piano. They put in a small crop or two. Though "never well," Clara did have farm experience. Kind neighbors helped. They made the house tolerably livable.[3]

And so it was into her father's romantic dream but actual poverty in rural Ohio that tiny—four-pound—Mary Evelyn Beatrice Longman entered the world. Late in the night of November 21, 1874, Henry called the children from the warmth of their shared bedcovers in the log house's cold, airy attic, and, holding two-year-old Louise's hand, Vally led them downstairs in their nightdresses to meet their new sister.[4]

Henry sent word for his and Mary Ann's teenaged daughter, Eva, to travel from Chicago to Ohio to help with the new baby. The name "Evelyn" had been chosen because it sounded somewhat like "Eva." As it would turn out, Eva would come as close to a mother as Evelyn would have.

Still an infant, Evelyn enjoyed music in the house. While she was learning to walk, she stood by a chair and followed the older ones in their singing, keeping time with her body, and when she could talk, she had her own lyrics to "Jesus Loves Me": "Jesus loves Eva'n Me."[5] The countryside was beautiful; the children had rich, fresh milk and vegetables in the summer. There was a grape dell, a cold-water spring, and their father had a cider press.[6]

Henry, whose artistic leanings also included drawing and painting, made a rendering of the two-story home with outbuildings and surrounding flora. Three oil paintings thought to have been made by Henry depict pastoral scenes of houses in the country, ponds with ducks, children fishing, women doing chores, picket fences, and a white-steepled church tucked into trees in the background of one painting. Whether these were realistic or romanticized representations, the facts on the ground were not as pretty.

The family managed to eke out a living in the country for two more years. But debts accumulated, and in late 1876, they gave up Henry's dream of "landed gentry."[7] Eva went ahead to Chicago and found the family a cramped suite of rooms on the north side. Clara and Henry's youngest child, Cecil, was born there in 1878. Clara died in 1880, of a liver tumor and cirrhosis. She was buried in Rosehill Cemetery, a few rows away from Mary Ann, who had died the year before.

Evelyn was five.

A more sweeping chaos ensued. Following an eviction and another move, the children were sent to live with Clara's siblings on farms in Ontario. Once, when Evelyn and her older sister Louise were put on a train in Chicago to travel to Highgate, Ontario, to stay with their aunt Eliza Smith, they got off at the wrong station. By the time they realized where they weren't, the train had pulled out. The Highgate station was another ten miles up the tracks. Little Evelyn yanked up her bag and walked along the tracks leading from the station. Louise hurried after her six-year-old sister and protested. Evelyn kept walking, her bag bumping her leg at every step, until Louise convinced her that hiking through the countryside was not a good idea. It's unknown whether they waited at the station for the next train or someone delivered them to Highgate.[8]

Louise and Evelyn shared a garret bedroom at their aunt Eliza's. It was cold in the winter, hot in the summer, drippy when it rained. "Evy," as her siblings called her, enjoyed the outdoors; a duck friend followed her around like a puppy; mice who had run of the garret and skittered over her at night became friends as well.[9]

One morning Evy and Lou, hands tightly clasped, walked along the road in front of their aunt Eliza's house, kicking up dust with their laced-up shoes. They had heard the whispers; they were wise to the adults' behavior; they knew what was up: transparent to them was why Evelyn alone was to be shuffled off to a neighboring farm to spend the day with a playmate. By now the sisters knew the pain, the uncertainty of sibling separations: their three oldest siblings and their two-year-old brother had been deposited around the countryside at relatives' farms. This particular separation was especially hard, for the sisters would be separated from each other for the first time—it was only Louise who would be taken to the train station, bound for their father's place in Chicago.

Determinedly stoic, the sisters said their goodbyes, and Louise watched Evelyn, well-aware that this was a diversionary tactic, trudge down the road to a playmate's nearby farm, not daring to look back "lest the grief that was overwhelming us should prove too much for us to bear."[10]

As the lonely months wore on, Evelyn, age nine, declared to her aunt Eliza that if they did not send her back to Chicago, she would run away and walk there. Eliza evidently believed Longman would try. Her father sent for her.

"I can dimly see a slight dark little maiden, with a good deal of straight dark hair, and unabashed dark eyes and clay skin," Louise would recall in a letter. "Rather an imperious little miss with an air of knowing what she wants, and, notwithstanding the difficulties of those early days, an assurance of seeing her wishes carried out."[11]

Life in Chicago was problematic. Henry Longman remarried in 1884, to Alice Williams, thirty years his senior. She was not fond of his children. Evelyn was the only one who could live in Henry's household for long, though sometimes she took a break and stayed with Louise, after she married, or with Louise's mother-in-law, both of whom lived in Chicago.

Evelyn found a kindred spirit in her father; like him, she wanted to create beauty, in painting or music. She later told a newspaper reporter, "I inherited the love of my art from my father. He was a musician by profession, but he was also an amateur artist, and he inspired me with the desire to create things of beauty."[12]

Her father taught her piano, voice, and drawing. There is a stunning piece of evidence that at a young age, Longman had the capacity to create meaning in beauty. When Louise had gone back to Ontario, Evelyn wrote to her on March 19, 1886.[13] The words were that of a girl, though her beautiful penmanship was more that of an adult.

> Dear Louie,
>
> I was very glad to receive your letter, and I was also glad to hear that you were coming to see me, after not seeing you for so long, but we were very disappointed when you did not come after all, and we will expect to see you on Saturday.
>
> I have passed for fifth grade, have you done so too? If you have, will you please bring it down when you come on Saturday, and then I will tell you about my average mark, and my marks in reading, writing, Arith., etc. I am up to Gracie Fog now, and she is in room 8 you know, I think she was in that same room when I first went to that school, and then I was in room 13, and now I have caught up to her.
>
> Come early on Saturday so that we can have a nice long day.
>
> Your loving sister,
>
> Evy

Not unusual for a young girl, she included drawings beneath the message. A few flourishes would not have been surprising for her age. Prophetically, this was not simply ornamentation for ornamentation's sake. The decoration meant something; it helped tell the story—in fact, the story beneath the story. Below the message, she's drawn a two-story house, with a tree beside it. The tree is interesting, considering it is drawn by an eleven-year-old, who might have swirled some leaves onto the tree; in her drawing, only a few leaves are barely scribbled around the outer edge of the curvy tree branches. One figure stands in the open door, her arms wide. Lettering is not beneath the image; rather, she writes it diagonally from the door down the page to the far corner: "Here I am waiting for you Louie." A hatted figure on the left walks toward the house. Reminiscent of her father's nostalgic paintings of the country, it is poignant because Evelyn's abode at this time would have been crowded rooms in urban Chicago, rather than a large house with a tree shading it.

Most amazingly—the prophetic evidence of unknown talent—before the *E* in her signature, there looks to be a fanciful curlicue. Upon closer inspection, it resembles a girl. After her signature, to the right of the *y* is another curlicue. This one seems to be a girl blowing in the Chicago wind, with leaves blowing around her. And beside her, in letters so tiny they can't be read without enlarging the image, is the word *Evy*. What appears to be a line under her signature is a line that connects the two girls symbolized by the curlicues.

Embellishment as a way of illustrating a story about a person's life came early to Longman.

Finished with her elementary-school studies, Longman was all set to advance to high school, but because she didn't have the money to attend a mandatory pre-graduation function, she was not allowed to graduate. Disappointed and without resources, instead of attending high school, the fourteen-year-old took a job doing office work in the warehouse of Wilson Brothers.

After a full day in the warehouse poring over ledgers, Longman dreaded the walk home along the windy lakefront.[14] As difficult as it might have been, she never lamented her childhood.

In June 1893, the year of the Chicago World's Fair, Longman visited her relatives in Dawn Mills, Ontario. Perhaps her older sister Vally, who on the one hand cussed and smoked, and on the other disliked statues of naked figures, was trying to dissuade her spirited little sister from her crazy idea of sculpting large statues. In any case, the entry Longman made in Vally's autograph book is significant.[15] Illustrated with a lovely drawing of Lily of the Valley are Shakespeare's words:

To thine own self be true.
And it must follow as the night the day,
Thou canst not then,
Be false to anyone.
Evelyn B Longman

She turned nineteen in November 1893. Despite her already legendary determination and the first indications of artistic talent, what chance in the world

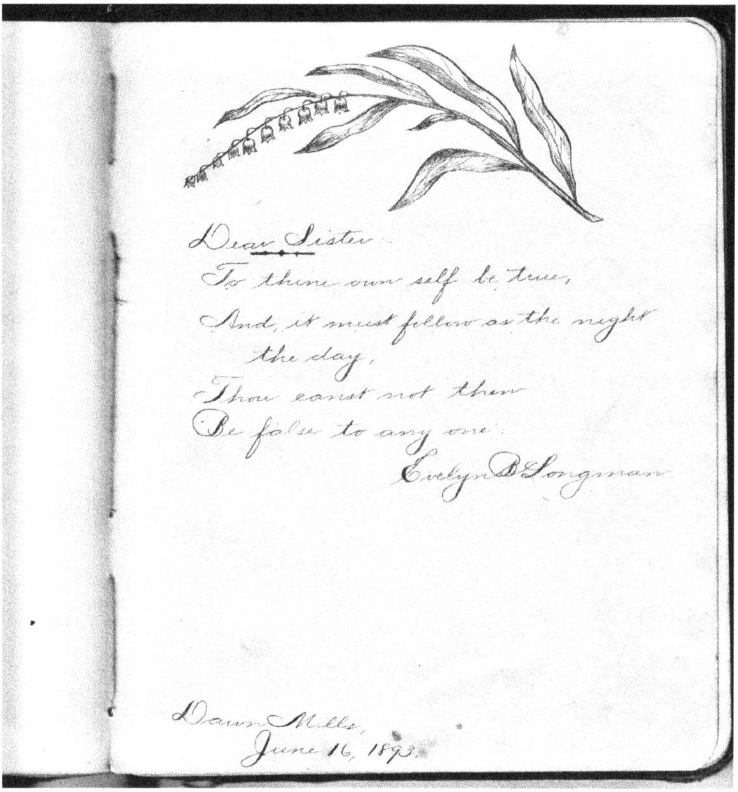

Figure 2.1 The page that 19-year-old Longman wrote and illustrated in her sister Vally's autograph book. Source/Credit: Bonnie French Collection

did a slight, poor, uneducated young woman (emphasis on *woman*) who wanted to create beauty in monumental statues (emphasis on *monumental*) . . . What chance in the world did Mary Evelyn Beatrice Longman have to live her dream? It seemed about as attainable as her father's hopes for the country life.

And if—miracle of miracles—she did find a way into society's wealthy stratosphere of bankers and industrialists, the ones who commissioned monumental works of art, would she be able to stay true to herself?

NOTES

1. Nathaniel Horton Batchelder, unpublished memoir, Loomis Chaffee.
2. Bonnie French, unpublished research and telephone interview, August 13, 1918.

3. NHB unpublished memoir.
4. Claude Longman, undated letter ("Sunday"), Loomis Chaffee.
5. Louise Longman Tewksbury, unpublished memoir, Loomis Chaffee.
6. NHB unpublished memoir.
7. Ibid.
8. Ibid.
9. Ibid.
10. Tewksbury, unpublished "Moving Pictures," Loomis Chaffee.
11. Ibid.
12. No author listed, "Little Girl Who Worked in Store Made Dream of Art Come True," *New York Evening Mail*, April 8, 1913, Longman scrapbook, Loomis Chaffee.
13. Bonnie French, personal collection.
14. NHB unpublished memoir, Loomis Chaffee.
15. Bonnie French, unpublished research and telephone interview.

Chapter 3

Nymph Fountain

Queen of Muscles and Bones.

—Students at the Art Institute of Chicago

Henry Longman's response to the commotion over his daughter's career-reveal at the Chicago World's Fair was to encourage her to take art classes.[1] When the Art Institute of Chicago opened in its new quarters following the Chicago Fair, Evelyn enrolled in a figure-modeling class taught in the evening by sculptor Hermon Atkins MacNeil. However, attending class from 7:30 to 9 p.m. three times a week after working full days proved to be too challenging. She dropped the class and continued working at Wilson Brothers until 1896.

After working seven years, and despite starting to save all over again after loaning her nest egg to a friend, she had saved $262. Enough: She quit her job and, at the age of twenty-one, moved in with her sisters Eva and Polly in Olivet, Michigan, so she could attend classes at Olivet College, where her brother Claude was already a student.

Olivet College was the second in the country to open as a co-ed institution (sister college Oberlin in Ohio was the first). It was the first place of higher learning in the state of Michigan to admit women and persons of color on an equal basis with white males. Its first graduates, in 1863, during the Civil War, were three women. With its philosophy of egalitarianism and charting the student's course based on the student's interests, Olivet College would seem a fitting environment for Longman, who had no secondary school education but was clear-eyed about her interest.

There is no record of the courses she took, though there is a story that she asked Alfred Wise, head of the art department, if she could take his beginning art class. He first told her she was too young, but, as the story goes, when he saw her disappointment, he relented, saying she could "try art." She entered as a "normal and special" student.[2]

The Burrage Library was a red sandstone building with higher and lower turrets on either side of a balcony with arched glass windows below. It must have been a moment out of her dreams the day Longman first climbed steps to the top of the shorter turret and opened the door to a small room with a high ceiling. There, a model sat perfectly still in a chair in the middle of the room while students working at long tables created clay likenesses of the model's head.

Before the end of her first year at Olivet, she had modeled a few pieces. A friend who knew Lorado Taft, sculpture instructor at the Art Institute of Chicago, took Longman to meet him. She showed him photographs of her work, and, just as importantly, fervently expressed her desire to sculpt. Taft invited her to enter classes—again, as a special student. To help with tuition, he offered her an evening job at the school library.

Never mind finishing coursework at Olivet: the Art Institute of Chicago! She leapt at the opportunity and left Olivet after a year. No doubt Eva, Claude, and Polly, sad to see her leave, and, knowingly, helpless to hold her back, must have celebrated her entry into one of the best art schools in the country.

Henry Longman did not live to see his daughter enter art school, though she would have shown him photographs of work she had done at Olivet on a trip she made to Chicago to visit him before he died, of an intracranial hemorrhage, in June 1897. Moving back to Chicago, Longman still had sixty dollars left in savings. Her sister Louise, who by then had two young daughters, welcomed her into her home. At times Longman again lived with Louise's mother-in-law, paying fifteen cents a meal and washing dishes, making beds, and pressing suits for board and room.

Just as at the academies of Europe, the Art Institute of Chicago provided a classical sculpture education. An extensive collection of plaster casts gave access to great works of antique art, for practice in drawing and modeling. Advanced classes used live models, both nude and costumed. Faculty taught anatomy, how to build an armature, cast in plaster, and chisel from a marble block. Daniel Chester French's brother William Merchant Richardson French, the school's director, lectured on anatomy, including a class on muscles and a class on bones. Taft's survey of modern American sculpture explored the life and work of Daniel Chester French.

Once again, Longman had found her way to the right place at the right time. Taft was one of a few teachers in the United States at that time to provide women serious training toward becoming professional sculptors. In fact, most of his students were women. Though he didn't consider women sculptors equal to their male peers, he supported their education and their careers.

Evelyn didn't buy into Taft's bias about male sculptors, but the two hit it off. Their personalities were compatible: he, charming, gregarious, zany; she, charming, buoyant, eager to learn, talented. Having attended the *École des Beaux-Arts* in Paris, Taft was steeped in the *Beaux Arts* style, the architectural design of the White City. He had contributed two groups to the Chicago Fair, for the Horticulture Building, not far from the Agriculture Building, where Longman had become enchanted with French's work. Most importantly, Taft was on a mission to celebrate the American values and ideals of that time in monumental public sculpture. And so it was that, at the Art Institute, Longman flourished, and by her second year, she assisted Taft—demonstrating sculpting procedures while he lectured.

Taft gave four thousand talks in his career, traveling 2,500 miles some years. One Dartmouth student who heard him speak told his father it was the most impactful lecture he'd ever heard. "He mixed wit and beautiful philosophy with his exposition," he wrote. "[Taft] . . . showed the whole significance of art—its parallel with life. It seems as if art *is* life."[3]

From Taft, Evelyn quickly learned how to create life in the form of sculpture. She was taking a heavy load of classes, and in the summers of 1898 and 1899, she also participated in the wit and playfulness of Chicago's artistic intellectuals at their summer camp. Named "Eagle's Nest," this small, isolated colony sat on a bluff overlooking the Rock River near Oregon, Illinois. In the tradition of artists' summer getaways—in Laguna Beach, California, and Provincetown, Massachusetts—Taft and his artist friends in Chicago sought a summer retreat from the city heat and first settled on a site in Indiana. After an outbreak of malaria there, however, a Chicago patron of the arts leased them fifteen acres in Illinois for one dollar a year and the promise that each member would give a free lecture in the area.

At the camp, Taft commonly wore a beret, women often wore their hair in braids, and everyone dressed in more casual, skimpier, summer clothing. Residents and guests stayed in tents, creating art and music during the day, and then enjoyed Taft's flair for fun at night. He borrowed models' costumes from the Art Institute and, with musician friends, led lively dances at the colony—as well as other creative moments gone zany. Friends and guests donned costumes for processions and dances in which flower girls added to the festivity and philosophers danced with *bacchantes*.

In his book *Chicago's Left Bank*, Alson J. Smith wrote that "on many a summer evening the whole colony would don the flowing habiliments of Attica and dance in and out of the trees along the bluff, fluttering the draperies in the silver moonlight and crying to one another: 'On such a night Pan and the dryads dance in the moonlight. Come, let us join him in the dance.'"[4]

One day Taft showed up for the morning swim in a Greek helmet, carrying a saw for a makeshift sword and wearing a red blanket in lieu of a white toga. Another time, residents built a skiff and a toboggan slide to launch it. After dedicating it with a bottle of root beer, they sent the new vessel down the slide and into the water, where it sank.[5]

Taft converted a small wooden barn into his studio. Its high, sloped roof allowed him to create large works; light poured through a skylight. Longman assisted him in his studio, where he also created portraits of friends who were members of the colony.

Though more academic, the school also promoted spirited play. Initiation ceremonies included pie-eating contests and duels with paintbrushes as weapons, palettes as shields. There were yearly rituals, like a Mardi Gras costume ball. And sometimes, on no occasion at all, students raided the costume room and donned the outfits used by models.

While frolicking in the water at Eagle's Nest in the summer of 1897, Taft came up with an idea to bring public art to Chicago. He was on a mission to convince Chicagoans that public sculpture was essential, as beautiful expressions of American values, "morally uplifting and . . . a tangible and permanent statement of American culture."[6] And so Longman, in her third year at the school, had the opportunity to create her first monumental figure: one of ten nude nymphs, the central figure in what would become the Institute's infamous *Fountain of Nymphs*.[7]

An outdoor area at the Arts Institute served as a studio for Taft's project. Ten women students created the nymphs, each at least seven feet tall. Wooden barrels held materials for plaster castings of the nudes, to be positioned in a forty-foot-wide fountain, playfully splashing each other. Plaster-splashed students worked for months creating the larger-than-life-sized nudes. Four nymphs in the center were splattered by the six nymphs around the circumference of the fountain.

Longman created the central standing figure. Rather than repelling the water aimed at her, her figure was laughing, holding her arms open to enjoy the splashes—revealing her full figure. Others in the center tried to avoid the spray; one held on to the waist of Longman's central figure as if she might fall off. Longman's nude was the most daring: in no way was she hiding her voluptuous body; rather, she was not only exposing it, but relishing in it.

Graduation was the sixteenth of June, and that night the nymphs were placed in the fountain that had been built amidst trees on the south side of the Art Institute. Nudity was the test, and, as evidenced by the trampled grass and resulting mud around the fountain the first day, Chicago came to look. The mayor, arriving on his bicycle, liked it, declaring it "beautiful and artistic. . . . The man who made these figures should be proud of them." When someone

Figure 3.1 Longman, on ladder, sculpting the central nymph at Art Institute of Chicago. Source/Credit: IMG 0010850, Women on Ladders Working on Large Nymph Sculpture, c. 1899. Allen S. Weller Papers, Record Series 12/1/20, Box 7, folder Nymph Fountain 1899. University of Illinois Archives.

reminded him the figures were made by women, Mayor Carter Harrison said that Professor Taft should be proud of his students.

The school's president defended it, saying, "There can be no objection to those figures. They are of the sort of art Chicago has been lacking in. I hope to see more of it. It is such beautiful adornment of public places that should be contributed by our artists. I do not see how anyone can find fault. I feel sure no one will who pauses long enough to see the higher motive in the conception."[8]

Others found fault. The national secretary of the Women's Christian Temperance Union said, "The nymph is not an intellectual goddess, therefore how can it type intellectuality or high ideas. It stands for nothing related to high or noble mental accomplishments."[9]

Though the nymphs were planned as a temporary, thirty-day installation, they remained on view until the morning of August 13, when it was discovered that the fountain and its nymphs had been destroyed by an unknown crew of workmen. The broken-up concrete pool and the mutilated female figures were dumped in the lakefront basin.[10]

Assisting Taft, while also carrying a heavy load of classes in which she surpassed classmates, Longman finished the four-year program in three years, graduating in June 1899, with honors. In keeping with the school's wacky ways, student peers dubbed her the "Queen of Muscles and Bones"[11] and—pointing to her beguiling charisma, which would always serve her well—first in the hearts of her teachers.

In a photo taken during her last year, she is surrounded by four friends, as if they are modeling for a group sculpture that features Evelyn. As some in the group look at her, she looks straight into the camera with the same compelling, direct gaze she had in second grade, plus a smile. Her right arm extends to the shoulder of the woman beside her, and though she indeed looks quite young, she holds a deeply rooted smile, an air of consummate confidence, ease, and belonging. Yet, snug in this charmed circle, Longman was ready to move on.

The summer after her graduation, in addition to a stint at Eagle's Nest, she taught children at the Art Institute. But she was determinedly New York City–bound, her mind set on assisting Daniel Chester French. Taft encouraged her to remain in Chicago, on familiar ground. But she thought too many were depending on him.[12] Her family wanted her to stay in Chicago—and find some other line of work. Again (perhaps they'd seen newspaper accounts of her nymph) an aunt and uncle came from Ontario to try one more time to

Figure 3.2 Friends at Art Institute of Chicago (Longman is in the center). Source/Credit: Photograph from the collection of the Loomis Chaffee Archives, Loomis Chaffee School, Windsor, Connecticut USA Photo by John Groo

dissuade her from a career connected in their minds with "sin." Knowing she knew no one in New York City, Chicago friends bought her a return train ticket, expecting her to run out of resources.

Longman was undeterred. She had forty dollars and, most critically, letters of recommendation from Taft and Daniel French's brother Will. That was enough, despite the fact that Daniel French notoriously had said he would not work with women assistants because, ever the New England gentleman, he didn't want to have to take the time to be polite.

Her sister Louise saw her off, "a slight dark-haired young woman wearing a little gray coat on the steps of a train. There are tears and some anxiety in her eyes. . . . Nevertheless, there is courage and confidence in her bearing."[13]

Challenge her muscles, hardship her bones, Evelyn Beatrice Longman headed to New York City.

NOTES

1. *New York Evening Mail*, April 8, 1913, Loomis Chaffee.
2. "Research Completion Form for Evelyn Beatrice Longman and Family," Olivet College Hosford History Center and Lawrence Archives, November 2020, 3.
3. Alson J. Smith, *Chicago's Left Bank* (Chicago: Henry Regnery Co., 1953), 157.
4. Ibid., 158.
5. "Lorado Taft and His Camp," *Kansas City Star*, September 19, 1897, 13.
6. Margaret Samu, "Establishing a Career in Public Sculpture: Evelyn Beatrice Longman" (For Honors in the Art Department, Wellesley College, April 2001), 10.
7. *Arts for America*, viii, no. 9, July 1899, 471. Allen S. Weller notes at University of Illinois Archives.
8. "Nymph Group in Favor," *Chicago Tribune*, June 17, 1899, 1.
9. Ibid.
10. "Lakefront Nymphs Are Gone," *Chicago Tribune*, August 18, 1899, 1.
11. Bob Vickrey, "World Famous Woman Sculptor Works Hard in Windsor Studio," unknown Connecticut newspaper, March 20, 1921, Loomis Chaffee. "She finished that four-year course in two years, with 'honorable mention and everything,' the other students saying of her, on account of her aptitude in anatomy, 'she is first in bones, first in muscles, and first in the hearts of the committee.'"
12. Batchelder.
13. Tewksbury.

Chapter 4

Louise

Well, it is necessary to tell you a thing only once.

—Daniel Chester French

Longman was twenty-six in the fall of 1900, when she arrived in New York City, found a room for three dollars a week, and toted her reference letters and portfolio to sculptors she liked, hoping to land an assistantship. Daniel Chester French was at the top of her list.

In a feathered hat that curled around her ear and drew attention to her captivating dark eyes, late in the year Longman met both Daniel and Mary French at their home, a town house at 125 West 11th in Greenwich Village. Entrance into the reception room heralded an exotic new world for Longman. A frieze depicting Grecian maidens French had made in his first studio in Concord spanned the fireplace mantel. Above, hanging on the Cordova-leathered chimney, an oval Grecian shield. Left of the fireplace, on a pedestal, a plaster bust he had modeled of his wife, Mary Adams French.

In a cozy corner to the right of the fireplace, a yellow Chinese parasol and a Japanese lantern hung above a divan covered with an oriental rug. Teakwood, stained glass, fans, an Italian primitive painting, and a gilded chandelier fitted for gas—all French's decorative touches.[1]

The older sculptor, in crisp white shirt, suit, vest, and bow tie—sometimes beneath a working apron—must have greeted Longman in that room, and perhaps he led her through sliding doors, onto a small balcony with wooden stairs and railings that took her down to his studio.[2] The wood-floored, green-walled, high-ceilinged studio was spacious, even considering the clutter of smaller pieces of plaster models on shelves and large plaster sculptures atop benches and tables and pedestals.

He had no intention of taking her on as an assistant. Perhaps out of politeness, he may have looked at her portfolio. Certainly, he took the letters of recommendation from Taft and his brother Will before he dismissed her, with the suggestion of another artist she might visit.

She did not approach French's suggested sculptor, but had found her own way. Isidore Konti and Hermon Atkins MacNeil both brought her into their studios to assist them as they prepared monumental pieces for the 1901 Pan-American Exposition in Buffalo, New York. Longman already had met MacNeil: he taught the Art Institute modeling class she had briefly attended while working for Wilson Brothers some seven years earlier. He and his wife, Art Institute alumna and "white rabbit" Carol Brooks, had established a studio in Cottage City, Queens, on the East River.

MacNeil and Konti had known each other since the World's Columbian Exposition days in Chicago. Born in Hungary, Konti studied in Vienna and Rome, before coming to the United States. He worked with fellow Austrian Karl Bitter and with MacNeil on sculptures for the Chicago Fair. In addition to other works for the Buffalo Fair, Konti and MacNeil were working on companion pieces that envisioned "The Age of Despotism."

Notable for its rainbow-themed buildings—to be distinct from Chicago's White City—the Buffalo Fair's art and architecture would be overshadowed by the shooting of President William McKinley at the Temple of Music on September 6, 1901. He died eight days later. MacNeil would one day create a monument to the twenty-fifth president for the Ohio statehouse.

Daniel French, who also was working on sculptures for the Buffalo Fair, visited Hermon MacNeil in his studio in December 1900. He wrote to his brother Will soon after: "Miss Longman presented herself to me with your and other letters—a very attractive woman. She has been and is working for McNeil [sic.] I saw some of her work at his studio the other day and it entirely vindicates your recommendation. I recommended her for something, but her place with McNeil is better."[3]

It wasn't long before French reconsidered and invited Longman back for a second visit. When she agreed to do the lettering for the Boston Public Library doors, which he had long avoided, he took her on.

It was a fortuitous moment. Daniel Chester French, of *Minute Man* fame . . . the man who created the sculptures she'd first admired at the Columbian Expo . . . Daniel Chester French, who had never employed a female assistant (and would never hire another), had asked Mary Evelyn Beatrice Longman, born in a log cabin, motherless at five, friend of mice and ducks, with spotty schooling . . . Evelyn Beatrice Longman, who knew she could do what Daniel Chester French did before she even tried and, given the headway she had made at the Art Institute of Chicago, now stepped across the threshold of what was perceived as her wild and scandalous dream.

Mary French wrote in her 1928 book, *Memories of a Sculptor's Wife*, about that morning:

> She was young . . . took Mr. French's eye, quite as much as the reputation she had already acquired as to talent. He had never had any young women working in his studio and always insisted that he would never have one . . . but he did take Miss Longman, who assisted him, and later advised him, and became our dear friend for life.
>
> She used to seize upon me sometimes and say, "Are you sure that I am a real help to him, that he didn't take me just out of kindness? I wouldn't stay for one minute if that were true." So I reassured her that he couldn't live without her—artistically. This was what she wanted; although I have always suspected that it was two thirds—her eyes![4]

For Longman, the possibility of fulfilling the life her father encouraged—of creating beauty—and her own hopes, inspired by Taft's vision of doing it big and for the public, looked bright. Determined to make it (French paid her two to five dollars a day), she would not use the return train ticket to Chicago. As she had been required to do all her life, she continued to live frugally. Budgeting herself scrupulously, breakfast and lunch, for years to come, consisted of Triscuits and milk—a quart for two meals. Supper cost fifteen cents at a nearby restaurant.[5]

Neither was she daunted by the fact that she was a woman entering a man's world. The livelihood, the artistic discipline into which Longman had set foot, would propel her into a strange new world—a completely foreign social milieu, and in spite of Taft's influence, a vocation for men only. Furthermore, large monumental sculpture or sculpture of any size was only an emerging creative medium, unseen by most North Americans (albeit, briefly, Chicagoans). Until relatively recently, U.S. sculptors had been considered artisans rather than fine artists, and there had been few schools in the country to train them.[6] North American sculptors, including French, had studied in Europe—Italy and France. Returning to the States in hopes of promoting sculpture as a respected profession, the European-trained artists connected with wealthy New York industrialists, who could commission public art to decorate their new buildings.

To support and recognize artists and architects through exhibitions, the National Academy of Design had been established in 1825. In New York City, with the creation of Central Park in the late 1850s, leaders began discussing whether public parks should be "refuges for elite or playgrounds for the masses."[7] Not until after the Civil War had public sculpture found a secure place in civic life in the United States—in the South, to reaffirm the Confederate cause with commemorative monuments of Confederate generals.

It was a coalescing moment: Great fortunes had been built in the Gilded Age at the same time a group of influential professional architects emerged to design the industrialists' buildings, often in the *Beaux Arts* style. The country's most successful foreign-trained sculptors evolved into a core group that included Frederick MacMonnies, Augustus Saint-Gaudens, and Daniel Chester French. From these movements in business, architecture, and sculpture emerged connections that helped promote the development of civic art in New York City.[8]

Longman, raised in itinerancy and poverty, planned to work in this male world of wealth and privilege.

Though French was not raised with great wealth, Longman's new teacher had been raised with privilege—the second son of Harvard-educated attorney Henry Flagg French and Anne Richardson French, whose father was also a New England lawyer. With interests in agriculture as well as the law, Henry French became a judge, assistant secretary of the U.S. Treasury, and the first president of Massachusetts Agricultural College, which would become the University of Massachusetts Amherst. He invented the French drain.

The family had lived on a farm at Concord, Massachusetts, at that time a community of creative intellectuals. Henry David Thoreau's Walden Pond was on the outskirts of town. The Frenches' closest neighbors were Ralph Waldo Emerson and the Alcott family. It was watercolorist May Alcott, sister of author Louisa May, who first gave Daniel French modeling clay and tools.

Encouraged by his father, who hoped there would be an artist in the family, Daniel French spent a month in the New York studio of sculptor John Quincy Adams Ward. He then studied drawing with two Boston artists, all the while modeling portraits of family members, but he was still a novice—this was before his first trip to study in Italy—when Emerson and others in his hometown commissioned him to create the *Minute Man*, commemorating one of the Revolutionary War's first battles, in Concord.

By the time Longman went to work in French's New York City studio, he was among the most respected and most popular sculptors in the United States. In addition to the *Minute Man*, he had modeled the *Milmore Memorial—The Angel of Death Staying the Hand of the Sculptor*, exhibited at the Chicago World's Fair (now in marble at the Metropolitan Museum of Art); *John Harvard* for Harvard University; *Ulysses S. Grant* in Philadelphia; a marble group for the U.S. Post Office and federal building in Philadelphia; *Thomas Gallaudet Memorial* in Washington, D.C.; *General George Washington* equestrian for Paris; and *Alma Mater* for Columbia University. Civic sculpture was becoming popular ornamentation for public buildings, and by 1903, Cass Gilbert asked French to create four groups representing four continents—Asia, America, Europe, and Africa—for the U.S. Custom House in New York City.

It was a felicitous time for Longman to be present in French's studio, during "one of his greatest bursts of creative intensity."[9] Working on many projects at once was the elder sculptor's way, as it would become Longman's. Between 1901 and 1904—her dedicated time in his studio—he had several works in progress, including another project with animal sculptor Edward Clark Potter, an equestrian monument of General Charles Devens for Worcester, Massachusetts; also a reworking of *Quadriga* from the Chicago World's Fair for the Minnesota State Capitol—*The Progress of the State.* French and Potter were also creating a replica of their Paris equestrian *General George Washington* to be installed in Chicago.

Assistants helped with enlarging clay models, building armatures, and lettering, as Longman did for the Boston Public Library doors. She surely worked on the commission French undertook creating the four groups for New York's Custom House.[10] French and his assistants made small-scale clay models of the allegorical pieces, then plaster maquettes for each. Alongside assistants, French, glancing back and forth at the small maquettes, built quarter-size clay versions, then half-sized models. Come early summer, the clay sculptures were shipped by rail to Chesterwood, French's summer home and studio in Stockbridge, Massachusetts. It featured rails under the removable floor so assistants could roll out massive sculptures into the daylight. There, French and his helpers refined the Custom House groups before shipping them back to New York, and eventually to the Piccirilli brothers in the Bronx, who would carve them in Tennessee marble.

In 1901 Bacon had redesigned the colonial revival farmhouse, with its porch's magnificent view of the Berkshires' Monument Mountain, into an elegant country villa befitting one of the country's premier sculptors. The Frenches resided there from May to November. It was becoming a busy country gathering place for many of Mary and Daniel's family and friends, as well as their daughter Margaret's chums.

During his two years studying in Florence, French had enjoyed music, so when no one in his immediate family took up an instrument, he invested in a Victrola and records of many musical genres. "Dan would hang out Chinese lanterns in the garden, lemon-colored ones, on slender bamboo poles,"[11] and put on music for dancing. He built a tennis court, where guests, including Longman, played tennis in interminable tournaments.

In addition to assisting French, Longman fit well into the lively ambiance at Chesterwood, and the Frenches increasingly sought her companionship. She became a regular guest at their country home, as well as in their New York City residence. Twelve years older than Margaret, Beatrice (as the Frenches, and all her friends, called her) was becoming like an older sister.

Every August for Margaret's birthday, Mary and Daniel held a gathering for the children of nearby Stockbridge. They posted an invitation in the post office, and dozens of children showed up for ice cream, photographs, and a show in the barn. It must have recalled the Eagle's Nest days for Longman, though a tamer version. One year, Daniel and his brother Will orchestrated a pageant of Mother Goose stories. Dan and his friend, writer Newton Mackintosh, performed a puppet show, with Dan pulling the strings.

A smiling Fat Lady wrapped in pink paraded about for the children, as did Margaret, as Little Bo Peep. Longman, in red cloak and peaked hat over her long black hair, rode out on a broomstick. Will French mounted paper to a wall and illustrated with colored chalk his recitation of "The Pied Piper of Hamlin." Cobbled streets, gabled houses, flying horses, the pied piper, and legions of rats produced delighted cheers.[12]

Without a studio of Longman's own, in the summer of 1902 French had workers convert a small barn into a studio for her.[13] It was across a meadow, near the "red house," where the superintendent and his family lived. It was there, while Longman was modeling a portrait of French's young cousin Louise, that she received enlightenment from the master. "Make the concaves bigger," French told her. "Write it large on the wall!"[14]

It was a watershed moment for Longman, who would report to Margaret some years later when Margaret was writing *Journey Into Fame*, a biography of her father: "My work changed from that moment, technically."[15]

Louise's hair is parted off-center and piled a bit higher on her left side. The left eye is slightly more open than her right. Concaves in her hair are

Figure 4.1 Louise. Modeled in 1902; carved in 1910. Source/Credit: The Metropolitan Museum of Art, Rogers Fund 1920.

deep. Less-deep concaves around her nose, mouth, and chin create shadows. A slight smile and the focus to the left add intriguing aspects to what might have been simply a lovely face.

The next time French came to look in on Longman at work in the barn studio, he was pleased with her improvements. "Well," he said, "it is necessary to tell you a thing only once."[16]

Probably because she had artist friends who lived in the Union Square neighborhood with its cheap rents—an area dubbed "a nursery of genius"—Longman sought her own studio space there, at 11 East 14th Street, half a block from the square and a five-minute walk to French's village studio.

The old brownstone offered generous front steps. Formerly the home of a millionaire, it had a ballroom, concert hall, drawing room, a magnificent chandelier, and an air chamber in its center. Brass-lined steps led to the upper floors. Many rooms had been converted into artist studios, and at the top of the building, four flights up steep stairs, Longman, in 1903, found Studio 17: a large space with a wide cornice above north-facing windows—for the next decade, her studio and home. Choosing to go it alone rather than share studio space with other women sculptors, she slept with a loaded gun under her pillow.[17]

Activity in the neighborhood became more interesting, if not safer, beginning in 1908, when D. W. Griffith made the ballroom at "11" into his first Biograph movie studio. In her memoir, *When Movies Were Young*, Griffith's star actress and first wife, Linda Arvidson, mentioned Longman as one of the artists with a studio in the building.[18] Longman would have been friendly with her interesting, moviemaking neighbors. ("She loved people . . .")[19]

Though she found cheap ways to relax occasionally (a roof seat on the Fifth Avenue bus to the end of the line and back; once in a while, a row on the pond in Central Park), Longman was a workaholic. "Her ambition had been so long thwarted that it broke all bounds, and was at this period the be-all and end-all of her existence."[20]

The Frenches were the center of her life, and from there her social network expanded—though not far, and always in a way that was related to her work. There are no indications that she was close friends with women, other than Mary and Margaret French, though she undoubtedly knew other women sculptors, and eventually, women patrons.

She knew soon enough that in order to function in a man's world, in a career dominated by men, she would have to labor very hard: always doing her best, never missing a deadline. Socializing would take time away from her work; marriage was out of the question. Women sculptors who married weren't doing large public sculpture, and some put even their smaller, more domestic sculpting on the back burner after their marriages.

From the first, Longman relegated her time to be with the artists and architects related to her projects, and those were men: men doing the monumental public sculptures, men designing the buildings decorated with sculpture. And so it was that, besides Daniel Chester French, her most frequent companions became architect Henry Bacon and painter Milton Bancroft.

Raised in Wilmington, North Carolina, where his father was an engineer, Henry Bacon, like French, experienced the opportunities of privilege. He showed such promise at the prestigious New York City architecture firm of McKim, Mead and White, that he won a traveling scholarship that allowed him to study in Europe, making his way through France, Italy, Greece, and Turkey. His brother Francis had worked in Assos, Turkey, as the chief draftsman for Harvard archeological expeditions, and, while there, Henry made sketches for his brother's project. It was in Assos that Henry met Laura Florence Calvert, whose father had been the British consul. Henry and Laura married in Turkey; Francis married Laura's sister. At the time Longman met Henry Bacon, he had left McKim and partnered with James Brite, who had traveled with Bacon in Europe. In 1903, the friends dissolved their partnership, and each went out on their own.

Longman wasn't only learning about sculpting from her master teacher, French; she was also learning about the collaboration of sculptor and architect. In the process, she and Bacon became friends.

Longman may have met Milton H. Bancroft, a painter, illustrator, and teacher, through French or Bacon, as they were all three friends. Or she may have met Bancroft before she met either French or Bacon, as Bancroft was a friend of both MacNeil and Konti. It might have been Bancroft who told her about the studios on Fourteenth Street, as his was down the street, at "30."

Bancroft, whose English ancestors settled in the Massachusetts Bay Colony, was born on New Year's Day, 1866. He attended the Massachusetts Normal Art School in Boston and the Pennsylvania Academy of the Fine Arts in Philadelphia, then taught art at Swarthmore College, founded by the Society of Friends. Margaret Corlies Moore, a Swarthmore student, married Bancroft at her family's farm, Norwood, in the small Quaker community of Sandy Spring, Maryland. To the displeasure of the Moore family, not only was Margaret marrying a financially struggling artist, but the couple was moving to Europe so Milton could further his studies.

He studied at the *Académie Julian* in Paris, and after three and a half years in ateliers and museums in France, he, Margaret, and their first child, John, returned to the United States. In the fall of 1898, Bancroft established a studio in New York City. Margaret and John, and later two more children, lived at Norwood, her father's home in Maryland. Milton and Margaret wrote letters to each other several times a week, as Milton struggled to make a living creating illustrations and teaching, frustrated that he had little time to paint.[21]

In the summer of 1901, Margaret's father rented a cottage for Milton and Margaret on Shelter Island, Long Island, New York, so that Milton could escape the city heat and spend time with his wife and children. Eventually establishing their own summer home on Shelter Island, Margaret and the children spent summers there, with Milton visiting a week or two at a time—as did Longman.

While Longman's relationship with French is well documented, nothing has been written of her friendship with Bacon or Bancroft, nor of Bancroft's influence on her work. Teaching boys at the Mechanical Institute of New York City, Bancroft also was teaching his eager friend Longman. "His figure studies from his *académie* years in France show that he would have had valuable insights to share about figurative art, and he probably discussed art that he saw in Europe while he studied there."[22]

In her own hand, Longman wrote in a note that it was Bancroft who taught her the most about painting, and art in general.[23]

In 1903, Longman sculpted a plaster bust of Milton Bancroft and a tinted plaster of young Margaret French. The next year Bancroft painted a pastel portrait of Longman in a bonnet sitting in the garden at Chesterwood, which French hung in the Main Hall of the residence.

Her new life, a circle—the Frenches, Bancrofts, Bacons—was forming around her. Talented and accomplished themselves, these men would not be intimidated by her achievements—a sure way to lose friends for some gifted women. Other pitfalls for women in areas perceived as men-only included needing the entrée they could provide, while maintaining one's own style and expression. Longman had her work cut out for her.

NOTES

1. Margaret Cresson French, *Journey into Fame. The Life of Daniel Chester French* (Cambridge, MA: Harvard University Press, 1947), 162.
2. Ibid.
3. Daniel Chester French (DCF) to William Merchant French, December 30, 1900, French Family Papers, Library of Congress.
4. Mrs. Daniel Chester French (Mary Adams French), *Memories of a Sculptor's Wife* (Boston and New York: Houghton Mifflin Co., 1928), 187–88.
5. Batchelder.
6. Michele H. Bogart, *Public Sculpture and the Civic Ideal in New York City 1890–1930* (Washington and London: Smithsonian Institution Press, 1997), 17.

7. Ibid., 18.
8. Ibid., 27.
9. Holzer, 214.
10. Dana Pilson, "'Write It Large on the Wall!' The sculptors Evelyn Beatrice Longman and Daniel Chester French," *Fine Art Connoisseur*, 18, no. 3 (June 2021), 105.
11. Margaret Cresson French, 239.
12. Ibid., 238.
13. DCF's Garden Notes, June or August 1902, 71: "Jack made over the little barn at the red house into a studio for Miss Longman this week."
14. Evelyn Beatrice Longman (EBL) letter to Margaret Cresson French, Chesterwood Archives; Chapin Library, Williams College, Gift of the National Trust for Historic Preservation/Chesterwood, a National Trust Historic Site, Stockbridge, Massachusetts.
15. Ibid.
16. Ibid.
17. Batchelder.
18. Linda Arvidson, *When the Movies Were Young* (New York: E.P. Dutton and Company, 1925), 5.
19. Batchelder.
20. Ibid.
21. Donna Cashdollar, curator University Museum, Indiana University of Pennsylvania, "Gilded Age to Great War: Milton Bancroft and His Art," 2016. Interview and email, July 2020.
22. Ibid.
23. Batchelder.

Chapter 5

Making It Her Way: *Victory*

Don't you worry about that; she model like hell.

—Vincent Russo

Ten years after she stood before French's *Corn Maiden* at the Columbian Exposition's White City and declared she could make that if she had the chance, Longman got the chance. The first international exposition in the United States since the Chicago Fair, the St. Louis World's Fair, celebrating the centennial of the Louisiana Purchase, aimed to show off U.S. development since 1893. Designers planned sculpture, fountains, and ornately decorated buildings just as in Chicago, but this time on a bigger campus set in a hilly landscape—out west.

Karl Theodore Bitter, chief of the Department of Sculpture, planned allegorical statuary that would meet the fair organizer's goals, "expressive of purely joyous and festive ideas, such as naturally associate themselves with an exposition designed to celebrate an event so fraught with jubilation as the extension of the sway of liberty from the Atlantic to the Pacific."[1]

Bitter planned three allegorical *Victory* statues, each atop a building, to help create that sense of jubilation. He gave the sculpture assignments to students recommended by veteran sculptors. In an undeniable vote of affirmation of her talent and skill, as well as his confidence in her ability to do the work, Daniel French, who was on the Exhibition's New York Advisory Committee for Sculpture, as well as the selection jury, recommended Longman. She was invited to submit the *Victory* that would crown the Varied Industries Building.

A classical Greek allegorical figure often shown holding a laurel crown, *Victory* was traditionally a winged female figure: a messenger of the gods sent to lead an individual to triumph.[2] In addition to considering that classical tradition, Longman must have thought about the cultural dynamic at play for the St. Louis Fair.

At the beginning of the twentieth century, there was a widespread feeling, including from President Theodore Roosevelt, that the upper classes were becoming soft. Young American men were being encouraged to do athletic training and compete, spawning an expansion of the Young Men's Christian Athletic Association. This athletic movement led to the modern Olympic Games in Europe in the late nineteenth century. The first Olympic games to be held in the United States would be at the 1904 St. Louis World's Fair.[3] (Indicative of Longman's era, women were not allowed to compete in the 1904 Olympics, except in archery.)

Longman would have been familiar with classical renditions of Nike, the Greek goddess of victory—especially the headless, winged female Nike of Somathrace, having viewed the plaster cast at the Chicago Institute of Art. All allegorical Victories were winged and female. Until Longman's.

A lithe, virile young man stands on a globe, tiptoed, his arms raised, one hand holding the classic laurel wreath, his mouth open in a triumphant shout. He has no wings. Longman's *Victory* is a real guy, ideally fit, his face animated. In his stance, there is an explosion of physical action and emotional exuberance—not a stodgy god, but a firmly grounded human, art historian Margaret Samu explained in her analysis.[4]

This would become classic Longman: doing the traditional thing, and also something fresh, unexpected; going at least a bit against the grain. Here, she used a classical idea, but changed it to reflect her time as well as the context of the figure's placement, in this case, the vitality of a modern and most human man, *sans* divinity. Risky though it might have been, it seems doubtful that she had any temptation to do the expected thing, to go thoroughly traditional on her first public piece.

Her boldness, her divergent interpretation worked. The sculpture committee (including French, MacNeil, and the preeminent American sculptor at the time, August Saint-Gaudens) approved Longman's visionary work.

To ensure the quality of the production process, Bitter invited sculptors to bring their maquettes to a workshop in Weehawken, New Jersey, where they could enlarge their sketch models into the massive sculptures that would stand atop buildings. Using pointing devices, the artists transferred their small-scale pieces into larger sculptures made of staff, a mixture of plaster and hemp fiber and coated with a waterproofing solution. From the workshop, located on a railroad line, the huge sculptures were hoisted directly onto cars and sent to St. Louis.[5] After the Fair, the sculptures would be destroyed.

Bitter was so impressed with Longman's *Victory* that, instead of installing it on the Varied Industries Building as planned, he decided to honor it with a

Figure 5.1 *Victory*, Longman's first public monumental work, for the Louisiana Purchase Exposition in St. Louis. Source/Credit: Photograph from the collection of the Loomis Chaffee Archives, Loomis Chaffee School, Windsor, Connecticut USA.

more prestigious placement: at the main intersection, atop Festival Hall, the center of the fair. The three-foot plaster model she created won a silver medal in the international competition in the Great Sculpture Court of the Palace of Fine Arts. The chief of the Department of Art said it was "one of the most beautiful pieces of sculpture in the American exhibit."[6] This, her first solo public work, would become her most reproduced.

Samu explained the impact of Longman's *Victory* at the time of the Fair:

> Longman's work . . . fused a traditional representation of the human form with turn-of-the-century artistic tastes for dynamic movement and elongated figures. This fusion made it appealing to both hard-line classicists and those with more progressive tastes. In addition, it spoke to a general audience that knew little of artistic traditions. Its exuberant athletic form represented a popular image of American masculinity at the turn of the century, and in doing so, it expressed the Exposition's central message of "triumphant progress." An analysis of the work reveals how Longman was able to bring together ideas from these disparate artistic and popular sources to create a sculpture that had meaning to a wide audience.[7]

Longman's intentional absence of wings brought *Victory* down to earth, wrote Samu. He is not bringing victory to someone else, as the gods did, but is seizing it for himself. "Longman's decision to depict a personal experience rather than an abstract idea shows her interest in appealing directly to the viewer's emotion. . . . By expanding the tradition of academic allegorical figures, Longman created a *Victory* that spoke to viewers of her day."

Longman created "an embodiment of a universal emotion," wrote Samu.[8]

There seems to have been little public discussion of her breaking with tradition and portraying a male figure, although one critic, who called her an insurgent, suggested her decision was to honor male victories. That seems doubtful.

Samu wrote that Longman was certainly calling into question conventional gender roles, in her very subtle—distract-them-with-beauty—Longman sort of way. Historically, sculptures were done by men who saw men as "real and concrete, while they perceived women as ideal and abstract."[9]

To those who assumed that because she was a woman and unknown, some other (male) sculptor helped her, Vincent Russo, Daniel French's plaster caster and a lithe Italian who probably sat for Longman's *Victory*, said, "Don't you worry about that; she model like hell."[10] From the start, Longman didn't spend much time focused on insults or patronizing comments or other dynamics around the woman thing: she just did the work.

Over time, her iconic bronze *Victory* was recast, in smaller scale, more than thirty times. A four-foot bronze was installed at the Art Institute of Chicago; another in the reception room at the Union Club in Chicago. Replicas in museums include the Metropolitan Museum of Art, Brookgreen Gardens, the St. Louis Museum of Art. One became the trophy for the U.S. Navy's North Atlantic fleet; another, a memorial to a soldier at the University of Virginia.

Longman's sister Louise attended a reception at the Art Institute of Chicago, where *Victory* was exhibited, and reported to Longman:

> [I] went up and spoke to Mr. Taft and asked him where I could find your work. His reply was "Wherever you see a crowd around a piece of sculpture."
>
> . . . In the centre of one . . . was "Victory" surrounded by palms, and facing it on either side were the beautiful busts of the French girls "Margaret" and "Louise." That was all there was in that room in sculpture, except a tiny figure of Ruskin. . . .
>
> You were decidedly the whole thing in sculpture. In the first room we entered was the fine strong bust of Mr. Bancroft . . . introduced me to Mr. French [Will] and I expressed my appreciation of that which the Art Institute did for you. But he would hardly listen to that, said you were an honor to the Institute. I also expressed my gratitude to Mr. Taft for what he did for you, but he would not hear anything of the kind either. The substance of what he said was that your work there was entirely . . . beyond anything which he could have taught you.[11]

She had daringly created a vibrant, voluptuous, very human nymph playfully splashing in the Chicago fountain. And she didn't seem to hesitate to take a risk in her own first public monument: going against the grain to create a wingless male *Victory*. Perhaps that early experience freed her—or perhaps her confident, brazen nymph was, allegorically, a self-portrait of a risk-taking attitude gained in a chaotic childhood. In either case, Evelyn Longman summoned her I-can-do-that aplomb for her next audacious attempt at creating a monumental work.

NOTES

1. Karl Theodore Bitter, "Sculpture for the St. Louis World's Fair," *Brush and Pencil* 13.3 (December 1903), 166.
2. Samu, 27.
3. Ibid., 31.
4. Ibid., 25.
5. Ibid., 23.
6. Ibid., 34.
7. Ibid., 25.
8. Ibid., 30.
9. Ibid., 29.
10. Batchelder.
11. Louise Longman Tewksbury to EBL, October 28, 1905, Loomis Chaffee.

Chapter 6

Woman Gets the Prize

I am pleased, of course, but I care more for my art than I do for the renown.

—Evelyn Beatrice Longman

Into Longman's life now entered the first from the world of wealthy men who commissioned monumental art: Robert Means Thompson. After his graduation from the U.S. Naval Academy in 1868 and stints on two ships, Thompson resigned his commission in 1871 and entered Harvard Law School, from which he was graduated in 1874 (the year Longman was born). Investigating legal titles of Canadian mining firms led the gregarious Thompson to a managerial position and then the presidency of a mining company, where he made his fortune.

Devoted to his alma mater, Thompson never missed a June graduation week in fifty-five years. In 1900, as a member of the Academy's Board of Builders, he encouraged a review of the institution's physical campus, and enlisted *Beaux Arts* architect Ernest Flagg to design a master plan for the complete rebuilding of the school, including, at the center of campus, a new chapel. Domed, with a crypt for the bones of John Paul Jones, the chapel's bronze doors, reminiscent of Ghiberti's Italian Renaissance bas-reliefs at Florence's baptistry, would open into a stained glass–windowed, Greek-cross sanctuary. The doors would be twenty-one feet high and ten feet wide. Midshipmen would know they'd been to chapel.

When Flagg's four-hundred-thousand-dollar budget for the chapel proved inadequate, and resulting cuts included scrapping plans for the enormous doors, Thompson donated the funds for them, with the stipulation that they would be dedicated to his 1868 graduating class. To find a sculptor,

Thompson enlisted the aid of the National Sculpture Society. The Society generally disapproved of competitions because competing artists put in so much time and money making the required models without any compensation unless they won. The Society joined with Thompson to ensure fairness and professionalism, and in late 1905, they sent a call to artists to submit designs for the bronze doors.

The prize was fifteen thousand dollars. As was the custom, from that amount the artist would be responsible for the cost of executing and erecting the doors. Estimates were that the sculptor would clear five to six thousand dollars, a whopping amount for an artist at the time (close to two hundred thousand in today's dollars).

It was a blind competition—the only way Longman or any other woman had a chance at winning a commission. The artists identified their unsigned work by a cipher; their name and address sealed in an envelope with the emblem on the outside. Even if Longman's model was chosen, she wasn't guaranteed the commission. Sometimes women who won blind competitions were not allowed to create the sculpture once it was discovered the winner was not a man.[1]

The jury was formed of representatives of both the Naval Academy and the Sculpture Society: Ernest Flagg; *Beaux Arts* architect Ernest Chambers; sculptor Charles Grafly; and Robert Thompson—though he asked Colonel G. M. Colocoresses to vote in his stead. Colocoresses was a Naval Academy alumnus who taught drawing at the Academy and designed a monument to a naval officer buried in the Academy cemetery. Chairing the committee: Daniel Chester French.

By this time Longman had finished her apprenticeship with French. To mark the occasion, someone, perhaps Margaret or her father, snapped a memorable photograph of Longman waving a handkerchief farewell—Longman, walking away, head tilted and looking back, with a mischievous smile, as if she would show up again any second. The photo marked a poignant moment—not an end, but a shift in her situation. She was no longer French's assistant; she was becoming a colleague. Their relationship and circle of friends were at the heart of Longman's personal and professional life. In the winter months, when the Frenches were in New York City, Longman often went round to their home, frequently joining other dinner guests, such as stage actress Mary Lawton. Will French was at table when he was in town, as was Longman's oldest brother, Claude, from Chicago.

Guests sometimes took to card games after dinner, and family birthdays were celebrated with special suppers and guests. Margaret often walked over to visit Longman in her apartment for long talks or walks.[2] With Margaret, Mary, and/or Daniel French, she attended art openings and plays. Once when Dan French was sitting for Milton Bancroft, Longman and the Frenches went along to Bancroft's studio. There were days when they took long walks to Bronx Park.

Longman wrote to French in February 1904, while he and Mary were vacationing in Mexico City. In his response, French began with a slight flirtation, as was often his way, and in the letter referred to Longman's *Victory*, which was in St. Louis for the Exposition.

> Dear Longman!!!
>
> There can certainly be no impropriety in this at so long range and you certainly are "a dear" to send me such a long delightful letter as the one I received this morning. It not only told me what I wanted to know, but your gentle art of flattery as practiced in it has made me feel in a state of elation all day. . . .
>
> I can't tell you how much I appreciate the kind things you say about the "Alma Mater" and the Carnegie figure. I have really felt more troubled and disappointed over the failure of the gold statue than I have confessed, but I think it likely that your fine intuitive sense may have told you what I thought I was keeping to myself. It was very sweet of you to reassure me,—and I needed it. Yes, we must do something to the gold in the spring. You very modestly say nothing about your own statue at the Exhibition. I am sure that looks all right compared with anything there.
>
> Your letter sounds very gay indeed. I am glad you are having such a good time. . . .
>
> Affectionately,
> DANIEL C. FRENCH[3]

The developing Longman-French colleagueship would be rare, and it presented a thorny situation, as far as competitions were concerned. The world of sculptors was a small sphere: They all knew each other—notable ones encouraged younger, talented ones and often sat on juries in which younger ones competed. A year earlier, French had written to Saint-Gaudens, on the issue of bias: "as Miss Longman [is] an assistant of mine, [I] shall probably be accused of favoritism. In any case, somehow the enemy overlooks the fact that we are interested in these people because of their extraordinary talent."[4]

Though French knew that Longman was preparing a model for the U.S. Naval Academy chapel doors competition, there is no doubt that they both wanted her to compete in the competition on her own merit. As they visited each other's studios regularly, it became standard practice when she was working on a piece for a commission for which he was a judge, that she kept her work covered when he came to call, including during the first three months of 1906, when she worked on the model for the chapel doors.

Up to this time, Longman had created a few busts, *Victory*, and a bas-relief for the Storey Memorial at the cemetery in Lowell, Massachusetts. Too busy to take the commission himself, French recommended Longman, who was working on a larger-than-life-sized bas-relief angel for Louisa Maria Wells's cemetery monument, also in Lowell.

Wells had been one of many New England young women approached by "recruiting teams" to work in Lowell's textile mills. She came from Vermont, at nineteen, in 1836, to work in the carding room for the Lawrence Manufacturing Company. After a year, she left, perhaps returning to her Vermont home. In 1866, she came again to the Lowell area and must have brought her mother with her. Nancy L. Wells died in 1872 at the age of eighty-two. Louisa purchased a lot at the Lowell cemetery where her mother was buried.

The quiet cemetery provided a relief from the relentless rhythm of the deafening machines at the mills, and the women who worked there often spent their days off among its trees. Ten years after her mother died, Louisa, who had never married, died at the age of sixty-eight, "from a disease of the heart."[5] In her will she requested that after her debts were paid and a few legacies given, she wanted the rest, which turned out to be about eight thousand dollars, used to pay for a monument to be built on the Wellses' lot, at the edge of the cemetery.

Her cousins objected to the provisions of Louisa's will. Litigation took twenty years and was finally settled in Louisa's favor by the Massachusetts Supreme Court. All those years her savings grew, and after a local judge executed the provisions of Louisa's will as she had directed, there were "a number of thousands of dollars" left with which to build a monument.[6]

In *Mill Girl*, Longman portrayed Louisa sitting, eyes closed, left hand holding her weary head; contented smile, seemingly glad for the rest; weaving spindle ready to drop from her right hand; thread broken in her lap. A draped angel, head wreathed in poppies, eyes lowered and focused on Louisa, holds the wisp of a kind and knowing expression; wide wings enfold them both; her right hand ready to touch Louisa's shoulder and grant her eternal rest. The inscription: "Out of the fiber of her daily tasks, she wove the fabric of a useful life."

Though *Mill Girl* was Longman's largest bas-relief to that point, it was not near the size, style, or complexity of the proposed Naval Academy chapel doors. And though she had worked on the lettering for French's Boston Public Library doors, this project was far from anything she'd done herself.

The model she created for the Naval Academy chapel doors breathed allegory; every inch uttered symbolism. In her words:

> The two main groups in these doors represent respectively "Peace" and "War."
>
> In the former is seen a figure symbolizing "Science"—an old man seated in an attitude of deep thought in the act of pointing out to two youthful students

the explanation to some difficult problem. The students wear the costume of the Training-School. One stands, holding a pencil in one hand, while the other supports the chart or parchment which is the subject of attention. The other student sits upon a pile of books, on which are inscribed the names of some of the branches of study taught in the Naval Academy. In one hand he holds a small model of a man-of-war; under the other is seen a draughtsman's triangle. In the background appear ships and a light-house.

In the group called "War" the principal figure represents "Patriotism." A female figure has been used as being symbolic of the "home," the protection of which is the great underlying reason for the existence of the Navy. Under the voluminous draperies appears a coat of armor. One clenched hand rests upon a cannon; the other points off to the distance where rise the masts of ships, showing that the destination of the marching figures in the background, wearing the uniform of the naval cadet, is the sea. One of these turns for a moment and waves his cap in farewell. In response to the call of Patriotism, a youth strides to her side ready to follow as she is directing him to do. Near the cannon appears a pile of cannon-balls.

In the upper panels of the doors are festoons supported by shells. These are of oak leaves in the panel over "War," and of olive or laurel leaves in that over "Peace." In the lower panels winged children support wreaths (of oak leaves on one side and olive or laurel on the other) in which appear names of men famous in our naval history. Between the three panels will appear on either side inscriptions suitable to the respective motifs.

The dedicatory inscription to the Class of 1868 will appear on the transom, with a design of dolphins and trident at either end.

The group above the transom represents "Fame." Two laurel-crowned figures sit upon either side of an altar-like pedestal bearing a shield with inscription to John Paul Jones, and surmounted by a tripod; the fire symbolizing enduring fame. One figure leans forward and points to the inscription on the shield, while the other is on the point of writing upon the stone tablet she holds. On either side stand attendant winged boys bearing the anchor and sword, symbols of naval warfare.

For the moldings, conventionalized rope and sea-shells have been used.[7]

Entries were due to the National Sculpture Society on West 57th Street, by March 19, 1906. The jury met at the Society's rooms and viewed thirty-three models, marking their first round of votes using the cipher of the artist whose model they judged to be the best. When the votes were counted, the first ballot was unanimous. The judges opened the envelope containing the cipher of the winner. It was Evelyn Beatrice Longman. A woman.

One judge wanted to change his selection. Though Colocoresses voted in his stead, Thompson was present in the room and insisted that they accept Longman's submission.[8] When members of the Superintendent's Committee in charge of the building project were told who had been selected, they were "amazed to find that the winner of the unanimous verdict was a nineteen-year-old girl!" It was impossible, they said, that such an important order be given to a young and inexperienced girl. Thompson defended the jury's decision and Longman's submission: having fulfilled every requirement for the competition, she was entitled to acceptance.[9]

"Nineteen-year-old" Longman was actually thirty-one—and the only woman to compete. Of the thirty-two men, some were well-known sculptors. The jury awarded small cash prizes to the sculptors whose designs came in second, third, and fourth.

Longman made headlines:

"Woman Vanquishes Men in Race for Coveted Sculptor's Prize"

"An American Woman Sculptor Wins Over Thirty-Two Men"

"Woman Gets the Prize"

"Woman Sculptor Wins. Triumphs Over Men"

The *New York Times* stacked headlines for April 7: "Woman Sculptor Modest. Winner of Contest for Design for Bronze Doors for Naval Academy Chapel Takes Her Victory Quietly. Her Work Remarkable for Its Atmosphere, Suggesting War and the Sea Without Actually Showing Them."[10]

The lead in that story: "From out of the West has come a slender, pretty little woman whose chief characteristic is her extreme modesty, who has taken away from sculptors of this city, and in fact, of the world, one of the most coveted awards made in the art world this year."

Daniel French was quoted in the *New York Tribune*:

> The votes of all five jurors were cast for Miss Longman's model on the first ballot, but it was not known to any of us until after the award was made who the winner was. I did not even recognize Miss Longman's work myself, though I am very familiar with it.
>
> I consider Miss Longman to be one of the most promising of our younger sculptors.[11]

In another newspaper article, French was quoted as saying: "Miss Longman's achievement in winning this competition has been equaled by few, if any, sculptor of her sex in this country. Her success did not surprise those who are familiar with her previous work, for in several instances she has given evidence of great ability."[12]

That newspaper reporter emphasized the historical import of the moment: "The award of this prize to a woman is said to be an unprecedented event in the artistic history of the country."

Longman was not a suffragette, and she never entered the public debate about women's right to vote. But the writer in an article from Brooklyn's *Standard Union*, evidently unaware of the men's behind-the-scenes discussions, made the argument that was also Longman's way: Show them that women can do what men do.

> Women's rights women will find a lesson in the award, after severe competition, of the designing of the bronze doors for the chapel of the U.S. Naval Academy to Miss Evelyn Beatrice Longman. The jury of award, presided over by Daniel C. French, was composed exclusively of men, and the other sculptors in competition were all men. Yet the men gave a unanimous decision that the woman's design was the best shown. The inference is that in this instance, at least, there was no attempt to override the rights of a woman artist merely because she was a woman. And there is a lesson of equal value for the opponents of those who insist on the quality of the sexes. They have been maintaining that woman can copy, but cannot create, and a jury of men, of unquestionable authority in art matters, negates this proposition.[13]

Having won the opportunity from an all-male jury to build the doors for the Ernest Flagg–designed chapel at an all-male institution, Longman was quoted in an unidentified Detroit newspaper: "I am pleased, of course, but I care more for my art than I do for the renown. . . . I am glad the jury of award liked them."[14]

On the wave of this success, it was that spring that Olivet College awarded Longman an honorary master of arts degree.

To appease the building committee at the Naval Academy, Thompson offered to advance Longman the money to travel to Europe for a year to learn more about creating the doors. She went almost immediately and stayed only four months. Her brother Claude, aware of the gravity of his little sister's accomplishment, and to mark the occasion, sent photographs and memories in an April 16 letter she received aboard ship. Brimming with affection for his sister, he wrote: "I don't care to see New York again till you return. . . . Perhaps I may be there on your home coming to be the first to pull you back ashore and the first to welcome you home. That would be romantic if I were not your brother, and is kind of any way."[15]

She was aboard ship, on her way home, when Daniel French wrote to her on August 18:

> Dear Evelyn Beatrice,
>
> Your postal cards have enabled us to follow you in your wanderings and to imagine the delight with which you have viewed the wonders of nature and art that are stowed up and down the fair land of Italy. . . . I am so glad it has impressed you so much—and you really did take my advice! How I wish I might have been with you when you first went to the Medici Chapel! I am curious to

> see what effect all of this is going to have on you when you get home. Do you suppose it is going to make you despise, my "Law," for instance!

French looked after Longman's studio while she was away, and as did Claude, he awaited eagerly her return.

> I was in New York week before last and, among other things, I called on Mr. G. I could see through your transom that there was lots of light in your studio. . . . I have failed to find a suitable place for myself . . . and shall probably occupy "125" as usual this next winter. I guess you and I will have to buy some real estate and build to suit ourselves another year.
>
> I have forgotten when you are coming home—I mean exactly—but you are to come up and report to us in full as soon after that happy event as possible. As Margaret would say, I am wild to hear all about it. . . .
>
> Affectionately yours,
> Daniel C. French[16]

Post-Italy, Longman made some changes in her design. "Science" holds up parchment, opening the view of his chest and beard. She relaxed the drapery over his chest; he seems a little younger, more engaged with one of the students. One of the two boys standing next to the wise teacher has moved closer and changed positions and holds out the model of a man-of-war, while the other is now in the background.

The action in the "War" panel did not change. Here is insurgent Longman again: using a woman, in armor, to depict war—poignant and agonizing, the call to leave home to protect home. As one reporter wrote, "There is the tale of a thousand battles in the figure of the woman who sends forth her sons to war. The sense of life and action is seldom found in sculptured doors as it is in these."[17]

Gone are the names of historic naval heroes and, instead, those panels hold door pulls, making that space more handsome and less cluttered. Though she has layered symbols liberally, including a flaming urn, tridents, spears, and serpents, the highly stylized elements create a cleaner look.

The most dramatic change is the space above the transom. The two cherubs are gone, and the two women are larger now and bare-breasted. They point not to an urn of John Paul Jones's remains (perhaps Longman got word that it would be a few years before Jones's sarcophagus would be installed), but to an altar. The front is inscribed, in Latin, at Thompson's request (and approved by the Navy Department), "Not for self but for country." Sitting atop it, wings spread wide, is a magnificent eagle.

The panels all work together for the overall sense of action: the study of war, a patriotism that speaks to love of country, even to the point of sacrifice to protect it. And the clear message—with tridents, dolphins, shells, and anchors on the hems of robes of both Science and Patriotism; ships in low relief in the background; and the nautical rope framing and connecting every panel—is that these doors celebrate the work of the Navy.

Longman would be both celebrated and criticized for her abundance of symbolic ornamentation. It was a defining characteristic of her work. There's such a rich story to tell: How do you do that in sculpture? For Longman: You get the image and character of the person exactly right; you choose meaningful symbols and the best possible words.

In 1908, James Spencer Dickerson wrote for *World Today* magazine:

> Whoever sees the design which Miss Longman has produced for Annapolis cannot but be impressed with its dignity, on the side of sentiment and relation to its environment; and its beauty of line and form, its admirable balance of composition, its sane adaptation of sculptural means to aesthetic ends, on the side of artistic accomplishment.[18]

Margaret Samu wrote that Longman's "intelligent adaptation" of early models for her design of the Naval Academy chapel doors "shows her belief in artistic tradition as well as her sense of innovation. By drawing on the works of . . . acknowledged masters, Longman boldly placed herself in the lineage of Michelangelo, Ghiberti and Filarete."[19]

As Longman took herself to be a serious professional, Samu wrote, so would the world.

Longman sent the completed full-scale models of her chapel doors to the Gorham bronze works in the spring of 1908. Fittingly, after such a massive accomplishment, she celebrated by hosting an afternoon reception in her studio/apartment. Mary French poured tea.[20]

A year later, Longman and Dan French traveled to Providence to see the bronze doors. Afterward, French wrote to Ernest Flagg: "She has done even better than I expected with all my confidence in her ability; in fact, I know of no one else in the country who could have done this work better, if indeed as well."[21]

Also in the spring, Longman and Margaret French boarded Robert Means Thompson's houseboat in Florida. There, Longman modeled a portrait of him. It was exhibited at the Naval Academy during commencement week when the doors were dedicated. To transport guests to the Naval Academy for his presentation of the chapel doors, Thompson ordered two private trains, one from New York and one from Washington, outfitted with sleeping and restaurant cars. Longman was invited onto the train from New York, and she again asked Margaret to accompany her.[22]

There was a full day of celebration on Wednesday, June 2, 1909, at the Academy, beginning with graduation ceremonies in the morning. Guests arrived in be-hatted finery; cadets and officers were in dress uniforms, some in white. Members of the Academy class of 1868 were present for the festivities.

Midafternoon, a gigantic U.S. flag rigged with pulleys hung from Doric column to Doric column across the entrance to the chapel, which was set high with a view across the center of campus down to the Severn River. In an historic photograph taken that day, Longman stood between gray-mustached, waist-coated Thompson and bow-tied, vested architect Ernest Flagg, both with hats in hand; Flagg with a hand on his hip. Longman wore a flower-covered hat with ribbons in the back and under the chin; an empire-waist, floor-length dress with embroidered vining flowers; and above-the-elbow white gloves. Covered completely on what must have been a warm, sultry June afternoon, she looked the epitome of elegance and competence. Her head tilted slightly, she cast a modest smile.

At 4:30 p.m., the brigade of midshipmen lined up in front of the chapel with the Naval Academy band behind them. Thompson made a presentation speech. Superintendent Badger accepted the doors in the name of the Academy. Thompson's grandson, seven-year-old Robert Thompson Pell, in white Navy outfit, pulled the cord that lowered the flag as the Academy band played "My Country 'Tis of Thee." Spectators cheered. After the unveiling, members of the class of 1868 were the first to enter the doors into the chapel.

Longman's bust of Thompson is housed in an exhibit case in the lobby of the fieldhouse, along with a trophy given in his honor. The Academy named the stadium after him. He was the first president of the American Olympic Association and chair of the U.S. Committee at the games in Stockholm in 1912, and Paris in 1924.

Margaret Samu put Longman's chapel doors in context:

> The impact of the Naval Academy commission on Longman's career cannot be underestimated. In the sculpture world, it took her from being a talented studio assistant to a full professional in her own right. It proved that creating a significant large-scale sculpture was not just a fluke for her at the World's Fair, but a consistent and attainable goal—one on which she could found her career. Finally, it gained her the respect of the male sculptural establishment by winning a competition against a group of men, judged by men, for a male institution, and by earning a significant sum of money, she established herself as a prominent public sculptor according to the standards by which male sculptors measured their own success.[23]

For years, tour guides at the Naval Academy maintained the myth that the huge, intricate doors were created by a nineteen-year-old girl. Eventually the Naval Academy corrected her age.

Figure 6.1 Naval Academy chapel doors. Source/Credit: Photograph from the collection of the Loomis Chaffee Archives, Loomis Chaffee School, Windsor, Connecticut USA.

As Longman earlier had sailed for Europe to study the masters' works, French wrote to her:

> June 17 1906
> Glendale, Mass
> Dear Evelyn B.
> This is just to bid you godspeed and to wish you the best time you ever had in your life. And I believe you are going to have it. To be launched in Italy with as thorough a preparation for all its wonders of art as you have, assures you're enjoying it to the utmost. Would that I could be with you to enjoy your enthusiasm which I can see in imagination bubbling up and running over in smiles and tears at every corner you turn.
>
> I believe you are just the right stage to make the most of it. I was so young—not in years, but in experience—when I first went to Italy that most of it was an unknown language to me, but you will absorb art at every pore and I envy you the joy you will take in the process. And you have earned the right to your enjoyment. You have been the "industrious apprentice," sure enough and you merit all you have won of honor and fortune and happiness and as much more as can be showered upon you.
>
> But don't become so enamored of foreign lands—or even of a foreign man!—that you won't want to come home. In the first place I don't believe it would be good for your art and in the second place it would be well nigh fatal to mine! The fact is that I have come to lean on you so hard, to trust your judgment about my work so much and, more than all, your high ideals and aspirations and your buoyant enthusiasm are such an inspiration to me that I—well!—that I hope some other fellow will not deprive me of them. Moreover, you know, you are very dear to me just as a fellow mortal and my admiration for your brave, little self equals my respect for your ability as an artist. (Don't you wish you knew what those blank spaces stood for?) So please come back, content to stay a few years, at least, in New York and help me, as I will try to help you, up to the top of Parnassus.
>
> Do write me, if only a postal, from time to time, and let me feel that I am in touch with you on your triumphal progress.
>
> Goodbye and God bless you
> With sincere affection
> Dan. C. French[24]

This letter, Longman read and reread the rest of her life, hand-writing a note on it to Margaret French Cresson years later: "Perhaps you can imagine what it meant to me, a beginner and comparative nobody, to have a man of Mr. French's character and high standing write so to me. Then, all through the years since, it was and is an inspiration to me."

French's shadow evidently was not a concern for self-assured Longman. She obviously deeply appreciated his generosity toward her and her career, learned from him, and, in that world dominated by men, needed him. But increasingly it was apparent as well, that he needed her. Staying true to herself, following her own lead, she had found exactly the right place: she had been woven into a small circle of friends and colleagues who provided support professionally and personally; friends, colleagues, who, more and more, respected and relied on her as well, professionally and personally.

A newspaper reporter would one day describe Longman as "one of the interesting personalities in the art world, or among the artists, although little of the personal finds its way into print concerning her because she devotes herself steadfastly to her art, confines herself to restricted circles of friends who do not balk at art's first place."[25]

Embraced by French, with his family and friends, this close-knit circle had become her home—a safe, loving, small community of artists and art-loving friends who supported her and wished to see her continue "up to the top of Parnassus."

NOTES

1. Samu, 38.
2. Margaret French, childhood diary, 1905–1909, Chesterwood Archives; Chapin Library, Williams College.
3. DCF to EBL, February 23, 1904, Loomis Chaffee.
4. DCF to Augustus Saint-Gaudens, July 6, 1904, Chesterwood Archives; Chapin Library, Williams College.
5. Harry C. Dinmore and Lewis Karabatsos, "Louisa M. Wells. The story of her monument in the Lowell Cemetery," Lowell Cemetery, 1978.
6. Ibid.
7. *The American Architect and Building News*, Vol. LXXXIX, No. 1582, Saturday, April 21, 1906, 138.
8. Secretary's Notes, "II," 83, U.S. Naval Academy Nimitz Library, Special Collections, l.
9. Ibid.
10. "Woman Sculptor Modest," The *Times* Special Service, Saturday, April 7, 1906, U.S. Naval Academy Museum, Annapolis, MD.
11. "Woman Sculptor Wins," *New York Tribune*, March 29, 1906, Longman file, U.S. Naval Academy Museum, Annapolis, MD.
12. "Woman Gets the Prize," Unidentified Detroit newspaper clipping, U.S. Naval Academy Nimitz Library, 1.
13. *Standard Union*, Brooklyn, NY, March 29, 1906, U.S. Naval Academy Museum, Annapolis, MD.

14. "Woman Sculptor Modest," unidentified, undated Detroit newspaper, Loomis Chaffee.

15. Claude Longman to EBL, April 16, 1906, Loomis Chaffee.

16. DCF letter to EBL, August 18, 1906, Loomis Chaffee.

17. "An American Woman Sculptor Wins Over Thirty-Two Men" unidentified Detroit newspaper, Longman scrapbook, Loomis Chaffee.

18. James Spencer Dickerson, "A Western Girl Who Has Become a National Figure in Sculpture," *World Today*, Volume 14, January–June 1908, 530.

19. Samu, 45.

20. DCF letter to Harriette French Hollis, April 21, 1908, Chesterwood Archives.

21. DCF letter to Ernest Flagg, May 3, 1909, Loomis Chaffee.

22. Margaret French, childhood diary, June 1 and 2, 1909, Chesterwood Archives; Chapin Library, Williams College.

23. Samu, 50.

24. DCF to EBL, June 17, 1906, Loomis Chaffee.

25. "Art Gossip," *Sun*, December 24, 1911, 32.

Chapter 7

The Husbands

I am a better man through you—It's a great gift you have—the one of making such steadfast friends.

—Henry Bacon

On Christmas mornings, Longman packed a bag containing her evening clothes and, with great enthusiasm, hastened to 125 West 11th before breakfast. She spent the day in the French studio lending a hand as Daniel and Margaret decorated with extravagant flair. They set a gilded statue in the center of a round tabletop and circled it with a huge wreath of gold-laced fruit and magnolia leaves. French had the table made just for these gatherings; it would seat twenty.[1] Henry Bacon had painted the place cards.[2]

Mary French supervised the festive food preparation. The much-anticipated culmination of the day followed dessert, which was *dolci* from the Piccirillis, an immigrant Italian family of stonecutters (and fine cooks).[3] Then, with champagne in hand, the toasting and roasting began. Carefully written jokes, rhymes, and toasts inspired laughter and lively banter. Daniel French went all out, picking up gifts from the five-and-dime related to the verses for the people he toasted.[4]

He received friendly roasting as well. One year *Life* magazine founder John Ames Mitchell, also a *Beaux Arts*–trained architect, was at table and offered a verse suggesting a gold statue of French for Central Park. The following year, Henry Bacon countered:

Last year we all heard of a statue of gold
The gold to be solid—the figure quite nude
To be placed at the entrance of Central Park West
Without trousers or vest—showing French at his best.

Now that was the story—so don't think me rude
I'm repeating exactly only what we were told.
Now I would suggest that this laudable plan
Though all must approve—can't be carried out
For take all the gold ever mined in the earth
Timed from Diplodocus' birth—there would still be a dearth
Of this metal, I'm sure, we all have no doubt
To fitly portray this remarkable man.[5]

Longman found Bacon's rhyme "particularly funny from such a source about such a man!"[6]

She did not escape the roasting/toasting. Some rhymes were quite tame, including this one, probably from Marguerite Bush, the wife of Daniel French's relative and financial advisor Robert M. Bush.

Ere since the world first began,
Would you believe a Long man
With a face like a dream,
Was a sculptress supreme,
And second only to Dan?[7]

Not so tame, from Peggy French:

When Beatty was in Paris
She as Parisians did.
She parley voused
She trouble brewed
And lifted off the lid.
But when she strikes Manhattan
She hits a different pace
To outward view
She's good way through
But just observe her face.[8]

Maybe it was Daniel French who offered this one, with a five-and-dime gift:

Perhaps Helen of Troy used this ancient whorl
Which we now present to a talented girl
Who models in clay and in plastolene——
If such is the case it is twice owned by beauty
And we deem it a pleasure and also a duty
To say we are glad you're the one we've seen.

More pointed were verses about her relationships with friends Daniel French, Henry Bacon, Milton Bancroft—called her "husbands," because they all had wives. Margaret delivered these:

> To Evelyn.
> Beatty has husbands by the score
> Architects, painters, artists all
> Other girls' husbands to be sure
> But hers to come at her beck and call.
> Art to the artless—Here's to you? {"Here's to you" is scratched out.} It is true.
> We spell it heartless, dear, for you.

And:

> Beatrice—
> In this little birch canoe,
> It is surely built for two.
> Yet Beatty, she will paddle it alone—
> They all worship at her shrine,
> Architects and painters, fine.
> But our Beatty of these fellows will have none.

Daniel also wrote of her "ganders."

> Sweet Evelyn had a flock of geese
> —-Or ganders,—all into
> And everywhere that Evelyn went
> The ganders went also.
> They follow you too often dear
> These geese in human shape
> For if their mates "catch on," you'll see
> Sweet Evelyn wearing crepe.

Years later, Longman wrote a note at the bottom of this one: "Read at one of the Xmas parties which included some of the 'ganders.'"[9]

If they knew of their husbands' designations, the ganders' wives had varying responses, but remained friends with her. Mary French, unperturbed by French's flirtations with younger women, accustomed to models in his studio, and hearing the Christmas toasts, was a steady presence for Longman.

It's unknown whether Margaret Bancroft knew her husband was one of Longman's. Troubled by Milton's proximity to Longman in the city, Margaret continued to invite Longman to their home on Long Island and to her family farm in Maryland. Some years later, Milton's kindness toward Longman at the expense of attention to his wife would cause a breach in their marriage, which healed, over time.

Laura Bacon, who often traveled to Turkey to visit relatives, sometimes included her good wishes in Henry's letters to Longman. It seems impossible that she wouldn't have had some knowledge of Bacon's extensive travels with the young woman sculptor, but there evidently was not complete transparency. Daniel Chester French seemed to encourage the Longman-Bacon relationship, however it was defined. In a postcard during a voyage to Panama in February 1913, French wrote to Longman that he wished she "and Henry" had been with him and Mary. Earlier, when Longman was traveling in Europe, Daniel French wrote from Chesterwood: "My very dear Evelyn B. Bacon . . . has been up here several times but Mrs. Bacon is expected day after tomorrow and that will be the end of his freedom. Make a note of this!"[10]

It was unusual, if not scandalous, for a single woman to travel alone with a man, yet there's no indication that Longman's reputation suffered. Perhaps it was their age differences—Bancroft was seven years older; Bacon, eight; French, nearly twenty-five. Perhaps it was her charm and perceived youthfulness or maybe the fact that they were working colleagues.

One wonders if Bacon and Longman, who called each other cousin—"Cousin Hal," "Cousin Trix"—were convincing as relatives. Longman's brother Claude also referred to Bacon as "Cousin Hal," and Bacon often accompanied Longman to Longman family swimming and boating gatherings during late summers at Claude's cottage in Lakeside, Michigan.

As a gift to Henry, Longman modeled a portrait of Laura in 1909, inscribing the dedication to her friend Henry Bacon on the back of the marble neck.[11]

Despite his initial hesitancy to employ a woman, French's letters to Longman show he had grown accustomed to, seemingly reliant on, her presence and her opinion of his work.

> September 2 1907
> Glendale, Mass.
> Dear Evelyn B.
> You <u>are</u> a dear,—and a jewel and a treasure and everything that's nice!
> . . . Yes indeed, we will have you in October if you will come. I have lots of things to show you and I want your criticism on my summer's work. . . .
> I have engaged Miss Anderson for this month, but if you should need her, there is no reason why she should not go down for a week or ten days any time, to pose for you. I am glad to hear that you have found the models you wanted.
> Affectionately and gratefully,
> Dan. C. French[12]

October Third 1907
Glendale, Mass.
Dear Longman,
The faithful John brought the package, up from the station this noon and Margaret and I opened it in the studio with much merriment and applause. We were properly impressed by the inscription which shall be followed rigidly. Thank you very much. Why is E.B. Longman like ginger? Because she is smart and sweet!!!

. . . I miss you constantly and need you, if not every hour, at least a good many of them. In spite of my impatience to have you here again, I have decided, if it is equally convenient to you, that I would rather have you come somewhat later than the fourteenth. I want to get the Palmer relief farther along and, what do you think, I was so disgusted with the head in the Melvin Memorial when I saw it in plaster, that I am making another in clay and I want to have this to show you too.

I have to be in New York on the 21st to attend a Metropolitan Museum meeting. Perhaps you could return with me on the 22nd?

It is needless to say how much I enjoyed your visit. I made no secret of my enjoyment.

Affectionately
Daniel C. French[13]

In a letter she received from French while she was alone and homesick in Europe, before Jacob Schmidlapp, a businessman, friend, and supporter, joined her on his annual trip, French wrote: "When are you coming home? I find that I miss you all the time. I feel quite mortified to be so dependent on anyone! Remember, you are coming right up here as soon as you land."[14]

July 21 1912
Glendale
You poor little feller!

We are awfully sorry to hear that you have been ill. O, dear! You need somebody to take care of you and I am married and if you married anyone else, ten to one he would be a sick one and you would have to take care of him.

. . . I am to be in New York on Tuesday, but I suppose there is no chance that I see you.

. . . We will make no plans about your visit to us. When you are ready, just come! I shall be greatly disappointed, however, if you do not come at all.

The fox sends his love; the rest of the family are off in the "Loco!"

Affectionally
Daniel C. French[15]

November 3 1914
Glendale
Dear Beatrix-Sculptrix
Bless you and thank you for all the trouble you have taken to have my statuette exhibited. I hope you will reap your reward somehow.

. . . I hoped you enjoyed your tiny visit here. I did immensely, and just think how you saved me from launching the statue with that clumsy bit of drapery as it was when you came.[16] I have gone even further in lightening it to its manifest advantage. "Frank" has been photographing it today, so you may see the effect of your criticism. I am expecting you to applaud the pine branch too.

. . . Poor little thing! Did it feel lonely? I thought you looked on us as your family and on "Chesterwood" as home. I wish you would. Your own kin could hardly be fonder of you than we all are and what you are to me is no secret, even to you.

Affectionately,[17]

Two French biographers have written about the Longman-French connection, stating, primarily, that there was one; that the famous sculptor respected as a colleague the rising-to-fame woman sculptor Evelyn Beatrice Longman. This was unusual, indeed, unheard of at the time, wrote art professor Michael Richman. He described Longman as French's friend, colleague, and confidant and their "three-decade professional collaboration unique in American sculptural history."[18]

Current speculation about a romantic relationship was inevitable, considering the hours they spent in studios together—and considering French's saucy correspondence. Harold Holzer, in his 2019 biography of French, *Monument Man*, called Longman French's "dear friend" and considered whether their relationship went further. Describing French as "a passionate, somewhat repressed, deeply sensitive" man, Holzer ultimately concluded that "however flirtatious he might be in private, French could neither abandon his conventional public facade nor compromise his notion of artistic probity."[19]

In the brief notes Longman made on letters others wrote to her and a few extant letters she authored, it seems that, for her part, Longman held immense respect and platonic affection for her beloved friend, "Mr. French."

When Margaret French was writing her book about her father in 1945, Longman sent Margaret copies of French's letters to her and wrote:

> He was truly Christ-like in character. Some thought him <u>too</u> mild; I did, at times, but he was firm as Gibraltar when necessary,—and always full of humor—quaint, spontaneous, clean—never acrid or tawdry—pure gold. I frequently thought, and said, that, if he had a fault I had not discovered it in all our years of friendship—except that of over-leniency toward others. He saw so clearly what was <u>good</u> in both the work and character of his fellow-men that his own

beautiful soul magnified it. While over his own greatness he threw such a garment of simplicity and modesty that little souls were misled and baffled, and sometimes formed no conception of the depths beneath.

I send everything he had ever written me in his own hand (as far as I know). There were many others, as the long gaps will indicate, either typed by himself or dictated to a secretary which I did not keep—though I wish now that I had kept all; but, at the time, the writing in his own dear hand seemed so much more precious.

. . . The other precept I have also quoted many times as it seemed needed: "It is almost as necessary to avoid the appearance of evil as evil itself." How many times I quoted that. . . .

Peggy darling, the foregoing are only a few thoughts, among the many which come thronging. . . . May you make a book—I was going to say worthy of him but I don't think that is possible—so I will say a book full of some reflection of his beauty.

Beatrice[20]

The few letters in Longman's hand that exist from her early years in New York were saved by Milton Bancroft. By August 1907, even for the happily hardworking Longman, the pressure and the heat overwhelmed; it was time to get out of the city. Longman escaped to Shelter Island, off Long Island, and the Bancrofts. Not only was it cooler, but there was a distinct change of pace with Bancroft family summer fun. Vacation at "Shelter" with the Bancrofts was evidently so enjoyable that returning to the city brought on an attack of "the blues." Back in her studio in mid-August, the heat was worse, her work was not going well, and Longman was lonely. Longman's letters to Milton Bancroft express a vulnerability in her early years in New York City that isn't otherwise apparent. She wrote on August 21, 1907:

Dear Folks at Shelter:

I wonder what delightful thing you are all doing at the present moment, two-thirty. I am so tired and "blue" and discouraged and warm that I am nigh to tears. Yesterday and to-day have been awfully hot, whereas while I was away it was delightfully cool, like September, Mr. Kiefer says. My head ached, so I am trying to write instead of working now. I am utterly discouraged over the work anyway; it does not seem of much use to work on it. It looked {indistinguishable word} to me when I got back.

I just took a little recess to have a good cry. I am feeling too blue and lonesome for words. Please excuse this, I feel that I must "let out" to someone, but shall now stop bemoaning my fate and try to be more cheerful. But that "Folks at Shelter" does not "go" now. I would not be willing to let everyone know that I am so foolish. So please keep my little skeleton in the bosom of the family. Isn't that a pretty phrase!

I could hardly stay on the boat while she was at Prospect and again at Manhasett. We took on two hundred barrels of potatoes at Greenport and four hundred and forty-six at Orient, disturbing my would-be slumbers at the latter place. Do you remember what a glorious night it was! In fact, it was too beautiful for it made me "blue" and lonely and I went to bed early to avoid this same fit which I felt coming on.

. . . I spent the morning of my arrival at Piccirilli's laying out an inscription on a tablet in one of Mr. French's groups. His letter, I am glad to say, could not have arrived before Saturday, so the work has not been waiting very long. It came from Concord, Mass., whither he and Mrs. French had gone for a few days. They want me to go up to Glendale very soon. Mr. French had been up to St. Gauden's funeral. He says: "It was held in one of the studios and was very impressive and very simple. Cox made a little address that was one of the finest, tenderest things I ever heard. What a strange mixture he is!"

You cannot know how much I wish I were at Shelter Island this minute. I am so sick of being alone here this summer that I guess I'll have to get married; but now that Mr. K has lost that commission and Mr. R. has lost his heart to Miss Nichol's possessions there does not seem much hope in that direction either.

I am looking forward to Mr. Bancroft's return so that I may have his valued criticism on my work. It needs it badly—and I need encouragement. I hope Mrs. Bancroft has quite recovered from her "indisposition." Love to Mrs. Moore.

Yours,
Evelyn B. Longman[21]

It seems possible that Bancroft's and Longman's feelings for each other were more than platonic. At one point she pressed him to burn one of her letters so that Margaret wouldn't see it since he had written to Longman before he gave certain news to his wife. She sometimes wrote in his Quaker vernacular—addressing him as "thee," as in a letter she sent him when he was in San Francisco painting murals for Henry Bacon's Court of Honor for the Panama Pacific World's Fair: "Beloved Friend . . . I miss seeing thee every day, as I always do when thee is away. . . . Dear 'Jitterbug,' do take good care of thy health! Won't thee?"[22]A few weeks later, she wrote, "It seems as if thee had been away a very long time—and NY does not seem the same with thee not in it."[23] She included news of friends: "Bacon is down in Florida for a two weeks rest;—left last Friday. Last evening I dined with Mr. French and went afterwards to the theater."

In one letter, she told Bancroft that her brothers Claude and Cecil had been in town. "Cecil and M. Bacon had dinner here with me last evening, afterwards going down to the 'Players.' Cecil, Mr. Schmidlapp, and I lunched today at the 'Vanderbilt.' Bacon called for us there before we finished and took Cecil and me up to his office to see the Lincoln Memorial model, then Bacon and I went up to the Architectural League, Ex., and saw a lot of poor sculpture and painting."[24]

In a letter to Margaret in 1910, Milton Bancroft spoke of meeting the out-of-towner in Longman's circle of friends: Cincinnati businessman and philanthropist Jacob Schmidlap.

> [Schmidlapp] . . . with whom I lunched earlier in the week. I went and found the people very pleasant and homely and after it was over Mr. Schmidlapp said to me "Now you have found your way here you have an annual ticket." . . . It was very cordial and nice and I would like to do it but without knowing them better I should feel like an intruder I fear.
>
> Miss L and her brother came to the studio in the afternoon and insisted on taking me with them to dinner with friends of theirs in Brooklyn which accounts for no Sunday letter. I feel like a fraud go-about so as it is only in the hope that work will or may come about thro' it if I keep it up but it is more pleasant than I would have thought. Dear love, Thine, Milton[25]

Whether or not Jacob Schmidlapp was considered a "husband," he was surely a dear friend, supporter, and included in, perhaps an outer ring, of the French-Bacon-Bancroft-Longman circle. A wealthy "capitalist," as he called himself, he founded a Cincinnati distillery, and with a talent for marketing, became quite wealthy. He formed a bank, and was a trustee for several Ohio companies. Like French, Schmidlapp was twenty-five years older than Longman—a widower whose wife, mother-in-law, and a daughter had all died tragically.

In February 1900, he; his wife, Emilie; their daughters, Emma, nineteen, and Charlotte, thirteen; and Emilie's mother, Charlotte Balke, were all riding in the last car of a train to Florida. Outside of Independence, Missouri, drifting snow forced the train to stop on the tracks, and a local train to St. Louis, going full speed, crashed into the Schmidlapps' train. His wife, daughter Emma, and mother-in-law all died of their injuries within the month. Jacob and Charlotte were injured but survived. Six years later, nineteen-year-old Charlotte was killed in a car accident in Arles, France.

Schmidlapp never remarried. He was often in New York City, where his son Carl worked as a banker. He gave generously to the University of Cincinnati, funding buildings named in honor of his wife and daughters. He built a housing development in Cincinnati for African Americans that W. E. B. Du Bois championed. When he died, he left a million dollars for charity.

He also championed Longman and her family, hosting and chauffeuring Louise and her daughter, who tried out for a music scholarship at the University of Cincinnati. Longman traveled with him and some of his Cincinnati friends to Europe in 1910 and 1911.

Besides the Frenches, it was Henry Bacon with whom Longman shared the longest and deepest friendship, perhaps even a love affair. A man of considerable *gravitas*, Bacon was held in high esteem as his architecture career soared toward the building of the Lincoln Memorial. His friend, art historian and critic Royal Cortissoz, in a speech delivered before the American Institute of Architects, characterized Bacon in two words: "embodied conscience."[26]

Margaret French Cresson, in her biography of her father, wrote of Bacon: "On the surface outspoken, hearty, and bluff, an intensely masculine personality concealed a wealth of tenderness, reverence, and kindness, while complete honesty and integrity were among his strongest characteristics."[27]

French's provocative but benign letters to Longman were nothing compared to Bacon's. For Christmas 1910, Bacon gave Longman a silver spoon of his design—engraved on it, the word *Trixina* and a laurel wreath. At the top of the accompanying handwritten poem, he'd drawn the spoon.

Oh yes indeed I think I'll risk it
A rhyme about dear Trix and Triscuit.
But first of all with Christmas greetings
And most sincere of heart's best beatings
I offer her a Christmas gift
Which every morning she will lift
With pretty hand to pretty lips
White milk with Triscuit mixed she sips
My gift each day thus gets a kiss.
Come Pegasus get out of this!
Lest me dismount—it's none too soon.
Lest envy seize me of the spoon.
Merry Christmas
1910[28]

He drew her a valentine poem in 1911:

Of all the gifts that Heaven sends
The best we have are loving friends
I know that Trix is one of mine
So I send her this Valentine
Come weak—Come Woe
She'll count on me
To the end of the Chapter one two three.[29]

A postcard from Denver, Colorado, in 1912:

Don't forget that
Every one & all
Are always in your
Reach and at your call.
To tell the truth

Really I must
I fear except I don't I lust
Xcuse the rhyme
I do it all the time
Naughty & uncouth
And yet I am your loving cousin
Hal[30]

A handwritten letter, undated:

Monday night.
Dear Piccola.
Here in a quiet place I have been looking over the photographs of your work very carefully and I am prouder of you than ever—I once said I was prejudiced in your favor and this will ever be true but if I were your bitterest enemy—and I shout aloud that you haven't one—still would I say your work is fine, and wish long life to your clever hands.

I think your clever hands are the least part of you, dear Piccolissima—clever as they are, and here's where Cousin Hal's prejudice may come in—but I don't think I'm alone in that prejudice—

At any rate my prejudice is a belief that you are a noble woman and your friendship is a great joy to me—

I am a better man through you—It's a great gift you have—the one of making such steadfast friends—Count me one forever . . . may the laurels rest on Trixina's raven hair—

Cheer up my lady—
Always your affectionate
Cousin Hal[31]

At the top of one handwritten letter, Bacon had drawn a slender moon, with Pegasus in the sunshine and clouds. Below the letter is Pegasus with a rider falling beneath. This was his birthday greeting to Longman in 1913:

Trixina's blessed birthday's here
Of course it comes but once a year.
Some ladies skip a year or two
To save their age—indeed they do!
But Trix is different from the rest
She's more than different—<u>She's the best</u>!
And if the truth must hold full sway
She younger grows with every day.
Born to the world to take a part
In loveliness and works of art
Triumph attends her whole career
And with it all, she's such a dear

That my poor heart —God bless my soul,
Don't speak of part—She takes the whole.[32]

And for her birthday two years later:

Nov. 21, 1915
God bless the day.
Beloved Beatrice.
The evening lights are coming out on your birthday and the Shell Camp is bravely shining on the street as I write— Such a beautiful glow dear girl, and so warm—just like the loving thoughts and good wishes that go with these words— Dear, brave old Trixina—with all her important works and plans, your Cousin Hal wants to be a help in them and make things easier for you in their execution— Work to do Piccola mine and it's going to be done well too!!!

{Drawing of a hand} There's my hand in it—I can draw a better hand—but I could never feel a better desire than the one in my heart—

God bless you Beatrice and as the years go on may everlasting happiness be your portion—always increasing—

Your loving Cousin Hal[33]

{Underlined four times}

Figure 7.1 An adolescent Margaret French, as a Bacchante. Longman also called this piece Peggy. Source/Credit: Photograph by A. B. Bogart. From the collection of the Loomis Chaffee Archives, Loomis Chaffee School, Windsor, Connecticut USA.

Longman made portraits of her friends: two of Margaret French, one as a *Bacchante*, also sometimes titled *Peggy*; portrait heads of Bacon, Bancroft, and Schmidlapp; and a large bas-relief portrait of Dan French. She also made an exquisite silver document box to honor Schmidlapp's family. French modeled a portrait of Longman in marble. Bancroft painted four, possibly five portraits of her.

In 1915, when Longman was hospitalized for an emergency appendectomy, Bacon, Bancroft, Schmidlapp, and her brother Claude all traveled to Washington, D.C., to see her. Daniel French received daily updates from Bacon, who attended her at bedside and wrote her this poem:

Dear old Trix
Sans appendix
We all love you dearly—and even more
Though a scarlet scar
May your tum tum mar
It's a trifle merely—we still adore—[34]

He seemed to be speaking for all the husbands.

NOTES

1. Margaret Cresson French, *Journey into Fame. The Life of Daniel Chester French* (Cambridge, MA: Harvard University Press, 1947), 240.
2. Ibid.
3. DCF to Newton Mackintosh, January 3, 1911, Chesterwood Archives; Chapin Library, Williams College, Gift of the National Trust for Historic Preservation/Chesterwood, a National Trust Historic Site, Stockbridge, Massachusetts.
4. Cresson French, 240.
5. DCF letter to EBL, December 25, 1914. The Christmas poems/toasts can be found at Loomis Chaffee.
6. Ibid. EBL handwritten note on letter.
7. DCF and EBL Correspondence. EBL handwritten note suggests the author might be "Mrs. Bush." No date. Loomis Chaffee.
8. Ibid. EBL note explains author was probably the "delicious humor" of Peggy French.
9. DCF and EBL correspondence, Chesterwood Archives; Chapin Library, Williams College.
10. DCF to EBL, July 23, 1911, Loomis Chaffee Archives.
11. Longman entered *Laura Bacon* in an International Exhibition in Rome and at the National Academy of Design Exhibition in New York, in 1911.

12. DCF to EBL, September 2, 1907, Chesterwood Archives; Chapin Library, Williams College.

13. DCF to EBL, October 3, 1907, Loomis Chaffee.

14. DCF to EBL July 23, 1911, Loomis Chaffee.

15. DCF to EBL, July 1, 1912, Loomis Chaffee.

16. This is a reference to French's *Spirit of Life*.

17. DCF to EBL, November 3, 1914, Loomis Chaffee.

18. Marilyn and Walter Rabetz, *Evelyn Beatrice Longman Batchelder* (Windsor, CT: Loomis Chaffee School, 1993), 14.

19. Holzer, 253.

20. EBL to Margaret French Cresson, 1945, Chesterwood Archives; Chapin Library, Williams College.

21. EBL to Milton Bancroft (MB), August 21, 1907, Milton Bancroft Collection, Manuscript Group 133, Indiana University of Pennsylvania (IUP), Special Collections and University Archives.

22. EBL to MB, February 16, 1914, Indiana University of Pennsylvania.

23. EBL to MB, March 9, 1914, Indiana University of Pennsylvania.

24. EBL to MB, February 16, 1914, Indiana University of Pennsylvania.

25. Milton Bancroft to Margaret Bancroft, 1910, Indiana University of Pennsylvania.

26. Royal Cortissoz, "The Architect," *New York Tribune*, February 17, 1924.

27. Margaret Cresson French, 267.

28. Henry Bacon (HB) to EBL, Christmas 1910, Loomis Chaffee.

29. HB to EBL, February 1911, Loomis Chaffee.

30. HB to EBL, February 16, 1912, Loomis Chaffee.

31. HB to EBL, undated, Loomis Chaffee.

32. HB to EBL, November 21, 1913, Loomis Chaffee.

33. HB to EBL, November 21, 1915, Loomis Chaffee.

34. HB to EBL, undated, on Hotel Occidental stationery, Loomis Chaffee.

Chapter 8

The Farther French Connections

I really know of no one man or woman in the country who would be likely to give you as satisfactory a result as Miss Longman.

—Daniel Chester French

At least two of Longman's pals—French and Bacon—were members of The Players, a gathering place for actors and artists, more accessible, and said to be more lively, than the clubs of the "titled, wealthy elite." Edwin Booth, a Shakespearean actor and brother of John Wilkes Booth, opened the establishment on New Year's Eve of 1888, partly to redeem the family name after his brother had assassinated President Abraham Lincoln. Booth's organizing partners included Mark Twain and General William Tecumseh Sherman.

The clubhouse was a Gothic-Revival mansion remodeled by architect Stanford White. Henry Bacon was then a draftsman in White's New York City firm. In 1903, Bacon joined the club; both he and French took Longman to dinner there from time to time. Welcome to accompany male members, women were not allowed to join until 1989.[1]

It may have been there that Longman met up with Kate Parsenow, a German actress debuting in her first English role at the Berkeley Lyceum in January 1906. Though in the throes of creating the plaster model of the Naval Academy chapel doors, Longman evidently was so inspired by Parsenow that she made time to model the actress. Eventually she had the bust carved in polychromed marble, creating an exquisite portrait of a woman with an indecipherable expression. One art historian later wrote that *Aenigma*, as Longman called it, has "generally been accepted as one of Miss Longman's masterpieces of character study."[2]

A year later, she entered the marble in the John Quincy Adams Ward competition for best portrait bust. Ward, the preeminent sculptor at the end of the nineteenth century, was Daniel Chester French's first sculpture teacher, briefly. (At nineteen, French left Concord, Massachusetts, and spent a month in Ward's New York City studio.) Founder and president of the National Sculpture Society from 1893 to 1905, and a member of the Advisory Committee of Sculptors for the St. Louis World's Fair, Ward was one of the original members of the Board of Trustees of the Metropolitan Museum of Art.

In other words, the Ward Prize was prestigious. That year it went to Charles Grafly, who had been one of the judges of the Annapolis doors competition. *Aenigma* received second place. Many years later, Longman would say it "is as good a piece of modeling as I have ever done."[3]

Longman's connection with Bacon and French, who both had extensive connections themselves, continued to result in work for her. John Stewart Kennedy, a wealthy New York City banker, served alongside French as a trustee for the Metropolitan Museum of Art. Kennedy gave some of his art collection to The Met, as well as funding for building Hamilton Hall at Columbia University. In 1906, Longman and French arranged for an aging Kennedy to negotiate the four flights of stairs to Longman's studio, where he sat for her. Upon his death three years later, The Met, which had received $2.5 million from Kennedy's estate, commissioned Longman to create his portrait bust. Her *Kennedy*, which expresses more kindness and humanity than those of other artists, who portray a more somber, stern Kennedy, was installed in Hamilton Hall in 1912.

Sculpting wasn't going so well for Longman in August of 1907, as she alluded to in her letter to the Bancrofts, but as was her nature, Longman persevered—no doubt continuing to practice her habit of first tenaciously doing the hard part of whatever work lay before her.[4] A lot lay before her. Besides the Naval Academy chapel doors, she had a commission for a bas-relief tablet, the *Mary Elizabeth Ryle Memorial* for the Danforth Free Library in Paterson, New Jersey. It was her first collaboration with Henry Bacon, who had designed the Danforth Library, where the *Ryle Memorial* would be installed. He designed a thin, elegant Vermont marble frame to hold Longman's tablet.

In her artist's conception, she wrote:

> The design represents Memory, which is depicted by a stately winged figure, who presents to the holder a portrait in relief of Mrs. Ryle. The latter is treated in a very simple style, in low relief, showing little more than the head. In the upper corner of the portrait tablet appear the dates of Mrs. Ryle's birth and death.

And the symbols:

> The lower portion bears the winged wreath enclosing an hour glass, symbolic of enduring fame.
>
> Memory, calm and benignant of mien, is clothed in a richly embroidered robe. The halo and double pair of wings remove her from the earthly and bespeak an eternal existence. She stands upon a tablet having the inscription, "Erected by the Citizens of Paterson, in grateful memory of Mary Elizabeth Ryle, the donor of this building. MDCCCCVII"
>
> This inscription is enclosed by two cornucopias overflowing with flowers and fruits symbolizing the life of Mrs. Ryle.[5]

The *Ryle Monument* was dedicated on November 15, 1907, with hundreds in attendance at a ceremony in Paterson.

The next spring, Longman traveled to Boston to meet up with Dan and Margaret French for the unveiling of French's portrait of Wellesley College's first president, Alice Freeman Palmer. Connections Longman may have made during that trip are unknown, but two years later, in 1909, following the installation of the Naval Academy chapel doors, Longman was invited to create similar doors—the Horsford Doors—for Wellesley's Clapp Library.

Eben Norton Horsford was a beloved friend of Wellesley College founder, Henry Fowle Durant. Descended from farmers and missionaries to Native Americans in New York, Horsford studied civil engineering, then taught math and natural history at Albany Female Academy, where he fell in love with a student. Her father wouldn't allow them to marry unless Horsford improved his lot in life, so he set as his goal a teaching position at Harvard. Toward that end, he studied agricultural chemistry in Germany, and when he returned, he landed the Rumford chair at Harvard's new scientific school—and married his love, Mary L'Hommedieu Gardiner.

Though he was a teacher, his focus was on industrial applications of chemistry. He invented baking powder, naming the company that produced it Rumford, after his chair at Harvard. He also devised a "compact and nourishing ration" for Union soldiers; patented the perforated postage stamp; manufactured a carbonated fruit drink; and built an extensive model farm.[6] Employees in all his companies could participate in profit-sharing.

Horsford's involvement with Wellesley was legendary. In business together when Durant started the women's college, Horsford sent him a list of his female Harvard students so Durant, who had requested the list, could interview the women for teaching positions. Horsford served as chair of the advisory Board of Visitors at the women's college from its early days until his death in 1893. He paid special attention to the science department and the library, offering advice teachers sought of him and making donations.

Wellesley houses a collection of thank-you notes to Horsford, for a myriad of favors, including tickets for two young instructors in Greek and Latin to attend a play in New York; student tickets for an electrical exhibition in Boston; an easy chair for President Alice Freeman's study; sabbaticals for the professors; and stays at his guesthouse on Shelter Island. From members of the class of 1886, who would later honor him with the bronze doors, there are thank-you notes expressing appreciation for the potted hyacinths he sent to each person at Christmas. The class president characterized Horsford as their "honorary member," "a big brother to us; big in years, in generosity, in wisdom, in courtesy, in strong kindness—he was big of soul."[7] When Durant lay dying, he told his wife to tell his best friend, Horsford, "I love him tenderly."

Some fifteen years after Horsford himself died, members of the Wellesley class of 1886 decided they wanted to honor their "big brother," Horsford, with bronze doors for the school library to celebrate the twenty-fifth anniversary of their graduation. Creating the memorial to this beloved man became Longman's next monumental work.

She was given only one mandate: the doors should bear the inscription "1818—In Memory of Eben Norton Horsford—1893." What else she did to design and build the two six-by-thirteen-foot bronze doors was up to her. In the transom, she carved the dedication to Horsford, the class ideal *To Kalon* ("The Beautiful"), and the college motto, *Non Ministrari Sed Ministrare* ("Not to be served but to serve").

Again, she combined classic symbolism with modern meaning pertinent to the life being celebrated. She chose two panels, one of Wisdom (*Sapentia*) and one of Charitable Love (*Caritas*). Typically, she did the unconventional gender appropriation again. As with her *Victory*, historically a woman she imagined as a young man, this time she made the classically female Wisdom figure male. He is portrayed as a bearded, older scholar with a proud and searching countenance, clutching his robe with one hand and holding a book in the other.

With twenty-first-century eyes, this choice may seem "a bit troubling" for a women's college, as Margaret Samu has written. But it was Horsford whom Longman and Wellesley grads honored in the doors. Indeed, one can imagine that Longman portrayed qualities of Eben Norton Horsford in both figures. Charity is portrayed as female, a heavily draped woman with weary eyes, her hands on the arm and curly hair of a young child standing at her feet, face buried in her robe.

In Longman's signature way, the doors abound in ornamentation and symbolism: The class motto is encircled by a wreath of laurel and daisies, the class flower. The thick border surrounding each panel is made of Horsford's favorite hyacinth blossoms, as well as the oak leaves and acorns plentiful on the Wellesley campus. Dogwood blossoms, which would become Longman's signature flower, decorate the corners. Small panels above each figure hold traditional symbols: the flame of knowledge burning inside an urn from which the serpents of wisdom emerge on each side.

Class members were reportedly delighted with the work. The doors were dedicated on June 17, 1911, with refreshments and orchestral music in the Rhododendron Hollow. Longman was in Europe at the time, with Jacob Schmidlapp and Cincinnati friends. In a letter to her, French reported that he saw her library doors at the bronze foundry "all set up and ready to swing. They looked fine."[8]

The French and Bacon connections extended beyond the East Coast. August R. Meyer, a mining engineer, cofounded Leadville, Colorado, and established the Kansas City Consolidated Smelting and Refining Company. After Meyer's company polluted the air in Kansas City, he sold the business and became a benefactor for cleaner air, helping fund Kansas City's park system and serving as the first president of the Parks Board. The inaugural sculpture placed in a Kansas City park, the Paseo, was a memorial to Meyer, with architectural design by Henry Bacon and sculpture by Dan French. Two large urns on either side of a wide staircase led to a small plaza, where French's lettering and bronze bas-relief were installed in Bacon's eight-foot Knoxville marble tablet.

Frank Faxon, owner of a wholesale drug store company and a member of the committee that commissioned French for the park statue, also asked French to create a portrait of his six-year-old daughter. Busy with other commissions for monumental works to be placed in Massachusetts, Ohio, and Minnesota, French recommended Longman to Faxon.

In a letter, French gushed (in a restrained New England sort of way):

> You may remember that I recommended Miss Longman B. Longman to you as a sculptor who has made some signal successes of portraits of some young people, and who, I am sure, would make a delightful statue of your daughter.
>
> I really know of no one man or woman in the country who would be likely to give you as satisfactory a result as Miss Longman.[9]

French informed Faxon about the possible price for the bust—nine hundred dollars for bronze; one thousand dollars for marble. While acknowledging he had no authority to negotiate for Longman, he predicted they could come to an agreement. In the summer of 1908, she took a train to Kansas City to model a portrait of Frances Darlington Faxon.

A heavy tapestry hung on the wall delineated a "studio" in a corner of the Faxon home. Using a variety of wooden boxes, tables, and stands to get heights just right, Longman set up a place for Frances to sit for two hours

Figure 8.1 Six-year-old Frances Faxon models a figure, as Longman models her, in Faxon home, Kansas City. Source/Credit: Chesterwood Archives; Chapin Library, Williams College, Gift of the National Trust for Historic Preservation / Chesterwood, a National Trust Historic Site, Stockbridge, Massachusetts.

each morning and two hours each afternoon while Longman modeled her. To keep the young girl relatively still and occupied, Longman provided clay so that Frances could model as well.

In an interview with the *Kansas City Star* during her stay in July 1908, Longman gave a shout-out to French and voiced her critical opinion about public statues:

> Don't be sorry Kansas City hasn't a bunch of monuments—be glad. With the *A.R. Meyer Memorial*, by Daniel C. French, as the first public monument to set the pace for any future efforts, Kansas City has a clear field for art development with nothing to regret.
>
> Kansas City is lucky not to have its beautiful parks and boulevards marred with a horde of unsightly statues and monuments. There is no getting rid of a monument when once it has been erected, no matter how obnoxious it may be. There is always someone who would be dreadfully offended if it should be removed, generally one or more of the old and distinguished families of the city.
>
> Many cities in the United States would be glad if they could have a clean slate, as Kansas City has. They see their mistakes now. New York City, Chicago and practically all of the other old cities in the country have scores of 'mistakes,' unartistic monuments that mar the beauty of their parks. But in most cases they are to be an everlasting sorrow.[10]

Longman created two statues of Frances: in tinted plaster, and marble.[11] A year later, on May Day, 1909, she exhibited the marble *Frances* and two other pieces (the *Robert Means Thompson* bust and the finial of *Faith, Hope and Charity* she had recently made for the Foster Mausoleum in Lowell Cemetery) in an exhibition and reception that celebrated her election as an associate in the National Academy of Design, the high court of art and architecture. To have been made an associate member—at that time, there were no women sculptors who were full members—was a remarkable achievement. She had reached a new height on the challenging climb up Mount Parnassus.

But she was only partway there. As she had at age six, she picked up that suitcase and kept walking. Given ten more years, she just might make it to the top.

NOTES

1. See https://www.bkmag.com/2016/06/29/inside-players-club-and-the-history-of-american-theater/, accessed November 7, 2020.
2. Jonathon Rawson, "Beatrice Longman," *International Studio*, Volume 45, Numbers 177 to 180, 1911–1912, 456.
3. EBL to William J. Drake, Gorham Company, November 9, 1935, Loomis Chaffee.
4. Margaret Samu, from an interview with Nathaniel Horton Batchelder II.
5. "A Memorial to a Noble Woman," *Morning Call*, Paterson, NJ, November 16, 1907, 9.
6. Margaret Jean Taylor and Jean Glasscock, *Wellesley College 1875–1975: A Century of Women. The Founders and the Early Presidents* (Wellesley, MA: Wellesley College, 1975), 19.

7. "Garden Party and Unveiling the Library Doors Presented by the Class of 1886." Longman vertical file, American Art Museum and National Portrait Gallery Library, Smithsonian, Washington, DC.

8. Letter DCF to EBL, May 15, 1911, Chesterwood Archives; Chapin Library, Williams College.

9. DCF letter to Frank A. Faxon, May 26, 1908, Chesterwood Archives; Chapin Library, Williams College.

10. "No Monuments—Be Glad," *Kansas City Star*, July 16, 1908, 5.

11. The tinted plaster was purchased as a gift for the Wadsworth Atheneum of Art, Hartford, Connecticut, in 1927. The marble is in a private collection.

Chapter 9

Shades of Controversy

A murmur of satisfaction and pleasure arose from the vast concourse of people.

—Gloversville Morning Herald

In 1828, the upstate New York town of Gloversville was known as Stump City because so many hemlock trees in the nearby forest had been cut down to use for tanning leather; in fact, until 1950, 90 percent of gloves sold in the United States were made in, well, Gloversville. Leather manufacturer Thomas G. Foster, also a director of the local bank and head of the town's free library, had accumulated some wealth before his death in 1895. His will provided for two memorials to be placed in the town cemetery: a "vault," or "tomb," for him, his immediate family, and family members already buried there; and a memorial to his grandfather, Timothy Murphy.

Foster delegated his good friend Francis Olney Winslow, another leather manufacturer, to supervise construction of the monuments. Winslow had moved to Norwood, Massachusetts, and built a mansion called Oak View. There, he and his wife entertained many notables, including presidents such as William Howard Taft, who had been in conversation with Henry Bacon about the possibility of erecting a memorial to Abraham Lincoln in Washington, D.C. This may have been the connection to Winslow that led Longman and Bacon to create both the Foster Mausoleum and the *Timothy Murphy Memorial.*

According to Winslow's specific instructions for the mausoleum, atop the tomb was to be a statue of Faith, at least ten feet tall, cut from a single stone and of the same style as a figure of Hope, already on the cemetery plot. Faith was to be placed in the center and behind Hope, on the other side, standing next to a figure of Charity. Faith was to be one foot higher than the other figures. This was completely implausible to Longman: the statue of Hope, already in existence, was five feet, nine inches tall. It was to be part of a group ten feet tall. In addition, Hope had been sculpted to be a single statue, and Longman felt it couldn't be harmonized "in the same style" with the other two figures, as the will requested.

Winslow went to court in April 1909 to plead that Foster's will be changed; that Hope be removed and sold, arguing that creating a group with the current figure would defeat "the objects of proportion, harmony, perspective and aesthetic affect which the testator must be presumed to have desired and intended."[1] The petition was granted, and Longman was paid $4,500 to create the more-than-life-sized, three-person finial.

Longman's finial atop the mausoleum portrays three figures in white granite, as Foster envisioned, but *Charity*, not *Faith*, is in front, holding a baby; her face, lowered to the infant's face, expresses tenderness and protection. *Hope*, holding a cup, and *Faith*, a bouquet of lilies, are arm in arm. The pediment upon which they stand is decorated with a Greek meander motif symbolizing the bond of love and devotion, guardianship, and healing—the eternal flow. Beneath, a garland of fruit stretches around the pediment; ram heads signifying strength and sacrifice decorate the corners.

The mausoleum was completed before the dedication of the *Timothy Murphy Memorial*, just across the cemetery road from it at Middleburgh, on October 17, 1910, the day Thomas G. Foster's desire to have a memorial erected at his grandfather's grave was realized. Murphy was a Revolutionary War rifleman and Indian scout credited with the shooting of a British general and a baronet at the Second Battle at Saratoga, a significant defeat for the British. As a member of General Sullivan's militia, Murphy continued to seek out British Loyalists and sympathetic Native people, destroying Iroquois villages, murdering inhabitants, and forcing into Canada those who remained. At one particularly horrifying event, he defied his commander's orders to stop shooting at the British while defending the Middle Fort in the Schoharie Valley. His commander finally retreated from Murphy's onslaught, as did the British. Murphy's patriot status is based on his raft of killings, characterized as protecting citizens.

On a sunny fall day—the 130th anniversary of the Middle Fort attack—Longman and Bacon sat at table with Francis Winslow and other local dignitaries at an elaborate lunch in Middleburgh's Hotel Baker. At 1:30 p.m., hundreds of Middleburgh High School students, each carrying a small U.S. flag, their teachers, and school board members processed two-abreast to Main Street. There, they met up with the Middleburgh Citizens' Silver Band, the Grand Arm of the Republic (Union veterans of the Civil War), the Middleburgh Steamer Company, Mr. and Mrs. Francis O. Winslow, Bacon, and

Longman. Joining the group in the half-mile procession were city officers, officials of the historical society, members of the cemetery association, and descendants of Timothy Murphy. The parade marshal and his aide, dressed in the uniform of the Spanish American War, rode horseback. Businesses and residences along the route were decked in red, white, and blue.[2]

People had already assembled at the Upper Middleburgh Cemetery when the parade arrived. The groups gathered in front of the *Timothy Murphy Memorial*, draped in a large U.S. flag. The band played "Hail Columbia," then the great-great-grandson of Timothy Murphy took the cords that held the flag in place and revealed Longman's life-sized rendering of Murphy in bas-relief. "A murmur of satisfaction and pleasure arose from the vast concourse of people," reported the *Gloversville Morning Herald*.[3]

Following the unveiling, the president of the historical society gave a long telling of the Murphy story, and then Winslow took the stage. He explained how the monument came to be, including a description of Longman's finial atop the Foster Mausoleum across the way and "requested Miss Longman to step to the speaker's station so that the people could carry her image in their memories of the day. This she gracefully and graciously did, and was received and thanked with warm applause."[4]

Description of the *Timothy Murphy* statue is chilling to 2025 sensibilities. The *Gloversville Morning Herald* provides this depiction:

> [Murphy] is represented as of slight but athletic figure, clothed in the familiar suit of buckskin, the jacket belted down at the waist, the trousers fringed at the side, a coon skin cap on his head. In his right hand he holds a musket. . . . He is looking out in the distance. His left foot rests on a tomahawk. His hunting knife is in his belt on which his left hand rests. An arrow is represented as sticking in the earth behind his right leg. The relief is bordered by a tracing of pine needles and acorns. The following inscription appears on the tablet at the base:
> To the memory of
> 1761 Timothy Murphy 1818
>
> Patriot Soldier Scout Citizen who served in Morgan's Rifle Corps and fought at Saratoga and Monmouth and whose bravery repelled the attack of the British and their Indian allies upon Middle Fort Oct. 17, 1780, and saved the colonists of Schoharie Valley.
>
> In the center of the inscription is the head of a native man, eyes closed, symbolizing the extinction of the race.[5]

The newspaper reporter wrote: "The entire work shows great artistic spirit, genius of conception, harmony in its symbolism and is a triumph for the sculptor, Miss Longman."[6]

It's impossible to imagine what was in Longman's mind as she made this monument. Murphy's descendants had called for a work that honored him—an idea repugnant to some in our time, when public statues of racists are being taken down. One might conclude from this work that Longman was not far-sighted enough, or compassionate enough, or willing enough to go against the grain when it came to accepting commissions. Or, one might suggest that in this work Longman intended to expose Murphy's cruelty, rather than celebrate it—but that seems unlikely, considering the era, and her gruesome symbolism.

Longman made trips to Europe in 1910 and 1911. "It is a good thing to go to Paris and wake up," she told a reporter. "If an artist feels that she is getting stale, a visit to Paris, where she will see new things, will act like a tonic. I have run across two or three times lately, but I do this just as one goes to the seashore or the mountains for a vacation, where the recreation and the new surroundings restore and stir up the imagination. The atmosphere in Paris is delightful for an artist and she returns to America full of new vigor."[7]

In 1910, she joined Mary, Margaret, and Dan French in England to celebrate Margaret's twentieth birthday. An often-published photograph of French and Longman rowing on the Avon was taken during that trip, probably by Margaret.

While she was away in 1911, French took care of her studio and explored properties in hopes that each of them could have new studios.

> Century Club
> 7 West Forty-Third Street
> May 15, 1911
> Nothing of importance of interest to a Parisienne has happened since we pushed you out into the sea; this is only to show that I bear no malice!
>
> . . . I have not seen the interiors of the two houses yet, but I have worked out a tentative plan for alterations that looks attractive on paper. Mr. Bacon is quite enthusiastic over the proportions, but I suppose the whole scheme depends upon your willingness to inherit "125." When you have any views about this, let me know.
>
> Do write and tell us how you are fixed and what you think of Paris. I wish I could be there with you to go to the Salon . . . do be careful of your health and don't fall in love with a good-for-nothing Parisienne. . . . Tell me how you and Mr. Adams got on. You should be able to add him to your choice collection of husbands with a week at sea with him.
>
> With double-distilled Affection,
> D.C.F.[8]

Both summers she caught up with Jacob Schmidlapp and his friends from Cincinnati. As well as a side trip to Switzerland, the 1911 voyage with Schmidlapp included visits to artists' salons and an introduction to Frederick

William MacMonnies, an American sculptor who settled in Paris as a leading *Beaux Arts* artist.

She also may have visited Auguste Rodin's workshop, or some other place where she could have viewed his work. When she returned (followed by a recuperation period with the Bancrofts at Shelter), she created two torsos reminiscent of Rodin's torsos, and French's similar plaster of a truncated female figure, *Artemis*, which he created in 1896.

Different from anything else she sculpted, Longman's torsos could have been experimental sketches with the help of a particularly good model at the time. Very likely that was Hettie Anderson, a model Longman and Daniel French had engaged several times since at least 1907. The favorite model of Augustus Saint-Gaudens, who died in 1907, Anderson not only had a reputation as an excellent model, but Saint-Gaudens said she had the figure of a goddess.[9]

On New Year's Day, 1911, French, Longman, and others presented Anderson with a whopper of a check for that time—$580—and a box of flowers.[10] Models normally made $1.50 an hour for half a day's work. Longman would remain friends with Anderson for years, and when modeling ceased to be Anderson's primary work, Longman advocated for her to work at the Metropolitan Museum of Art because she thought Anderson would like being around art.[11] Later, when Anderson faced what were perceived as mental challenges, Longman offered friendship and advice.

Torso of a Woman is a truncated figure seated on a marble form and in a tilted position. *Seated Female Figure* is seated with crossed legs and twisted torso. Both are rendered in bronze: *Female* with a patina of dark brown with green highlights, and *Woman* with a black patina. Compared to other of her works, they are small, about twelve inches high, on marble bases.

Experiments or not, Longman must have liked the pair. At one point, she displayed both of them in her own apartment/studio. She exhibited them in the 1912 winter exhibition of the National Academy of Design; in 1913 and 1916, at National Sculpture Society exhibitions in Buffalo; and at the Panama-Pacific International Exposition in 1915. The Metropolitan Museum of Art now owns castings of both figures. The museum purchased *Torso of a Woman* in 1912, and Edward Dean Adams purchased *Seated Female Figure* for his personal collection and then gifted it to the Metropolitan in 1927. Adams, president of the company that built the first hydroelectric power plant in Niagara Falls, New York, was a trustee of the Metropolitan and treasurer of the special committee for the acquisition of casts and reproductions.

A onetime pupil and long-time friend of Longman's, sculptor Georg John Lober owned a *Torso of a Woman*. And there is another casting at Chesterwood, no doubt a gift from Longman. Longman made other casts of *Seated Female Figure*. Besides their residence at the Metropolitan, they are located in what is now the St. Louis Art Museum and in the collection of art dealer Joel Rosenkranz in New York City.

In addition to the torsos, that year Longman also created a bronze bust of Jacob Schmidlapp, perhaps her way of thanking her friend. One aspect of their friendship probably was a shared commitment to a work ethic and faithful follow-through, for it was written of Schmidlapp: "He could forgive a man for making mistakes, but not for doing nothing. So active was he in mind and body that it was difficult for him to overlook the inactivities of other people."[12]

No doubt at Schmidlapp's recommendation, Longman created a bas-relief of one of his friends, Civil War general Henry Corbin, who led one of the first regiments of the United States Colored Infantry. Corbin also led the 38th Infantry, a Buffalo Soldier regiment. As secretary of the Sitting Bull Commission, he participated in convincing the Lakota chief to return from Canada and surrender to the United States. A friend of Ulysses S. Grant, Corbin served in the White House with presidents Rutherford B. Hayes, James A. Garfield, William McKinley, and William Howard Taft. He was with President Garfield at a railroad station in Washington, D.C., when the president was shot, and he stayed with Garfield until he died a few days later in New Jersey.

Corbin and Schmidlapp were both Ohioans, both friends of President William McKinley, also of Ohio, and both members of West Point's Board of Visitors. Too, Schmidlapp's housing projects for African Americans (embraced by W. E. B. Du Bois) may have resonated with Corbin, who died in September 1909. Because he was buried at Arlington Cemetery, his friends (including J. P. Morgan, Andrew Carnegie, and Schmidlapp) arranged for a memorial to be installed at Corbin Hall, the building on Governors Island in New York Harbor that Corbin gave to the Eastern Division of the Army, of which he also was once commander.[13]

Upon the committee's invitation to build the memorial, Longman spent a couple of months creating the bas-relief, using an official photograph of Corbin in uniform. During the dedication on January 16, 1912, Jacob Schmidlapp presented the tablet. The general's daughter, Katharine Corbin Parsons, told the *Sun* that it was the best portrait of her father she'd seen. An unnamed Corbin friend complimented Longman for the "intense, life-like expression in the eyes."[14]

Late in the afternoon on Saturday, March 25, 1911, fire broke out in the Triangle shirtwaist factory eight blocks south of Longman's apartment and studio. Oil dripping from sewing machines onto piles of cloth created conditions ripe for a conflagration. Some doors were locked; other doors only opened inward; the city's firetruck ladders and water could only reach the sixth floor (the factory was on the sixth, seventh, and eight floors). Within a half hour of the initial spark, 146 of the five hundred immigrants working in the dress factory were dead. Thirteen of the dead were young men; the rest were young women, mostly Eastern European Jews and Italian immigrants, family breadwinners.

Unions were trying to improve working conditions in the shirtwaist manufacturing industry, though it was a struggle. In 1909, 150 Triangle employees had been fired for being union sympathizers. Strikes throughout the industry resulted, and Triangle workers gained a small increase in wages, but demands for fire escapes and open doors went unmet.[15] The deaths of so many young women, some in their teens, heightened the public awareness of unjust labor issues, including working conditions. The fact that the women were immigrants highlighted another social tension of the time, control of immigrant communities.

In the days that followed the fire, after families claimed bodies, seven remained unidentified. Labor unions requested that these bodies be released for a public funeral procession and respectful burial within the embrace of their communities. Fearing a demonstration of uncontrollable public outrage, the city refused to release the bodies to the unions.[16] When the city announced the bodies of the unknown would be interred in a private ceremony on April 5 in a city-owned plot at Brooklyn's Evergreens Cemetery, the unions organized a memorial parade. One hundred thousand people marched, while another three hundred thousand watched from windows as the people parade passed. Upon reaching Washington Square, they stood for six hours, in the pouring rain, beneath a sea of black umbrellas, from time to time cries of anguish piercing the hush.

A crowd of hundreds stood waiting at the gates to the cemetery, where eventually eight hearses (one carried the casket for unidentified body parts) brought the bodies that had not been identified to their final resting place. A rabbi, an Episcopalian priest, and a Roman Catholic priest performed memorial services. A quartet from the local Elks Lodge sang "Nearer, My God, to Thee."

Immediate relief efforts for the families came from the unions and the Red Cross Emergency Relief Committee, headed by industrialist Robert de Forest. In 1912, when donations had been distributed to families, the Committee reserved $2,500 to build a monument at the site of the burial of the "Unknowns." Longman and Henry Bacon would have known de Forest, a member of the Trustees of the Metropolitan Museum of Art, as was Dan French. When it was determined that a monument to those unidentified be built, de Forest was no doubt instrumental in commissioning Henry Bacon to design the monument "in collaboration with Miss Longman."[17]

Bacon's setting was simple: a slightly trapezoid pink granite slab. Longman's figure, set in the slab's upper half, crouches on one knee, bent in profound grief over a Grecian urn. Folds of cloth drape the woman and are gathered over the urn, her hands clasped among the folds, her head resting there as she seems to weep. The Piccirillis carved the monument.

Beneath the figure, Longman lettered: "In sympathy and sorrow citizens of New York raise this monument over the graves of unidentified women and children who with one hundred and thirty-nine others perished by fire in the Triangle Shirtwaist Factory Washington Place March 25, 1911." Inscription on the back acknowledged mayor William J. Gaynor's relief fund, administered by the Red Cross Emergency Relief Committee of the Charity Organization Society of the City of New York.

It was installed in December 1912 without any announcement or ceremony. By the second anniversary of the fire, activists were pushing legislation that would promote safety for workers. They also organized an annual remembrance of the tragic fire, a living monument to the victims, held to this day.

There is no mention of the Triangle monument in Longman's archival collection at Loomis Chaffee School. Typically, she had a photograph taken of her work in its plaster or plastiline or finished form. But there is no record or even the slightest mention of the memorial in her personal files. She did have the monument at Evergreens Cemetery photographed after it was installed, evidently a required part of her commission. But there are no photographs in her archives.

It is the only known public work that she didn't sign. Why she didn't will continue to be the subject of debate. The only indication she completed the commission are the letters she wrote to the committee explaining the photographer's problems with lighting. It wasn't until 2009 that anyone living even knew she did the work. Art historian Ellen Wiley Todd discovered the letters about the photography of the memorial in the American Red Cross archives.

In an article in *Smithsonian Magazine*, Todd considered Longman's possible intentions:

> I am suggesting that Longman found a way in these subtle components of her design, whether consciously or not, to satisfy all the mandates of the commission and still acknowledge the deeply conflicted conditions surrounding the fire and its victims, their lives and work, as well as to make a space for different constituencies of visitors to the monument.
>
> Longman found her way up a social and professional ladder precisely by exercising moderate, gracious, dignified behavior rather than by espousing any positions, such as the cause of working women, that would endanger her own status . . .
>
> So when asked to do the memorial, she responded by executing the design and remained untainted by the controversy that continued to surround the fire in 1912 . . .

> For Longman, there was nothing to do but mourn in a dignified manner and to show the figure in a guise acceptable to the commission and the sculptor herself. This was the overriding message of Longman's Evergreens Cemetery memorial even as she may have provided sympathetic nuances to complicate its terms and address multiple audiences.[18]

The Cemetery of the Evergreens in Brooklyn is astonishing . . . hundreds of thousands of gravestones and monuments, many thousands inscribed in languages other than English, cover its 225 acres, now a lovely park of sun and shade from the trees growing there since the cemetery was established in 1849. Today it is a respite for both dead and living, as urbanites walk its curving paths.

Longman's *Monument to the Unknowns* stands flanked by trees on the very edge of the oldest section. In the years since the monument was installed, the raised words on the back have weathered, and an identical set has been inscribed below the original words. The monument has become a sort of living memorial. Visitors have set dozens of small, smooth stones on the base, as well as a few trinkets: owls, a mushroom. And a few feet in front, there is a new, artless granite marker. Since 2011, those who were unidentified are now known: Josephine Cammarata, Dora Evans, Max Florin, Marla Giuseppa Lauletti, Concetta Prestifilippo, and Fannie Rosen.[19]

Longman's image of the grieving woman in pink marble still incites a somber reverence, a sadness that time has not extinguished. The memory stones, the modern-day trinkets, leave the silent, loud message that these now-knowns are remembered—and so are the political dynamics of the time, the labor issues that resulted in so many deaths of young people on March 25, 1911.

Considering this era of monuments and memorials, a hundred and more years later, calls onlookers to reflect on a compelling and universal question: How does one stay true to oneself amid cultural dilemmas—that shadow that hovers around us all until the just-before-sundown-sunshine that casts a golden light on our human goodness, our human decisions?

This consideration is for those of us who live now; Longman never looked back. And if she had, there would also be her next monuments to consider, those made when she stepped fully, gloriously, into the noonday sun.

NOTES

1. Court documents, Surrogate's Court, County of Fulton, Johnstown, NY.
2. *Gloversville Morning Herald*, October 22, 1910, Longman scrapbook, Loomis Chaffee.

3. "Statue of Tim Murphy was Bequest of the Late Thos. G. Foster of this City," *Gloversville Morning Herald*, October 22, 1910.
4. Ibid.
5. Ibid.
6. Ibid.
7. Isabel Stephen, "Women Who Have Won . . . ," McClure newspaper syndicate, 1913.
8. DCF to EBL, May 15, 1911, Loomis Chaffee.
9. Eve Kahn, "The Woman Who Was Victory . . . ," *Antiques*, September–October 2021, 169.
10. DCF to Newton Mackintosh, January 3, 1911, Chesterwood Archives; Chapin Library, Williams College.
11. EBL to Henry Watson Kent, October 8, 1917, Harriet [sic] Anderson file (An 2279), Office of the Secretary Records, The Metropolitan Museum of Art Archives.
12. "In Memoriam Jacob Godfrey Schmidlapp," funeral document, Loomis Chaffee.
13. *Army and Navy Register*, January 20, 1912, Vol. 51, 17.
14. "Seen in the World of Art," *Sun*, December 24, 1911, 3.
15. "Remembering the 1911 Triangle Factory Fire," Cornell University. https://trianglefire.ilr.cornell.edu/story/introduction.html.
16. Ellen Wiley Todd, "Remembering the Unknowns," *Smithsonian Magazine*, Volume 23, Number 3, Fall 2009, 61.
17. Emergency Relief after the Washington Place Fire, New York, March 25, 1911: Report of the Red Cross Emergency Relief Committee of the Charity Organization Society of the City of New York (New York: Charity Organization Society, 1912), National Archives, 67.
18. Todd, 75–77.
19. "Final Six Victims Identified in 2011," Cornell. https://trianglefire.ilr.cornell.edu/victimsWitnesses/unidentifiedVictims.html.

Chapter 10

Moving Uptown

We no longer speak of Miss Longman as doing good work for a woman.

—Daniel Chester French

Now came a call for entries in a blind competition for a statue that challenged Longman to continue to enlarge her skills and broaden her landscape. She designed an elaborate, multi-figured allegorical statue, to be installed far from New York—a memorial to U.S. Senator William Boyd Allison, for the Iowa state capitol grounds in Des Moines.

Notably, Dan French had nothing to do with it, except to cheer her on.

The fifty-thousand-dollar prize (equivalent to 1.3 million in today's dollars), "to him" who could best express the monument committee's hopes, must have also been a draw for her. As always, all expenses for building and installing the monument would come out of that amount. But Longman, should she win, hoped the commission would afford her a nicer studio/apartment.

In the summer of 1912, she set aside other work and began envisioning an "artistic expression of Allison's character and the meaning of his life," as the committee requested. Allison had represented Iowans in Congress for forty-three years; eight as a member of the House of Representatives and thirty-five in the U.S. Senate. A "Lion of the Senate," he was one of only a handful of committee chairs at that time: of the powerful Senate Appropriations Committee—for longer than anyone else, even to this day.

Two presidents asked him to serve as secretary of the treasury and another as secretary of state. He declined them all and stayed in Congress, working with Republicans and Democrats to accomplish many of his conservative goals, supporting U.S. business and industry through legislation. He died in 1908. His portrait still hangs outside the entrance to the U.S. Senate Chambers.

Grenville Dodge, a friend of Allison, was a civil engineer who worked for railroad companies, served in the Union Army during the Civil War, and helped establish military intelligence. He also served in Congress and then as Union Pacific's chief engineer in the building of the transcontinental railroad. After Allison's death, Dodge set to work to memorialize his friend.

Longman took the opportunity to create a model for an enormous, extravagant monument, with six larger-than-life statues on the sides, a bas-relief portrait of Allison in the front, and a huge *Republic* on top. It reeked with allegory, as she described in her entry:

> His portrait . . . appears on the front of the pedestal in bas-relief flanked on either side by the Victory of Knowledge and the Victory of Peace, the great actuating ideals of his life.
>
> Above, upon the pedestal is a statue of the Republic, laurel crowned, and holding in her left hand a staff surmounted by the American eagle and in her right a sheathed sword.
>
> "Knowledge" carries aloft in one hand a torch, in the other the sphere, symbol of the universe; on his breast are entwined the serpents of Wisdom. The figure is followed by "Legislature" and "Financial Prosperity," the former carrying the books of the law and the fasces, symbolic of power, and the latter holding a horn of plenty filled with coins.
>
> On the other side, Peace, with her symbol, the palm, leads forward Humanity, represented by the mother and child and the laborer carrying a sheaf of wheat and a scythe. The wheat is also the symbol of plenty and is used again in the ornamental border around the top of the pedestal.
>
> Above the plinth which supports the Republic is a conventional laurel design, symbolic of achievement. About the base of the pedestal is a design of oak and laurel symbolizing strength and success, and on it, in font, appears the inscription "Good citizenship is the foundation of a nation."
>
> At the side, below the group led by Knowledge is the motto: "Knowledge is the fountain of lasting prosperity," and on the other side, below the group representing Peace, is the quotation "Peace hath her victories no less renowned than war."

Henry Bacon designed its water setting: "The pedestal rests upon a flight of steps, in the top one of which is a bronze inlay of water-flowers, from the center of which the water is designed to bubble quietly and flow down the steps into the basin below."[1]

Longman worked through Manhattan's sweltering summer months designing the maquette, which cost her at least five hundred dollars. If it was selected, the seated *Republic* would be eight feet tall; the six figures around the base each would be almost nine feet tall—the entire piece, thirty feet tall and sixty-nine feet wide at the fountain's base. She sent the model by train to Des Moines before the October deadline. Her cypher in the blind competition was a four-leaf clover. She told her sister Louise she was afraid she wouldn't win.[2]

For the most part, the judges were unfamiliar: Grenville M. Dodge; Iowa governor B. F. Carroll; curator of the Historical Department of Iowa E. R. Harlan; E. L. Marquery of St. Paul, Minnesota; and sculptor Charles Grafly. Familiar with Longman's work, Grafly had judged the Naval Academy chapel door competition and competed with Longman in the 1907 John Quincy Adams Ward contest for best portrait bust.

There were at least twenty-five entries in the contest; among them "the best artists in the world," a Detroit newspaper reported when the winner was announced in October. "In giving the first place to 'Four-Leaf Clover' we were compelled to do so by its great artistic superiority over all other work shown, and by the most ingenious manner in which the different qualifications of statesmanship and personal characteristics were depicted allegorically, the highest form of plastic description, together with the rare charm that goes to make up a work of distinction."[3]

Dan French wrote to her immediately:

> Gosh!
> Eureka!
> Congratulations
> Billy-be-Gosh-gol-darn!
> Splendid
> What a girl you are!
> So glad I know you!
> Well, I'll be ____d!
> Wait till I catch you alone!
> Wow, wow, wow!
> The rest when I recover from the shock.
> Very respectfully,
> Daniel C. French [in tiny letters]
> TO EVELYN B. LONGMAN [in very big letters]
> October 24 1912[4]

Evidently French didn't have much faith in the Iowans' opinions, nor in Grafly's artistic sensibilities. He wrote again later in the day:

> Glendale, Massachusetts
> La min cara Sculptrice
> I sent you an exclamation mark this morning. This is a sober-minded congratulatory epistle. I have thought of your victory all day and I have told James and Russo and Contini and the ox and the ass and all that was within my gates about it and Mary and I have talked of it to a finish and I have been just as proud of the achievement as if I had any claims of kinship with you or any part in your success. It is great!

I really was surprised, not that I had much doubt but that your design would be the best presented, but because I had very serious fears that the competition would not be decided on the merits of the designs. That you had no friend at court to intercede for you makes the triumph all the greater. And I shall have a better opinion of Grafly's artistic perceptions from now on!

Those five hundred dollars were well spent and the expensive studio venture is vindicated. "Nothing is successful as success;" from now on you will doubtless be flooded with work. In fact you are, already, with seven big statues to do—and you just a little might of a girl! How much will you give me for my new studio to make them in? It looks as if it would be too expensive for me.

Mary and I leave here Monday for Concord, Mass and I expect to get round to New York Wednesday. You may expect to see me as early Thursday as it is fitting to call on a lady and if I do not observe the proprieties when I see you, well! It won't be entirely my fault.

What did "Henry" say? Mary sends her enthusiastic congratulations. I wonder if you can guess why, with my joy in your joy, there is a little thread of sadness running through it? Guess again!

Affectionately,
DANIEL C. FRENCH
October 24, 1912[5]

Figure 10.1 Longman's winning model for the Allison Memorial, surrounded by friends' celebratory signatures. Source/Credit: Photograph from the collection of the Loomis Chaffee Archives, Loomis Chaffee School, Windsor, Connecticut USA. Photo Credit: John Groo.

Friends used the *Allison* announcement for a double celebration. Somewhere—maybe at The Players—they threw her a thirty-eighth birthday party. Guests autographed a photo of her *Allison* sketch. On the mat at the bottom Longman had written, "Central Motif of Sketch for Allison Monument to be erected in Des Moines, Iowa. Evelyn B. Longman, Sc., 1912." At the top of the mat is the date "Nov. 21/12," her birthday. In the same handwriting just beneath the date is the signature "J.G. Schmidlapp." In Longman's hand, beneath Schmidlapp's signature is her own: "Evelyn Beatrice Longman." Beneath Longman's signature is that of Grenville M. Dodge.

More signatures: William A. Marburg, a Baltimore financier and philanthropist, and a friend of Schmidlapp's; they served together as officers in the American Society for Judicial Settlement of International Disputes. A Baltimorian, Marburg was a major donor to Johns Hopkins Hospital and owned an extensive art collection. Also present were signatures of Longman's closest friends: Dan C. French, Henry Bacon, Milton Bancroft, Margaret French, and Mary French.

"Without work—no life to my sister in art," signed someone whose name is indecipherable. And this from W. A. Day: "Words fail me."[6]

It was a keystone moment. It had been eleven years since Longman arrived in New York City. Not only had she launched a career in monumental public statues, she had developed a circle of friends who considered her a colleague. As Daniel French wrote in a ca. 1912 letter promoting Longman to create a Benjamin Franklin statue for Waterbury, Connecticut (which she evidently didn't get), "We no longer speak of Miss Longman as doing good work for a woman."[7]

A reporter for the *Sun*, expressing the implicit bias at the time that women must be feminine, wrote: "Feminine in everything but her art, she expects the woman to be eliminated when art is discussed, and indeed among the painters and sculptors alike, in private conversation, it is quite as often . . . 'Longman' as it is . . . 'Miss Longman' that . . . Longman Longman [is] spoken of in [her] profession . . . accorded [her] place as [artist] among the men."[8]

From French's October letter, it appears that before the *Allison* commission was decided, and despite her fear of rejection, Longman had already committed to a new studio and living quarters on the top floor of the remodeled Upper East Side mansion of Henry Marquand, a founder of the Metropolitan Museum of Art. The *Beaux Arts* brick and sandstone triple-mansion at the corner of Madison and Sixty-Eighth had been renovated into a luxury apartment building. The original architectural plans show a thirty-foot-square space on the twelfth floor, with a sitting room, dining room, bedroom, and casting room—living and working space specifically designed for Longman.[9]

A reporter for the *Evening Sun Times* who was allowed to tour Longman's new digs had expected a Bohemian artist décor. "There are no tight skin rugs, no languorous looking divans, no cigarette stumps, no futurist paintings, no pictures of nudes," the reporter wrote.

> The front door of the apartment opens into a hall. One way leads into the studio workroom, another to the living room. Here there is a big sofa, deep and comfortably tufted in a dark velour. A large and beautiful conch shell of the translucency and quality of mother of pearl, is set up on a rod and shades the light over the desk. No executive secretary for a business man could have a more orderly desk. On the floor are dark rugs, on the walls a few pictures. At one end of the hall a stairway, on Colonial lines, winds delightfully to rooms above. The workroom is enormous, with ceilings high enough to accommodate the great figures standing on pedestals. There is not a thing there but gives evidence of being needed.[10]

In April 1913, Longman had photographs taken of her new apartment. In one staged photo she sits on a seat below a large window reading the newspaper. Small sculptures, including a smaller replica of *Victory*, are arranged on the mantel of a fireplace next to her. A glass-fronted bookshelf holds not only books, but a vase and other small pieces.

Her small *Torso of a Woman* rests on the mantel in the living room. Another posed photo shows her at a dining table. Around the room are upholstered chairs and a glass-fronted breakfront with porcelain dishes inside.

Upstairs on the brick-floored roof in an open-air space made homey with potted vines and trees, Longman stands in front of arched lattice, dressed in long skirt and white blouse, arms akimbo. In several photos of the spacious studio space, a large, heavy wooden table holds the working model of the *Allison Memorial*. Longman stands at the top of moveable wooden stairs to work on it. The studio is immaculate—perhaps for the photographs, but evidently Longman was a tidy sculptor. Rather than using the long-sleeved smock covering her clothes as a place to wipe clay from her fingers, she kept a handkerchief in hand.

To celebrate her long-awaited move to a luxuriant living and working situation, she held a housewarming reception. A guest, the president of a large corporation who also had a—bigger—apartment in the building, told Longman that an artist shouldn't live in such luxury. When the Marquand apartments opened in 1913, monthly rent ranged from $165 (six rooms) to $580 (thirteen rooms). The story goes that Longman turned her "glowing eyes" on her guest and said something like, "It is good for an artist to have all varieties of experience. It is no better for an artist to live in a garret than it is for a businessman. I'll sell my apartment when you sell yours."[11]

Prominent in her new uptown bedroom were a triple-mirrored vanity, curtained window, and a four-poster bed covered in a bedspread festooned with garlands and wreaths. Every night Longman, who once slept with scampering mice under a dripping roof, now—the queen of ornamentation—safely tucked herself in under cover of garlands and wreaths.

NOTES

1. Allison Monument folder, Loomis Chaffee.
2. *Detroit Tribune*, December 1, 1912, Loomis Chaffee.
3. "A Remarkable Career," *Sioux City Journal*, November 17, 1912, 25, Loomis Chaffee.
4. DCF to EBL, October 24, 1912, Loomis Chaffee.
5. DCF to EBL, October 24, 1912, Loomis Chaffee.
6. Matted photograph with signatures, Loomis Chaffee.
7. DCF to Darragh de Lancey, February 10, 1911, Chesterwood Archives; Chapin Library, Williams College.
8. "Art Gossip," *Sun*, December 24, 1911, Loomis Chaffee.
9. Christopher Gray, "The Once and Future Marquand," *New York Times*, September 8, 2013, Real Estate Section, 9.
10. "Again a Woman's Work Is Awarded the Highest Place," *Evening Sun Times*, November 1, 1916, Loomis Chaffee.
11. Batchelder, unpublished memoir.

Chapter 11

Thee, He, and She Go West

I cannot tell how my work is progressing. Thee knows I never know when thee is not here to tell me—and that is no joke.

—Evelyn Beatrice Longman

With increased rent for her uptown studio and the unrelenting juggling act between paying project expenses and being paid in stages for those projects, Longman was uncertain she could swing a trip to San Francisco in the spring of 1914. She wanted to join Bacon and Bancroft at the Panama-Pacific International Exposition (PPIE) site to do the post-cast finishing on her *Fountain of Ceres*, which Bacon had commissioned for his Court of the Four Seasons. Bancroft was in San Francisco finishing eight murals for the Court; Bacon would soon travel there to supervise final construction.

It was probably Henry Bacon who helped her find a way west; in late April, the two took a train to San Francisco. For a week, "The Triumvirate," Longman called them, worked on their projects, housed in mammoth, hangar-like buildings at the yet-unfinished Exposition site, due to open in 1915. They visited with other artists and fair dignitaries—and then they went on vacation together.

Ceres was waiting for her outside the temporary sculptors' studio on the Expo grounds. As with all the thousands of groups of sculpture, the pieces for Longman's fountain were cast in plaster and tinted the ivory color chosen by Bacon's friend, Jules Guerin, director of color for the Expo. All buildings would wear the same muted ivory; this would be no glaring White City. Guerin also chose a palette of eight soft colors for everything in the park, including domes, murals, banners, flags, the guards' uniforms, and even the sand in the driveways.

Just as Chicago had organized the World's Columbian Exposition to show the world that it had recovered from its catastrophic fire, San Francisco mounted a campaign to host the 1915 world's fair to prove that the city had overcome the earthquake and fire of 1906. The PPIE would celebrate the completion of the Panama Canal, the four-hundredth anniversary of the discovery of the Pacific Ocean by Balboa, and current U.S. industrialization.

Sculptor Alexander Stirling Calder, chief of sculpture, hired thousands of assistants to add the ivory finish to the statues, which were molded in staff, a mixture of plaster of Paris and other materials, that would be destroyed at the end of the fair. Two assistants were assigned to Longman the week she worked on the *Ceres* pedestal, alongside monumental works-in-progress by many of America's most renowned sculptors.

Daniel Chester French's central contribution to this world's fair, *The Genius of Creation*, would be displayed as the main group on the Avenue of Progress. A hooded, spectacularly winged male figure extended arms beneath which Adam and Eve faced opposite directions, but held hands in the back of the monument.

When Bacon's Court was completed, it would be described as a place of relaxation:

> Toward the west, passing through a very characteristic avenue, in the style of the happiest phases of the Italian Renaissance to be found in Florence, one enters the Court of the Four Seasons. . . . The chief quality of this court is that of intimacy . . . a very happy combination of gardening effects and architecture, together with the interesting wall-fountains, screened by stately rows of columns, make for a picture of great loveliness. Of all the courts, it has the most inviting feeling of seclusion. The plain body of water in the center, without statuary of any kind, is most effective as a mirror reflecting the play of lights and shadows, which are so important an asset in this enchanting retreat. . . .
>
> As an Exposition feature, the Court of the Four Seasons is a decided innovation. At St. Louis, for instance, in 1904, everything seemed to have been done to excite, to overstimulate, to develop a craving for something new, to make one look for the next thing. Here, in the Court of the Four Seasons, one wants to stay. Most emphatically one wants to rest for awhile and give one's self over entirely to that feeling of liberation that one experiences in a church, in the forest, or out on the ocean. I could stay in this court forever.[1]

Bancroft's murals:

> The fountain niches of the Seasons in the Court of the Four Seasons are graced by Milton Herbert Bancroft's appropriate panels. Two of these, one on each

> wall of the fountain niche, are devoted to each season. One represents the pleasures that that period of the year brings forth for man; the other shows the duties it demands of him. In "Spring," we have the poet's conception of the time of blossoms and garlands, of young loves, piping shepherds and dancing maidens, while the goddess of the season dreams of coming glories. In the companion panel, "Seedtime," the waiting farmers attend her as she stands, sceptered with an Easter lily, and extends her benison on the land. "Summer" crowns the victors in athletic sports; while in "Fruition" the goddess of the season receives the tribute of the successful workers of the soil. The panel called "Autumn" is gay with the dance of the vineyard festival; three happy figures modeled with grace and much refinement are placed on a background divided into panels by a vine. But "Harvest" is quiet and serious; the goddess, bearing the torch of Indian Summer, receives the sheaves of the gleaners. So in "Winter," one panel shows Festivity, with the old bard, the Christmas garland and the gaieties of the home; the other, the distaff by the fireside, the huntsman and the wood-cutter.[2]

Bacon had planned Longman's *Ceres* to rise from the reflecting pool, but later moved it to the forecourt. The fountain had three components: *Ceres* stepped atop the world atop a pedestal decorated in bas-relief with dancing maidens above a base of garlands and masks, water shooting from the masks into a pool below. Smiling *Ceres*, wind blowing her skirt, carried a scepter of corn and offered a wreath of wheat. The eight smiling maidens in bas-relief danced gaily, skirts awhirl, carrying garlands of flowers and baskets of fruits and vegetables, some playing tambourines and pipes.

Once again, Longman had interpreted a classical figure in a new way. Stirling Calder wrote of Longman's *Ceres*, "Miss Longman has expressed her as exultant, regal, young—far less matronly than as conventionally pictured—glorying in her power to bless the cooperative labors of man and nature."[3] A photograph of Longman's *Fountain of Ceres* was published on the title page of the official catalog of public works at the fair.

Bacon, Bancroft, and Longman stayed in San Francisco's Kensington Hotel, and shared early-morning breakfast in the lace-curtained Paisley Cafe, on Geary Street. Longman dressed for work in long linen skirt, cummerbund, long-sleeved white shirt, and feathered hat; jacket at the ready. The three also dined at "our woodpile restaurant" on the shore at "Government Docks." They socialized with other artists and exposition officials and visited some of the local sites, including Golden Gate Park designed by John McLaren, landscape engineer for the fair. Longman met McLaren and photographed "some of McLaren's trees," the park's Tamalpais Trail cliff, and the Japanese Tea Garden—where Henry Bacon gifted her with a "topaz chain."[4] The two walked arm in arm at the park's "Buena Vista."

In response to correspondence she and Bacon sent to Daniel French, he replied:

> 125 W. 11th St.
> New York, May 4 1914
> Dear Wanderer,
> Your postals and "Henry's" have been very exciting and make us feel quite in touch with you. . . . You must be having a wonderful time and I am envious of the position of your courier.
> I feel as if there were little to report from New York,- nothing to rival the wonders you are experiencing. I have nearly finished the Saratoga figure and even the fastidious [painter Thomas Wilmer] Dewing, who was in today, thinks it is pretty good. . . . The "Creation" has gone along, too, and I shall have no trouble to finish it next week. I need your enthusiasm to key it up, however, and it wasn't kind of you to go away just when I wanted you!
> D.C.F.[5]

While in San Francisco, Bacon had made arrangements for a trip, writing out an itinerary and budget ("about $200").[6] Longman finished work at the Exposition at 5 p.m., May 10. At midnight, the triumvirate boarded a Santa Fe Railroad car and were in Merced, California, for breakfast, then lunched at El Portal on their way to Yosemite National Park. In the park, they stayed at the Sentinel Hotel, a two-story white-frame building with second-floor rooms opening to a balcony. Situated along the Merced River, it afforded a full view of the dramatic Yosemite Falls.

During their two-day visit, they took before-breakfast walks among the trees and meadows in Yosemite Valley, then hiked to *I'llouette* Falls and Vernal Falls. Their most arduous trek was with a guide on horses to Yosemite Falls. The three and their guide were photographed at Columbia Point. They lunched at the bridge over Yosemite Falls, and then Longman waited while the others mounted the last part of the trail up to the Falls.

The morning of their noon departure, on May 13, they hiked to Mirror Lake. In a beautiful photograph of the three seated on a rock outcropping, Mount Watkins is prominent behind them, mirrored with their images in the lake.[7]

After a train ride to the park's southern entrance, they arrived that evening at the Wawona Hotel, and early next morning the three helped each other up into the back seat of an open-air carriage pulled by four horses, for a drive through one of the giant Sequoias. Later Longman and Bacon ("T & H") were photographed beside the giant roots of the "Fallen Monarch." After lunch they returned by train to Merced, where they stayed the night.

It must have been at this point that Milton Bancroft headed back to New York, or Maryland. There are no photos of him during the rest of the trip.

Figure 11.1 Fountain of Ceres at Panama Pacific Exposition, San Francisco. Source/ Credit: Photograph from the collection of the Loomis Chaffee Archives, Loomis Chaffee School, Windsor, Connecticut USA.

Longman and Bacon took a daylong train ride to the Grand Canyon, stayed at El Tovar Hotel on the south rim, and visited a Hopi village across from the hotel. On a rock outcropping, at Grand View Point, Longman, in a half-sitting, half-lying position, stretched her body to look over the edge; in another photo at the same spot, Bacon sat upright, legs crossed, looking at the camera. That afternoon, accompanied by a cook, "Slim" Shankland, and a guide, "Mr. Brinckman," they began a descent into the canyon on the Hermit's Trail, a seven-mile, sometimes twisty, sometimes steep journey—walking or aback mules.

They stayed overnight on the canyon floor at Hermit Camp, a relatively luxurious encampment nestled beneath breathtaking, towering, stratified red limestone cliffs. Operated by the Harvey Company, cabins with wooden sides and a canvas roof were set on rock pilings and furnished with comfortable beds, fresh linens, Native American rugs, chairs, and small woodstoves.[8] Chefs prepared hearty breakfasts, tea along the trail, and gourmet dinners at the end of the day. Bacon drew a map of the camp with their accommodations, his and Longman's cabins side by side. Longman photographed the sunrise from Hermit Camp on May 18 and was photographed at 5 a.m., when she stepped from her cabin ready for breakfast.

Photos of the walk on the trail reveal a happy, relaxed Longman, sometimes hatless, which was unusual. She looks calm and at ease in every photo, a bit flirty in some (perched on her tummy, her legs kicking up behind her as she leans over the edge above the Colorado River); playful (her skirt raised enough to show off the leggings beneath, "Ready for first trail"); holding back a curtain at a hotel window, which she captioned, "Dust of trail removed before leaving El Tovar" at the end of their Grand Canyon visit. Even Bacon joined her in hamming for the camera (she more hammy than he), eating cherries at a train station. She must have thought it unusual for him to do so, because she made note in the caption, "He ate too."[9] Individual photos of them at a train station show Longman leaning against a luggage cart with a sassy, cocked-head smile and Bacon in front of a train car, without tie or hat!

Photos taken on the long train trip back to New York, via Chicago and Toledo, show Longman looking dreamily out the window while Bacon looks into the camera.

In Chicago for the day, Longman and Bacon met up with her siblings and their spouses. Cecil, Claude, Longman, and "Hal" photographed each other in front of Lorado Taft's Fountain of the Great Lakes on the Art Institute grounds. It is reminiscent of the fountain of the nymphs Longman had helped to create her last year at the Institute. They toured Claude's Acme Steel company, made a stop at the University Club, and shared corned beef and cabbage with other family members at "The Works." In photographs taken at the family table, Longman's face is stunning: tan, bright, relaxed, laughing. In one she is thoroughly engaged with the photographer (Bacon, presumably) in a way no one else at the table is.

This photo and the ones in the Grand Canyon, as well as the fact that from this point there are no more "missing Thou" letters from Longman to Milton Bancroft, possibly indicate that Longman's and Bacon's time together in the Grand Canyon had marked a shift in their relationship. A vacation can make or break an alliance, in ways everyday life doesn't, or bring it to a new place. Away from anyone else they knew, completely removed from work, sharing the grandeur and monumental beauty of the natural world, negotiating travel challenges together. . . . Indications are that during this trip they established a deeper and more comfortable familiarity, a more confident connection, a more affectionate companionship.

Arriving home on May 22, a letter from the ever-faithful Dan French, at Chesterwood for the season, greeted Longman. In it French indicates his familiarity with the Longman-Bacon relationship and expresses his response to their time together.

May 20 1914
Dear Evelyn B.
Your postal from Casa del Desierto {in Barstow, California} has helped us to open the season here this morning.
I wonder if it is possible that you will drive home today as it says? I intended that you should find a letter from me to bid you welcome upon your arrival. You certainly have been good to me to send me so many postals in your progress, and these proofs that Bacon had not entirely crowded me out of your thoughts has pleased me greatly, but I still feel regretful that I could not show you all the wonders of the world and so be associated with your memories of them always. I am "crazy" to see you and to hear all about everything! I hope to hear that you found your work reproduced to your satisfaction.
It is perfectly beautiful here today. The cherry and pear trees are white with bloom and the apple trees are just coming out and all the foliage is of the tender and varied greens that make this one of the fairest seasons of the year.
I do not know when I shall come down to earth, but when I do you will not escape me!
Affectionately,
Dan. C. French[10]

The PPIE opened in February 1915. Daniel and Mary French made their way to San Francisco to see it in the spring. On April 9, Daniel sent Longman a postcard that pictured her *Ceres*. And at the end of April, he sent a postcard from Yosemite, reporting as well on *L'amour*, a small marble group she entered in the international competition.

Hotel del Portal
Yosemite April 27 1915
We have come from San Francisco today. . . . The Exposition is magnificent and your fountain is beautiful. You and Fraser lead "the bunch," of course, with me not far behind! Your marble group gets lots of bouquets,—and deserves them. We are due home about May 15.
D.C.F.[11]

At this point in her life, Longman could track the development of her career by world's fairs. 1893: The nineteen-year-old warehouse clerk caught a glimpse of her destiny, admiring French's sculptures outside the Agriculture Building at the World's Columbian Expo in Chicago. 1903: Having trained with French, Longman's first public monumental sculpture was chosen to top Festival Hall at the center of the Louisiana Purchase Exposition in St. Louis. And now 1915: Just as Longman's youthful Ceres, the goddess of fertile ground, stepped a foot deftly and confidently on top of the world on Longman's thirty-foot fountain, so did Longman herself arrive, alongside her pals, in San Francisco, a confident, talented, mature sculptor of monumental work.

In fact, shortly before she left New York, she was one of four sculptors (the only woman) who received an invitation to submit a model for consideration of a statue to top the tower of a new 434-foot-tall Western Union building on Fulton Street in New York City, the second-highest peak in the city. The top of Parnassus.

NOTES

1. Eugene Neuhaus, *The Art of the Exposition.* http://www.books-about-california.com/Pages/Art_of_the_Exposition/Art_of_the_Expo_Chapter_2.html.
2. Ibid.
3. Ibid.
4. Henry Bacon to EBL, 1918 postcard of tea garden and EBL handwritten note recalling the earlier visit, Longman scrapbook, Loomis Chaffee.
5. DCF to EBL, May 4, 1914, Chesterwood Archives; Chapin Library, Williams College.
6. Longman scrapbook, Loomis Chaffee.
7. Trip photos, Longman photo album, Loomis Chaffee.
8. See https://nplas.org/hermitcamp.html.
9. Longman photo album, Loomis Chaffee.
10. DCF to EBL, May 20, 1914, Loomis Chaffee.
11. DCF to EBL, April 27, 1915, Loomis Chaffee.

Chapter 12

Consecration

To each one who sees this work its message will be different, but I think it will always be one of beauty and purity.

—Evelyn Beatrice Longman

When Longman moved uptown in early 1914, she continued to rent her old studio for a month so she could finish the plastiline model and cast in plaster one of her "ideal" pieces—noncommissioned works that expressed her values. Begun in 1903, while she was still working on busts of young Margaret French and Milton Bancroft and making the study for *Victory* in the little barn at Chesterwood, it was the earliest ideal piece she would create—this first one was her take on love.

Originally named *L'amour*, then *Consecration*, the marble statue is of a nude man and woman embracing. He is taller, tenderly holding her shoulder with his right hand; kissing her crown, he enfolds her head with his left hand. Her face tilted up toward him; she rests her head and left hand on his chest, embracing him with her right arm. He stands strong on both legs; one of her legs is bent. Their eyes are closed. He seems absorbed in her, protective; she looks safe, content.

On her own since she was five, working since she was fourteen, determinedly finding her way in a world dominated by men, alone in New York in 1903, she easily could have been tempted to envision the kind of love and support for herself that she began to portray as ideal in her sketch of *L'amour*. Other moments in her life suggest considerable ambiguity.

Through the years, in interviews, Longman spoke of a woman artist's dilemma over love, marriage, and career, her views changing over time. In 1909, when she was working on her portrait of Frances Faxon and *L'amour*

Figure 12.1 The marble *Consecration*, Longman's first ideal work. Source/Credit: Photograph by A. B. Bogart. From the collection of the Loomis Chaffee Archives, Loomis Chaffee School, Windsor, Connecticut USA.

had been set aside while she tended to commissions, a *Kansas City Post* writer reported her saying, "Work is not enough to fill a woman's life. Women who complete the life unmarried and without having come to motherhood cannot know perfect happiness." Asked if she would give up her career if she met the right man, she said, "Yes, if I loved him. I should never hesitate.

"When real love comes, it far overshadows all else in life—and the seeming sacrifice comes easy. I love my work; my life seems wrapped up in it now. People tell me I have a wonderful career, yet I would give it up if real love came into my life."[1]

In 1911, under a headline "'Don't Wed If You'd Succeed.' Girl Sculptor Gives Sage Advice," a reporter quoted her advising female artists to "remain unmarried; you can't do two things at the same time and do both well."[2]

In a 1913 *Des Moines Register* article, reporter Ada Patterson and Longman had a conversation about love and marriage:

> "Professor Theresa Labiola, the first woman admitted to the Italian bar, has been leading a strike of the telephone operators in Rome," said Patterson.
>
> "The Government wants the girls to choose between work and husbands. They want both, and Professor Labriola says a woman is entitled to both love and work."

"I agree with the Italian Portia," said Longman.

"But Rosa Bonheur . . ." the reporter says.

"We know her work, but we do not know whether she was happy. I am willing to wager that if we knew her real life we would know that she was not a happy woman, and she was not completely successful, for success includes happiness. No one's life is a success unless she is happy!"

"And work isn't enough?"

"No, indeed, I don't believe any woman who completes her life unmarried dies or lives happy. No woman who has not children is happy. The greatest happiness is in children, and greatest art is sculpture in human flesh."

"So far you—"

"I know. I have stayed single, but I wouldn't if the right man came. Would you? Would any woman?"

"You would give up your career for marriage?"

"Yes, if I loved the man."

"Suppose a woman were hesitating between work and marriage?"

"She would assuredly have to make that choice if she married while young, for the object of a marriage while one is still young is children, and children will push any art into the background and should, but they would be worth the sacrifice. If a woman marries late in life that probability is not to be considered. Then she might continue with her art or professional business and meet her husband in the evening. That's the way men do, isn't it? Meet their families in the evening?"

"Meet them rather grumpily."

"Yes, the grumpiness is likely to follow a hard day. But if a woman can endure it in a man a man should be as generous."[3]

Sometime in 1909, when she had found two exceptionally good models, she went back to work on the love group. The female model was Audrey Munson, who modeled for Konti, French, and many other sculptors. Referred to as "Miss Manhattan," Munson was the figure on a dozen public sculptures in New York City. When Calder chose Munson as the model of choice for the Panama Pacific Exposition, Longman hired her for *Ceres*.

Munson posed for three-fifths of the sculptures created for the fair. In his 2016 biography of Munson, *The Curse of Beauty*, James Bone wrote: "Set like gemstones in her milky skin, she had questioning, slightly impertinent gray-blue eyes," and importantly, he wrote, she was unusually good at holding the perfect pose for hours, despite the pain in her muscles and nerves.[4]

Working on *L'amour* in earnest for the next three years, Longman finished the plastiline and cast it in plaster late December 1912, so she could move it safely to her new studio. Cutting on the marble began in the summer of 1914, following her trip west and after finishing the model for the Western Union competition. For several months, a "Mr. Horton" blocked the statue in a Greek marble, Seravezza, enlarging it by six inches. Longman then cut and polished the marble, often working late into the night with hammer and chisel, tweaking the piece.

Before sending it west to the sculpture competition at the PPIE, Gorham Company exhibited the group in New York City for a week in January 1915. In San Francisco, *L'amour* won a silver medal in the international competition. Alexander Stirling Calder wrote:

> There are few more complete examples of delicacy of feeling and of refined, caressing perfection of tooling than this exquisite marble group, "L'Amour." . . . The purity of its emotion, the tenderness and fidelity of its poignant pose, are surpassed only by the marvel of surface finish. The surface has been gone over so lovingly, so painstakingly, so repeatedly that the marble has taken on the soft, warm impression of living flesh. And the gentle unstrained modeling has the plastic grace of the human body. Miss Longman . . . is an earnest and serious artist of abundant talent whose work is treated with ever-increasing respect and admiration. . . . She presents Love in the group under discussion as a rarefied and inspiring emotion in which the physical and spiritual commingle and "sense helps soul" as well as "soul helps sense."[5]

Peter Thomson of Cincinnati, no doubt a friend of Jacob Schmidlapp, bought the group. A self-made millionaire, Thomson began his career at twenty as a shipping clerk for a bookstore. He soon opened his own bookshop, collected rare books, wrote *The Bibliography of the State of Ohio*, and made his fortune manufacturing paper, as president of the Champion Paper Company. Thomson acquired 150,000 acres of woodland, including an old-growth forest, which he cut, then replanted a pulp preserve. For his employees, he established a free medical clinic, offered free life insurance, and established commissaries where food and household supplies were available to them at cost.

When his wife, Laura, who wrote books for their five children, died in 1913, Thomson asked Longman to design her memorial. She simplified an image of an angel stepping out of the stone and holding a flowing drapery over her head that in 1908, French first used for his *Melvin Memorial*. She and French had modified it again for their *William Slocum Memorial* in Forest Hills Cemetery. Five years later, Longman shortened the image and, uncharacteristically, used no other symbols for Laura Thomson's memorial. Thomson later asked Longman to create a bronze frontispiece of the same image for the organ in his Cincinnati church.

After Thomson purchased *L'amour*, he asked Longman to write the story of the creation of the group, but she wasn't inclined to explain the motivations for her work. In August 1916, however, she complied with his wishes. Of all her works, it was the only piece for which she ever explained her personal motivations. By then she had renamed it *Consecration*:

> You have set me a difficult task in asking me to write you a description and history of the conception of the marble group "Consecration." . . . At first it seemed quite hopeless to attempt it—our inmost thoughts upon a subject of this kind seem too sacred to put on paper. I think, too, that the marble itself speaks clearly and in unmistakable language to those who understand. I shall try, nevertheless, to tell you something.
>
> The subject of this work, the love between man and woman, the greatest thing in human life, has been the inspiration of artists of every age. Most, if not all, of the results which I have seen, have expressed the lower form of the great passion, not the highest and noblest. It was from the desire to perpetuate the finest side, from the woman's standpoint, which inspired this work. While acknowledging the beauty of the physical side of love, I feel that without the spiritual side also, this passion is not worthy of representation through the noble medium of sculpture, or indeed through any medium.
>
> In this group I have endeavored to suggest self-abnegation and sacrifice, the test of true love, in the tender, protecting attitude of the man and the clinging surrender of the woman; self and all the grosser elements of human love are for the moment obliterated.
>
> It was not intended, however, to rob love of the fine physical side; the two figures, while refined, are strong, the man's whole form and attitude expressive of manly strength, the woman's replete with the noblest physical impulses—entire surrender to the man she loves combined with the natural shrinking of her sex.

The couple stands next to what looks like a tree stump, which Longman has lavished with symbols:

> All the symbols used further strengthen these ideas. That of the oak and ivy is well known—the symbols of masculine power and feminine dependence. The skull and serpent have been placed beneath their feet, symbolic of the triumph of supreme love over death and temptation. The winged children's heads, dimly emerging from the upper part of the rough block of marble, are suggestions of the innocence and holiness of such a love, and also, perhaps, of its pure and perfect fruits.
>
> The subject has been looked at from the woman's standpoint,—obviously the only possible thing for me to do,—and I have therefore placed the man upon a slightly higher level than the woman, not because he necessarily occupies this place in general, but because the one man always does—to the woman who loves him, in the same measure as he assumes the protecting attitude of strength toward her.
>
> You ask my reason for changing the name from "L'Amour" to "Consecration." I should prefer not to name a work of this kind at all; for intelligent people it hardly seems desirable; but for the purpose of cataloguing for exhibition,

it was necessary to call it something. The English word "Love" seemed too brusque for a title, and the French equivalent was therefore used at first as being more euphonious. But this did not satisfy me, chiefly because so many ignoble works have been given to the world under this name. So I finally settled on "Consecration" as being more expressive of the kind of love which this work depicts. The definition found in the Standard Dictionary for the word "consecration" is: "The act or ceremony of separating from a common to a sacred use."

What I have said does not do justice to my ideals, or even to the marble expression of them; but, as I said in the beginning, it is very difficult to do so. To each one who sees this work its message will be different, but I think it will always be one of beauty and purity.

Of course you understand I would not wish these sentiments published, as they are far too intimate and personal.

Sincerely yours,
Evelyn B. Longman[6]

Longman's letter to Peter Thomson *was* published, presumably with her permission, along with a photo of her, biographical information, and a list of her works, for an exhibition at Brookgreen Gardens in South Carolina. She had the piece cast in bronze, and in 1916, that version was exhibited in Buffalo, New York. In 1927, Hartford's Wadsworth Atheneum purchased it. At that time Longman summarized again the history and meaning of the piece. Her last paragraph: "I could write at much greater length as to the meaning of this group, but sculpture is, after all, my language, and I believe that all I would say is written clearly in the work itself—for those who understand; for others, more words would not help to clarify it, I fear."[7]

Longman later had two or three smaller, half-sized bronzes of the piece cast: for a Christmas gift, a swap with another artist, and a gift for a friend.[8] "Its reception by the public was a great joy to me," she had written to Thomson. "Nothing which I have ever done has received such favorable comment—from men and women alike—friends, acquaintances and many strangers."[9]

Longman turned forty-two in 1916. Past what was considered normal childbearing years, that fulfillment seemed to have slipped away. If *Consecration* was her "ideal" notion of a relationship between a woman and a man, it is hard to imagine she could achieve it. Had there been one moment in her entire life when this woman—who from six, when she trudged up a railroad track and later demanded to move from Ontario to Chicago, and still later broke through an all-male barrier—was ever "shrinking?" Ironically, it would be *Consecration* that would make its way into the heart of a man who would make the possibility of love and career, and the shrinking of one's self, the marriage, and children dilemmas less theoretical.

NOTES

1. *Kansas City Post*, Longman scrapbook, Loomis Chaffee.
2. "'Don't Wed If You'd Succeed.' Girl Sculptor Gives Sage Advice," unidentified newspaper and author, 1911, Longman scrapbook, Loomis Chaffee.
3. "Girls Entitled to Love and Work; Love First," *Des Moines Register*, 1913, Longman scrapbook, Loomis Chaffee.
4. James Bone, *The Curse of Beauty* (New York: Regan Arts, 2016), 2, 111.
5. A. Stirling Calder, "The Sculpture and Mural Deocrations of the Exposition: The Art of the Exposition," edited by Eugene Neuhaus (San Francisco: Paul Elder and Co., 1915). http://www.books-about-california.com/Pages/Sculpture_and_Mural/Sculpture_and_Mural_main.html.
6. EBL to Peter Thomson, August 22, 1916, *Consecration Booklet* (Brookgreen, SC: Brookgreen Gardens, undated), Loomis Chaffee.
7. Bulletin of the Wadsworth Atheneum, Vol. VI, No. 1, January 1928.
8. Longman later had two or three smaller, half-sized bronzes cast: a Christmas gift for Horton Batchelder; a swap of art pieces with Chauncey Foster Ryder; and one for Katrina Trask at Yaddo.
9. EBL to Peter Thomson, August 22, 1916, Loomis Chaffee.

Chapter 13

Electricity

I want you to come up Saturday afternoon - or any time before that - to inspect the San Francisco group which nears its finish. Can you? Can't you? Will you? Won't you pleeeease come? I have improved it lots, thanks to your critical aid, and it has a sort of homogeneousness that it lacked before.

—Daniel Chester French

When Evelyn saw "Joe," a bodybuilder pitching a patent medicine in the window of a downtown drugstore, she hired him on the spot to be her Zeus.[1] If she won the competition for *Genius of Telegraphy*, her towering, modern, gold-leafed bronze Zeus would stand tiptoe on a globe 450 feet above Fulton Street to crown the tower of the new twenty-six-floor Western Union Building, at 195 Broadway.

Despite the architect's order for a majestic, seated god, Evelyn envisioned another virile, handsome young man standing—holding thunderbolts in his left fist, his arm raised high above his head, à la her *Victory*'s raised wreath. A twirl of cables would encircle his plainly nude body; in his right fist, extended to the side, the exposed wires at the end of the electrical cables. This time, with classical Greek's magnificent wings.

William Welles Bosworth, designer of the Greek-inspired skyscraper for Western Union, had in mind a classical Zeus—a mature, bearded god. And specifically, the Zeus atop the tower was to be seated, holding a thunderbolt. Again, Evelyn did the unexpected, though she did incorporate a thunderbolt—certainly not because it was expected, but because it fit.

Evelyn didn't mix things up, do the opposite thing simply to be obstreperous. Rather, a woman's view, sensibility, and process were mostly unknown in the field of monumental public sculpture, so what she produced was unexpected. And although she was a classical artist, she considered the modern context. In this case, she gauged what the finial would look like from hundreds of feet below and determined that from the new subway station and for pedestrians coming down Park Avenue, a standing figure would be much easier to view than a seated one.[2] Also, a virile, young man with his strong jaw, and wavy, short hair communicated the tenor of the modern project: spirited, purposeful, strong, dynamic.

Whether the men who would judge the submissions would agree was, of course, the question. Once again, she took her chances. Should her figure tower above New York City's skyline, it would be a real-life-symbol—fourteen years after she came to New York City to sculpt beautiful, monumental public works—that she herself, at the age of thirty-nine, stood at the pinnacle of a most unlikely career.

Joe modeled for her until his untimely death. At that point, she engaged a professional model, Solomon Goldstein, who modeled under the name of Sol Padrone. Evelyn's Zeus would have Joe's upper body and Sol's legs.[3]

In her description of her design for the judges, Evelyn campaigned for the "preeminent desirability" of a standing rather than sitting figure. "In the composition the sculptor has aimed to create an interesting and spirited silhouette viewed from whatever angle or distance, and has paid special attention to the two main views from below—that coming from Park Row where the statue may be seen for some distance and the view directly in front where it will be seen at a very acute angle by crowds going to and from the new subway entrance."

Championing her contemporary figure, she wrote: "The subject should be modern in thorough keeping with the building, which, while Greek in detail, is thoroughly modern in its spirit and purpose."[4]

As she would explain to her sister Vally (some Ontario relatives still protested aspects of Evelyn's profession), the figure's nudity "represents a perfectly elemental, natural force [Evelyn's emphasis] namely electricity, and I cannot imagine any kind of drapery or clothing which would not detract from its force and simplicity."[5]

Judges were the president of Western Union, Theodore N. Vail; architect Bosworth; and, representing the National Sculpture Society, which directed the competition, Daniel Chester French. When Evelyn learned her teacher and friend was a judge, she was concerned that whatever his vote, it might be criticized, and she insisted that French request more judges. His request was refused. He wrote to Bosworth: "It was only her desire to secure absolute fairness and to avoid criticism that she made the suggestion that the jury should be increased."[6]

Visiting Evelyn's studio that summer wasn't an issue. French was focused on finishing *Creation* for the Panama Pacific International Exposition. Also, his brother Will fell ill.

2709 Prairie Avenue
Chicago, June 1 1914
My true little friend.
Your dear, sympathetic letter came to me an hour or two ago at the hospital where my brother lies mortally ill. Until yesterday it was thought that he would recover from the effects of the operation, but he failed rapidly in the afternoon, and it is thought that he will pass away very soon. It is really better that he should, for he may so be saved from a long and painful illness with no hope of recovery.

I have thought of you often during these long days and I intended to write to you because of your acquaintance with Will and, I guess, just because I was in trouble.

Affectionately,—and with deep appreciation of your beautiful letter,
Daniel C. French[7]

Evelyn wrote again a few days later, upon learning of Will French's death. Dan French responded:

Chicago, June 6 1914
Dear—
You have the gift of sympathy! The sweet little letter that was waiting for me when I came back from the cemetery yesterday afternoon seemed to say just the right things and conveyed in every line the kindness and sympathy and affection I needed, and made me more than ever grateful for the dear little friend who has been so much to me since she came into my life. I shall need you more than ever now.

The funeral yesterday morning at the Art Institute—in the auditorium—was quite beautiful and the evident sorrow of the host of people who attended it was most touching. After the cremation Mrs. French and Henry and Prentiss and a half-dozen intimate friends laid the ashes away in a really beautiful part of Mount Greenwood Cemetery, with the sunshine of a perfect June day about us. It was all quite as it should have been.

I start for home this afternoon and should arrive about five o'clock tomorrow. I wish I might find you there.

Affectionately,
Dan. C. French[8]

Evelyn spent three days at Chesterwood in late June and the Fourth of July holiday on Shelter Island with the Bancrofts. Though she was immersed in finishing the *Telegraphy* model, French begged her to return to Chesterwood to look at his group, *Creation.*

> July 6 1914
> Glendale
> Dear Evelyn Beatrice,
> It is probably very imprudent of me to send you this appeal when you have just returned from Chateau Bancroft because you will feel that you must not take another holiday. But, I answer, this is not a junket; this is business, and the fact that it is mine, not yours, makes no difference.
> This means that I want you to come up Saturday afternoon—or any time before that—to inspect the San Francisco group which nears its finish. Can you? Can't you? Will you? Won't you pleeeease come? I have improved it lots, thanks to your critical aid, and it has a sort of homogeneousness that it lacked before.
> Affectionately,
> Daniel[9]

In late July, he wrote, "Dear Sculptrix . . . I wonder if you will hate me if you don't win that competition? I guess you will win, though!"[10]

By July 25, Evelyn's model of *Telegraphy* was finished and photographed in her studio. Four days later, well before the deadline, all entries were delivered to the architect. The three judges viewed the models and unanimously voted for entry #3 (French saved his vote until the other two judges had voiced their choice) and when the envelope for entry #3 was opened, Evelyn had won the competition. "Mr. French probably thought he recognized my work, though, of course, I had kept everything rigidly secret from him," Evelyn noted at the bottom of Bosworth's letter awarding her the commission.[11] Bosworth later confessed to her that he thought the model they unanimously chose had been done by Robert Aitken.[12] Aitken's submission was the traditional respectable, bearded, curly-haired older nude and draped male—seated, holding thunderbolts in one hand and a staff with a flame on top in the other.[13]

Evelyn's standing Zeus was a hit. Bosworth wrote of her entry: "It is an inspiring and highly appropriate conception as regards subject and extremely happy in scale and in silhouette which is, of course, above all other things, of prime importance."[14]

Ultimately, rather than the seventeen-foot figure she designed, the figure would stand twenty-four feet tall and weigh ten tons. Cast in bronze, it would be daubed with a thin layer of gold and lit at night—a dazzling sight atop the city.

In her contract for *Genius of Telegraphy*, she agreed to "furnish all labor and materials and complete a full-size model in plaster . . . and personally

Figure 13.1 Genius of Telegraphy won Longman a place "at the top of Mount Parnassus."
Source/Credit: From the collection of the Loomis Chaffee Archives, Loomis Chaffee School, Windsor, Connecticut USA.

supervise and criticize the execution of the said full size model and the bronze statue to be made from the said model for the sum of $7,000" (equivalent to about $195,000 in 2022).

"I agree to complete the small-scale model of the said statue on or before June 1st, 1915, and I agree to complete the full-size model as rapidly as possible consistent with good workmanship, and in any event not later than October 1st, 1915."[15]

Evelyn had experienced a multi-month high: traveling to San Francisco and working amidst other artists at the Panama Pacific Exposition; vacationing with Bancroft and Bacon in the beauty of the Sierras and the Grand Canyon; winning the Western Union competition. And now she had mountains of work before her. Strong, tenacious, resilient, hardworking Evelyn came down from the high that summer, somewhat depressed. Vulnerable and transparent, she turned to the husbands.

Daniel French wrote to her from Glendale, cheering her on with shop talk about her helpful contributions to his work, a smattering of empathy, and teasing humor.

Aug. 16 1914
Dear Sculptrix,
So you were blue after you had won that competition! That's just reaction. I am almost always blue after great excitement or even comparative joy. I have no doubt you have settled down to reasonable satisfaction over the down-fall of your rivals. By the way, I see the Luxembourg has purchased one of Tonetti's busts! Don't you wish you were as great as he! The more I know about works that are acquired by L'Etat, the less I think of any of it.
I am going on with the Trask statue, having sent the "Spirit of Creation" off a week or more ago, and I am also at work on "Sculpture" over in the little studio. Miss Anderson is helping me and, I think, is enjoying being here.
I am expecting any time to hear from Piccirilli that the Longfellow is ready for me to finish and you may have me on your hands for a week 'most any time. Not before next week, however.
Give my compliments to the husbands and please give an occasional thought to the absent one who is always
Devotedly thine
D.C.F.[16]

By the time French arrived in the city, Bacon and Longman had escaped from the August heat and any fragments of depression and embarked on a working vacation, visiting cemeteries and monuments from Westchester County, New York, and points north; stopping in on friends in Kennebunkport, Maine; and visiting Evangeline's Well in Nova Scotia. Mid-September they were in Tarry Town, New York, where Longman photographed Saint-Gaudens's *Hall* monument in Sleepy Hollow Cemetery. She also photographed Henry Bacon, hat in hand, sitting on the base of the Davis Monument, which he designed. The two joined members of Longman's family at Lakeside, Michigan, for swimming and boating in late September.

Work awaited. The artistry of creating the seven-foot plaster of *Telegraphy* was one thing. The technical achievement of mounting a twenty-four-foot, ten-ton bronze atop the 434-foot tower was another. In November, she met in her studio with a representative from Roman Bronze Works, who would cast the final piece from the plaster; a representative of the electrical company that would light the figure; a fellow from the construction company building the tower; a steel anchoring engineer; and a member of the architecture firm.

The foundry representative expected to cast the sculpture in two or three sections. They took into account wind, other elements, and the small connection of the tall figure—only its toes—to its base at the globe, and they determined the thickness of the metal and how to make the figure rigid: by installing three-inch steel bars in both legs as high as possible and two horizontal two-inch webs in the globe. Longman agreed to put extra material under the feet of the figure so the steel rods could be placed in the legs. Discussions

Figure 13.2 Longman (left) and Henry Bacon at her brother's summer cottage, Lakeside, Michigan. Source/Credit: Photograph from the collection of the Loomis Chaffee Archives, Loomis Chaffee School, Windsor, Connecticut USA.

about lighting began, including Longman's hope that the piece be lit overall and her assent to add lights to illuminate the head and feet of the figure.[17]

But *Telegraphy* wasn't the only major, monumental, long-term work taking shape in her studio. There was also her ambitious *Allison* with its bas-relief, six larger-than-life-sized figures along the sides, and its grand figure of *Republic* on top. Then Bacon recommended that Longman sculpt his monumental memorial for the state of Illinois' centennial. And, in the offing, with Bacon and French, there was the Lincoln Memorial in Washington, D.C.

NOTES

1. "The Man Behind the Man Atop 195 Broadway," *Gentleman's Headquarters Quarterly*, 1955. Genius of Telegraphy file in Longman Collection, Loomis Chaffee.
2. EBL, "Description of Model," *Genius of Telegraphy* file, Loomis Chaffee.
3. "The Man Behind the Man Atop 195 Broadway."
4. EBL, "Description of Model."
5. EBL letter to Vally, Christmas 1938, Loomis Chaffee.
6. DCF to Welles W. Bosworth, May 2, 1914, Chesterwood Archives; Chapin Library, Williams College.

7. DCF TO EBL, June 1, 1914, Chesterwood Archives; Chapin Library, Williams College.

8. DCF to EBL, June 6, 1914, Chesterwood Archives; Chapin Library, Williams College.

9. DCF to EBL, July 6, 1914, Chesterwood Archives; Chapin Library, Williams College.

10. DCF to EBL, July 23, 1914, Chesterwood Archives; Chapin Library, Williams College.

11. WW Bosworth to EBL, July 29, 1914, Loomis Chaffee.

12. Ibid.

13. Brookgreen Gardens. https://brookgreen.pastperfectonline.com/Webobject/54611602-A816-498B-A311-990146143007.

14. WWB to EBL, July 29, 1914, Loomis Chaffee.

15. Marc Eidlitz to EBL, December 7, 1914, AT&T Archives and History Center, Warren NJ, box 127, 10 01 01.

16. DCF to EBL, August 16, 1914, Loomis Chaffee.

17. "Minutes of Meeting . . . Miss Longman's studio . . ." November 9, 1914, AT&T Archives and History Center, Warren NJ, box 127, 10 01 01.

Chapter 14

Bizzy-Izzy-Izz-She

None of us who were at the studio of Miss Longman for several hours together and so close together in earnest and enthusiastic consideration of the object of our conference, can ever forget it.

—General James S. Clarkson

No one could have imagined at the World's Columbian Exposition of 1893 that a rising architect, a sculptor of national import, and a young woman warehouse worker attending the fair would one day come together to work on one of the nation's most beloved monuments. But, indeed, one thing had led to another.

Henry Bacon and Daniel Chester French met at the Chicago Fair. Bacon was a junior member of the country's most prestigious architecture firm, in New York City, which had designed the Agriculture Building that featured four of French's sculptures—including *Indian Corn*—at its entrances. Bacon and his mentor, Charles McKim, served as members of the advisory committee with Daniel Burnham, the Chicago architect who, inspired by Europe's Neoclassical architecture, had created the striking White City, to which French contributed other central monumental works.

The extravagant display of *Beaux Arts* architecture in the White City had demonstrated that an urban landscape could not only signify a city's financial status, but it could also include aesthetic aspects for its inhabitants—thus, the City Beautiful movement. In 1900, the American Institute of Architects held its annual conference in Washington, D.C., to honor the centennial year of the city. They carried the City Beautiful idea forward by establishing a design commission to continue to develop the landscape and architecture in the nation's Capitol. A year later, McKim was named to the Senate Park Commission, also called the McMillan Commission.

With the City Beautiful philosophy and the *Beaux Arts* aesthetic in mind, the commission drew up the 1901 Plan for Washington. It envisioned a coordinated park system with an emphasis on a mall from the U.S. Capitol to the Washington Monument and included a new national monument to President Lincoln. In 1910, a federal Commission of the Fine Arts was named to carry out the plan. Burnham was chair; among its first members was Daniel Chester French.

In February 1911, the Fine Arts Commission created the Lincoln Memorial Commission to oversee the construction of the new monument. In August of that year, members of the Lincoln Commission brought on Henry Bacon as an expert advisor. By then, French had partnered with Bacon on several projects.

Two days after French introduced him to the Lincoln Commission, Bacon was solicited to submit his ideas for the Lincoln Memorial. There were months of fiery debate about a location for the monument, including the marshland along the Potomac River, to the south and west of the Washington Monument, at what would be the end of the mall. Perhaps the possibility of building a monumental building in a marsh was not as daunting to Bacon as it was to Washington politicians; when he was eleven years old, his engineer father, Henry Bacon Sr., had been responsible for building a barrier dam across the mouth of Cape Fear River near Wilmington, North Carolina.[1] If the Lincoln Memorial were to be built in the swamp along Washington's Potomac River, a sixty-five-foot-deep foundation would be required to get through the soggy earth to solid rock. After more than a year of contention, with Bacon's backing and French's lobbying (he was now chair), the commission chose the site in the marsh.[2]

Bacon had been sketching ideas for a Lincoln Memorial all along. The first sketch of his design of the majestic, Greek temple–styled, Doric-columned monument is inscribed in his own hand on the lower right side of the drawing, two years before the Fine Arts Commission would tap a Lincoln architect.

> Aug 6th 1911
> 1st Sketch for Lincoln Memorial.

Though Lincoln Committee members halfheartedly viewed designs by other architects, in January 1913, President William Howard Taft signed legislation appointing Henry Bacon architect of the Lincoln Memorial. He was given sole authority to recommend a Lincoln sculptor to the Lincoln Committee.[3]

Soon after his appointment, Bacon wrote to Longman from Chicago, where he and French were inspecting their Marshall Field Memorial. "Dear Trixina . . . isn't it splendid! HOORAY—Rejoice with me. . . . Think of a bolt like this from the blue depositing in one's lap such a prize—& without competition. . . .

". . . I was told the day before I arrived in Chicago (which was last Wednesday) that the Fine Arts Commission had unanimously recommended me—Voila! French and I were in Chicago together looking at the Field which is set up and looks well——— We had an hour with Claude into whom French . . . poured champagne in honor of my good fortune—"[4]

Bacon could not have known then that the edifice he sketched and would later proudly call "a majestic noble structure that breathes reverence and honor to the memory of Abraham Lincoln" continues, one-hundred-plus years later, to be an engaged space in the ongoing struggle for freedom and equality for all.[5]

Even from the day of dedication, when African Americans in attendance experienced one humiliating dismissal after another, ill treatment of African Americans would continue to play out at the noble building Bacon engineered to reverence the president who signed the Emancipation Proclamation. On that day in 1922, African American Robert Russa Moton, president of the Tuskegee Industrial School, after delivering the (censored) keynote address, was escorted from center stage to a cordoned-off area a block away to be seated with the other African Americans at the event.

Perhaps Bacon would have been surprised that this would be the place where seventy-five thousand people gathered to hear Marian Anderson in concert on Easter morning 1956, when the Daughters of the American Revolution refused to allow her to perform before an integrated audience in their Constitution Hall. . . .

The place where John Lewis and the Rev. Martin Luther King Jr. inspired hundreds of thousands at the March on Washington for Jobs and Freedom on August 28, 1963. . . .

The place where Barack Hussein Obama stood to address a crowd the evening before he was inaugurated, the first African American president of the United States. . . .

The place where National Guard troops dressed in camouflage and body armor lined up in rows across its front steps during days of nonviolent Black Lives Matter rallies in the nation's capital in June 2020. . . .

The place where visitors stand every day, in the hush of a sacred national space and in awe of an icon of the resolve, courage, and sacrifice that are required to summon and respond from "the better angels" of our human nature.

In conversations and during repeated trips to Washington with colleagues Bacon and French, Longman's input was sought from the start: the myriad decisions for Bacon's building, including the choice of marble; the long, agonizing process—in French's studio and at the memorial—creating and lighting the Lincoln statue; designing a space that elicited reflection and inspiration. Indeed, the only woman artist to work on the monument, she would fashion the ornamentation of the Lincoln speeches on the north and south walls, though, for decades, her name was not mentioned in National Park Services information.

Bacon gave his first sketch of the Lincoln Memorial to Longman, who at the time was working on *Consecration*, her ideal of spiritual love, and on *Ceres* for Bacon's Four Seasons at the Panama Pacific Expo. She had recently won the *Allison* competition. Inscribed in his handwriting in the lower left of the Lincoln drawing, Bacon wrote:

> To E.B. Longman
> from Henry Bacon. Oct. 1913

But his most tender inscription was for her eyes only, hidden and discovered decades later. A granddaughter of Longman's who inherited the sketch took it to a paper conservator, and upon inspection, he found tiny letters hidden in the bushes—so small, indiscernible, unless you happen to look for them with a magnifying glass: "To Beloved Beatrice."

In a low-key, groundbreaking ceremony on Lincoln's birthday, February 12, 1914, shortly before Longman and Bacon's trip to San Francisco, Bacon stood with a small group of over-coated, be-hatted men on what would become the northeast corner of the Lincoln Memorial and lifted the first shovel-full of frozen swamp.

Next, the architect's task was choosing a sculptor. It seemed inevitable that it would be Daniel Chester French; after all, French, who often had chosen Bacon to design the architectural settings for his monumental sculptures, had recommended Bacon as advisor to the Lincoln Memorial committee. By then the French-Bacon partnership and friendship were well-established; their ease working together became one of the rationalizations to choose French.

However, there were other opinions about a sculptor. The most challenging to Bacon was the suggestion that an earlier Lincoln statue by the then-deceased Saint-Gaudens be enlarged for the new memorial. This required the quiet, mild-mannered Bacon to stand up and speak up for his choice of French.

French had a challenge as well. To avoid a conflict of interest, he couldn't keep his cherished position on the Fine Arts Commission and be designated as the Lincoln architect. Nevertheless, in January 1915, the Lincoln Memorial Commission chose Daniel Chester French to create the Lincoln statue.

A month later, again on Lincoln's birthday, at three in the afternoon, Bacon was front and center during the cornerstone-laying ceremony. A time capsule had been intricately placed in a cavity inside the seventeen-ton, seven-foot square stone. African American workers stood on two sides to help guide the great stone into place after a U.S. flag–wrapped crane had set it on the northeast corner of the site. Bacon, Robert Todd Lincoln, and Washington dignitaries then stood atop for photographs. Dan French was not in the picture. It would be another two months, in April, before he resigned from the Fine Arts Commission.

A few weeks later, early March 1915, Longman and Henry Bacon traveled to Vermont to visit marble quarries. Photos in her scrapbook detail the trip. On March 6, Bacon stood in front of an unidentified memorial in Burlington, Vermont. At Barre, the two toured a granite quarry. On Sunday, March 7, they took a horse-drawn sleigh ride in the snow at Waterbury. They stayed at the Berwick Hotel in Rutland, Vermont, on March 8 and visited the Vermont Marble Quarry. Climbing steep wooden stairs, they viewed walls of marble yet to be harvested and a tumble of marble blocks in a snow-covered pile.[6]

The following day, Longman had an important meeting in her New York studio with a delegation of Iowa-connected people who came to view her plasticine model of the *Allison Memorial*. It went exceedingly well. Sculptor Charles Grafly, a member of the selection committee, wrote to General Grenville M. Dodge the next day that "The minor changes made in the restudied working model have greatly improved the scheme . . . and I am sure could you have been with us you would agree that no mistake has been made in the selection, and that your city will not only be proud of the Allison memorial but will 'set the pace' for future work of like character in cities of the west."[7]

Grafly also suggested that if Longman required more time for completing her work, "it ought to have the unqualified approval of your committee." General James S. Clarkson, an Iowan by then retired as surveyor of the Port of New York and living in New Jersey, was among the visitors to Longman's studio. His recording of the experience, in a letter to Iowa Historical Department curator Edgar Harlan, was rhapsodic: "None of us who were at the studio of Miss Longman for several hours together and so close together in earnest and enthusiastic consideration of the object of our conference, can ever forget it."

> To me, as I think it over, it seems as if Senator Allison himself must have been present, for in addition to the gifted woman who in this monument has given not only to Iowa but to all the world a new meaning and a new eloquence in art, there was Senator Clark, so great himself in the world of art, and Mr. Roberts who knew Senator Allison so well and so truly that writing a life of him is as much a duly [sic] on his part as Miss Longman's conception of a fitting monument to him was an inspiration to her, and Mrs. Clarkson who knew Senator Allison intimately and admiringly all through his long career—and all these thinking of him so intensely, actually made me feel as if their intensity had brought the Senator's own spirit at least into the meeting. I shall always regret that a camera [sic] was

> not taken of that group to which you called attention, when Miss Longman and Senator Clark, standing before the model, with Miss Longman standing higher than the Senator and both gazing upward at the statue.[8]

Former Montana U.S. Senator and "copper king" William A. Clark, who had lived in Iowa, collected art, and at the time lived in a mansion he had built on Fifth Avenue, wrote to his former colleague General Dodge of Longman's progress: "She certainly has displayed a great deal of ability in her grasp, of the spirit and scope of the subject, and has handled the symbolic grouping in a most forceful and intelligent manner that will, when completed, be attractive and impressive.

"The graceful characters that compose the group are replete with life and action, and the ensemble presents a scene of harmonious arrangement that cannot fail to impress the beholder with a sense of admiration."[9]

More pressing in early 1915 even than the *Allison* or the small-scale plasticine model of *Telegraphy*, due June 1, had been a smaller, presumably quick, but, as it turned out, another politically complicated project: designing a commemorative coin for the Panama Pacific International Exposition in San Francisco. The Fine Arts Commission, Daniel Chester French then as chair, recommended six artists, including Longman, to design five coins. Secretary of the Treasury William G. McAdoo selected Longman to create the $2.50 coin, the "Quarter Eagle." She and three other artists chosen to develop coins (Robert Aitken, Charles Keck, and Paul Manship) met with acting director of the mint, Dr. Frederic Dewey, in New York City. By January 29, all four had submitted bronze casts of their designs.

McAdoo sent the designs to the Commission of Fine Arts, whose members approved all. When McAdoo showed the designs to Charles E. Barber, chief engraver of the Philadelphia mint, Barber offered suggestions. So McAdoo asked the four to make alternative designs. On February 5, all four were sent rejection letters for their new ideas from McAdoo. Reasons seemed unclear; all four artists protested. Longman asked for an explanation and submitted four new designs—all declared "unacceptable." Bacon planned to introduce Longman to Secretary McAdoo in Washington so she could find out what to do next.

On the morning of March 12, Longman fell ill in her Washington hotel, and Bacon took her to Providence Hospital, where she had an emergency appendectomy. Astonishingly, McAdoo had a scheduled appendectomy at Providence Hospital that very day.[10] His and Longman's rooms were the same number, one floor apart.[11]

Longman dropped her efforts to design the coin.

Henry Bacon stayed with her during the surgery and for several days, making phone calls to Longman's family and friends and shepherding visitors when they came to Washington to see her—sometimes also taking them to the Lincoln Memorial site. During her two-week stay, visitors included her brother Claude, Jacob Schmidlapp, Margaret French, Milton Bancroft, and, separately, Margaret Bancroft. Most stayed for multiple days or, as was the case with Margaret Bancroft, who lived in nearby Maryland, visited more than once. Margaret French sent Longman something new every day, Longman noting later, "to amuse and entertain me. I have never forgotten it!"[12]

Illness had plagued her on and off, but this was a dangerous moment. Her pain would continue for several days following surgery. And though Bacon speculated that maybe this was the problem all along and now hoped she wouldn't have so many physical issues, frequent illness would continue to frustrate her.

Daniel French wrote to her from New York the evening of the day of her surgery:

> You poor, dear little thing!
>
> We are full of pity and sympathy for you. What a strange and lamentable and unexpected catastrophe it was,—and to hit you when you were away from home! It was cruel. At least we will be thankful that the faithful Henry—bless him!—was by and that you have had his resourcefulness and wisdom and devotion to see that everything was done for you that could be.
>
> Mr. Bancroft telephoned me this noon and again this evening. . . . I hate to think of the terrors of looking forward to the operation and of the pain and discomfort of it all, but I know how brave you are and how like a Stoic or a Christian you have gone through with it.
>
> In the evening paper we have found this about Secretary McAdoo. As you could not go to see him he has, apparently come to you. It is an odd coincidence, isn't it? I imagine you and the Secretary of the Treasury in twin beds, side-by-side, holding hands in mutual sympathy over the loss of your respective appendices!
>
> Good-night,—and may all good angels guard you!
>
> Always with deep affection
>
> Dan. C. French[13]

And on the 13th . . .

> Dear Beatrice
>
> Mr. Bacon has just been reporting the latest from you and I am grieved to hear that you are suffering so. I am sorry for you! . . . He also says that they attributed all your past ills to this one defect in your anatomy and that they predict better health for you than you have had in recent years. I pray that this may prove true, too,—and it seems reasonable to expect it, too; doesn't it? It may be a heavy price to pay for immunity, but when it is all over, we can all rejoice.

I had just been talking with Mrs. Bacon when Mr. Bacon called me up and she seems to think that "Harry" must stay in Washington as long as he could be of service to you and that his office was of no consequence in comparison. It is splendid that he can be there. He is a friend indeed!

This is only to assure you of our constant thought of you and to tell you again how sorry we are for you. You will be dearer than ever to us now because of our anxiety that opened our eyes to your dearness to us before. (I am not sure that this is English, but I hope it will convey what I mean.)

Good night and sweet sleep and a better day tomorrow.

Affectionately,

D.C.F.[14]

Daniel and Mary French were preparing for a trip to San Francisco to see the Panama Pacific International Exposition. He hoped to see Longman before they left.

March 18 1915

Dear Beatrice

I got the latest reports from Henry this morning by telephone. I am sorry to hear that you have had such continuous pain. I hoped that was all over . . .

Bacon says your brother is with you. I am glad of that and I wish you would remind him of my existence.

This isn't a letter, but only an outward manifestation of my constant thought of you. Bless you and good-night!

Affectionately,

D.C.F.[15]

Henry Bacon wrote to Longman from the Occidental Hotel in D.C. as he was returning to New York, probably March 16.

Dear old Beatrice—

When you read this you will be in the loving care of old friends and to make all of your many friends happy you must be careful from now on, for I hope a short time only—not to tax your rapidly returning strength— Soon you will [missing word] quite well again but it seems just yesterday that we were walking "through the valley of the shadow of death" together—at least that's what your old Cousin Hal thought and your angelic smile and trust in me through it all will always be an inspiration to me. Bless you my dear friend—It has been such a comfort to me to do what little I could—I wanted to sleep on a mat under your bed all the time—

Soon we will be trundling out to Sandy Spring and soon I will be leaving you but if ever anything was left with anybody there will be left with you loving good wishes and promise of all that is best on the part of your

Loving Cousin Hal[16]

He included the poem mentioned earlier:

> Dear old Trix
> Sans appendix
> We all love you dearly—and even more
> Though a scarlet scar
> May your tum tum mar
> It's a trifle merely—we still adore—

While the plan that she would recuperate at the Bancroft farm at Sandy Spring, Maryland, evolved, unexpected complications developed there, too, though it's possible Longman never knew of them.

On Monday, the 15th of March, Henry Bacon wrote from the New Willard Hotel in D.C., to Margaret Bancroft:

> First of all the appendixless one is feeling much better this morning though she still suffers pain; but thank goodness it's evidently diminishing.
>
> It's too bad I missed seeing you yesterday. I was with a friend at Chevy Chase walking over the links.
>
> I shall probably leave tomorrow at 3 p.m. for New York. Have just phoned Mrs. Bacon the news from here and she will transmit it to Banny, French et al. I have been keeping the Chicago people acquainted with events . . .
>
> Miss L. said this morning that she hoped you would come in to see her some time the first of next week . . .
>
> Mr. Schmidlapp was here yesterday and will be back Thursday night and will spend Friday here.
>
> I will be here in a week or ten days and take her back to "At Last."
>
> Bizzy-Izzy-Izzynot!
>
> Love to all.
>
> Yours Sincerely
>
> Henry Bacon[17]

Evidently unbeknownst to Bacon, and perhaps to Longman, was the fact that Margaret Bancroft's visit of March 14 had resulted in a great upheaval, a marital firestorm, a tragic breach. Bacon had invited Milton Bancroft to join him the day of Longman's surgery, the 12th.[18] Instead, Bancroft arrived at Longman's bedside the day after her surgery, on March 13. The next day, Margaret Bancroft made a first visit to Longman, during which Longman told Margaret how much she appreciated Milton's visit the day before.

This came as crushing news to Margaret, who lived with their children about a half-hour's drive from Washington, D.C., and who didn't like the fact that most of the year she and Milton lived apart. Now she had just learned that Milton had not come to see his family, nor even let his wife know in a telephone call that he had been so close to home, at Longman's bedside and at the Lincoln Memorial with Bacon, before returning to New York City.

Margaret's letters to Bancroft at this time shed light on the Bancroft marriage, their friendship with Longman and with Henry Bacon, Longman's illness and recovery, as well as Margaret's remarkable generosity of spirit and strength of character.

On March 13, the very day Milton Bancroft visited Longman in the hospital, Margaret wrote to him using language of her Quaker faith, reporting that, after a recent bout with the flu, she was "up and about but so weak and just longing for thee. I am so dependent on love & affection."[19] So ironic, her confessing her need for love and affection, having just been ill with her husband far away, while in fact he wasn't far away. He was thirty minutes away, visiting Longman at Providence Hospital and going with Henry Bacon to see the progress on the Lincoln Memorial.

After a visit to see Longman, Margaret's letter to Milton dated March 15 is heartbreaking:

> I went to see Miss Longman yesterday. She was frightfully weak, and seemed to think that she had been throu' a very hard time. I sat with her an hour in almost absolute silence, but she seemed glad to see me and I shall go again . . .
>
> I am almost myself again but for the really terrible pain I have suffered since I learned from Miss L. that thee was in Washington Sat. and didn't even call me up. I really cannot get over it. I do not know that I ever shall. I am glad thee came down, and only wish thee had responded to Mr. Bacon's first messages, and been with him during the operation.[20]

Relaying other details of the day's trip, including, with her children Tom and Nancy, a viewing of Saint-Gauden's *Adams* memorial in Rock Creek Park cemetery, she continued:

> This separation is about killing me spiritually, and when I knock up against such a blow as last Saturday's I weep inward tears which have scars. Thy letter tonight brought me some comfort, but dear how could thee do it; how could thee. On the way to the city Nancy said I wonder if Papa came down, and I answered so confidently "No, he would never have passed so near us without telephoning." I wondered if my remark occurred to her again after receiving thy letter, & doubtless it did for she handed me her letter with the observation "Papa did come down." Please understand I do not bear the slightest [indecipherable word] but I am so hurt so really hurt. . . .
>
> A Toi,
> Margie

If Margaret Bancroft ever was concerned about the relationship between her husband and Longman, and she evidently had been, she doesn't seem to be anymore. Her words indicate that she was not upset that her husband visited Longman (in fact, she admonished him for not going a day sooner), but she was upset that he was so close by and didn't let her know. It's likely this would have triggered prior concerns about her husband's and Longman's friendship, but if she was not overly concerned about that currently, it might have been because it was clear that Longman and Henry Bacon held each other in great affection. And that would indicate either the possibility that Longman's affections were not focused on Milton, or that Longman could hold friends in great affection without that attention and affection being a threat to others who loved them.

Margaret relayed her next visit to Longman in a letter to Milton, dated March 22:

> I went in today to see Miss Longman—found her in splendid condition. She sat up this morning for a short time, but is still too weak to enjoy it. I spent nearly two hours with her, and was so glad to be with her again, and find some of the old-time sparkle.

Before signing off with her usual "Hearts Love, Margie," she wrote: "I am trying to see things from thy point of view, but I would rather see thee."[21]

By the next day, March 23, Margaret seemed to have had a shift in spirit.

> My Sweetheart,
> I am glad thee let go, and I am glad I let go tho' as I look back on the intensity of my distress it seems very silly of me to have felt as I did, but I did, and I am glad that it is past.
>
> As to our life we have lost much that can never be made up to us, but think what we have, an abiding love for each other which has kept alive and vital in spite of separation; totally different environments, and necessarily somewhat divided interests. The children love thee dearly, and thy companionship is prized by them far more than that of most fathers. Thy work has been the lodestar of both our lives—without that I do not think that I could have borne things at all.

Margaret was open to the idea that when Longman was released from the hospital on April 1, she would come to Sandy Spring, for recuperation:

> Mrs. Moore wants Miss Longman to come out here for a little while after she leaves the hospital. I hope she will but I would not urge her. She said yesterday that she had not received a letter from thee and I think she felt it—do write soon.[22]

In a March 29 letter to her husband, Margaret wrote that she enjoyed her "little time with Mr. Bacon—he is so real. I was interested in the Memorial, and only wish that I could watch its growth from week to week" and expressed her hope that Longman would recuperate at Norwood.[23]

Bacon delivered Longman to Sandy Spring on April 1. Photographs taken the day of her arrival showed Longman, who was quite fond of Mrs. Moore (Margaret's stepmother), wrapped in a shawl and standing outdoors with her head affectionately on Mrs. Moore's shoulder while Margaret Bancroft, in white blouse, long dark skirt, and a skinny man's tie, stood somewhat apart from the two, smiling slightly at them.[24]

A proud and private woman, Margaret seems to have kept her current marital crisis to herself so that Longman and Mrs. Moore didn't know of her hurt feelings. What is clear is that Margaret Moore Bancroft was the one holding the Bancroft family together. She wrote to Milton the next day, April 2:

> My dearest,
> Miss Longman seems quite fine this morning—she slept better last night than she has for a long time; and has worked about the place with the children and me. She seems to like the idea of being here, and we hope that she will stay a long time. Dr. Bird is coming down tomorrow morning to be sure that everything is progressing well. It was lovely to have Mr. Bacon for even the few hours he could give us. . . . He is splendid. . . . We are counting on thee for next week.[25]

Indications are that Milton arrived at Sandy Spring sometime around the middle of April. A photograph of the triumvirate—Milton Bancroft, Henry Bacon, and Longman—is dated April 14. Bacon and Bancroft are pulling Longman riding in a wooden wagon, smiling into the sunshine. Longman's caption on the photograph in her scrapbook says "A Load of Nuts."[26]

On April 27, Longman remained at Norwood; Milton was back in the city. A letter from Margaret to Milton on that day related more news from home and an update on Longman.

> Miss Longman is still far from herself—she looks better but she is so delicate. This morning when every ailment seemed on the mend, she woke with a stiff neck and back.
>
> It is so sad for that splendid spirit to be housed in such a fragile body.
>
> She blames all her trouble on that first year of New York restaurant-fare, and not even then feeling sure of the next meal.
>
> There have been steps toward reconciliation.
>
> I was so glad to get thy letter last night. I wish thee had had time to write me about our talk, tho' I feel so much better since thy visit—so much more a

Figure 14.1 Henry Bacon (left) and Milton Bancroft pull a wagon full of Longman, during her recovery from appendix surgery at Norwood. Longman captioned the photograph: "A Load of Nuts." Source/Credit: Photograph from the collection of the Loomis Chaffee Archives, Loomis Chaffee School, Windsor, Connecticut USA.

part of thee and to thy life that talk between us is no longer needed, tho' always dear to me.

She related family news, and then:

I wish that Miss L. had gone back with [Mr. Bacon] the last time he was here. She was in better shape then than now. It worries me that she is so miserable—I feel responsible.[27]

Three days later, on April 30, she wrote to Milton:

Miss L. & Mr. Bacon have just gone, and I could not but feel awfully sad to have them go. Miss L. has been such a pleasure to me & it has done me a world of good to be thrown with artists again. Mr. Bacon says that he is coming back again in May with Thee which gives me two lovely things to look forward to.[28]

Longman had been at Norwood for a month. When Henry Bacon picked her up at Sandy Spring, they didn't return to New York City, but traveled the short distance to Washington, D.C., where Bacon showed her the progress at the Lincoln Memorial construction site. Sections of immense columns of Vermont marble lay about. Bacon photographed Longman with her arm leaning on one. They spent time at Great Falls, Virginia, outside D.C. The next day, they visited historic sites in Alexandria, Virginia, and the National Cemetery in Arlington. The following day, they toured sculpture around the city.

A few days after Longman left, tragically, Margaret burned the old letters Milton had sent.

> I spent a large part of yesterday destroying thy old letters—it nearly broke my heart to do it, but they were letters that I would not want others to see. They were so sweet and brave though so much to break one's spirit—that I would like the children to read them, and yet after all they were between thee and me, and could never mean to anyone what they meant & said to me so they are in my heart & memory only now.[29]

The marital wounding in the spring of 1915 seems to have brought the Bancrofts' spousal struggles to a crisis point. The longtime, ongoing separation was clearly hard for Margaret, and her husband's friendships with women artists, perhaps most decidedly with Longman, had added to the tension. One wonders how Margaret had felt about "the triumvirate" in San Francisco and their vacation together.

Fortunately, the reconciliation that the Bancrofts accomplished during the early spring of 1915 held. Though Milton traveled even farther, in 1919 to France near the end of World War I, to make illustrations for the Red Cross, a year after that it was to Norwood and Margaret that he returned, permanently. Though Longman kept in touch with her friends and continued to visit them at Sandy Spring and Shelter Island, by the time Milton returned from Europe, unexpected changes in Longman's life meant that soon her days at Sandy Spring and Shelter Island simply would be beloved memories.

Longman's full recovery from surgery came too slowly for her. She visited the Frenches at Chesterwood in May as flowers bloomed in the garden—the visit and the blossoms a boost to her spirits, as well as Daniel French's. Even though she was fatigued, and the hospitalization and long recovery added pressure to her schedule to complete the many figures of the Allison in plasticine and the seven-foot plaster model *of Telegraphy*, she was accepted as the sculptor for Bacon's *Illinois Centennial Monument*. Longman would create a bas-relief of the state's one-hundred-year history that would wrap around a circular base; rising above would be a seventy-foot Doric column with a ten-foot eagle on top. The monument would be installed in Chicago's Logan Square.

Lacking in stamina, she did what she always did: do the work anyway, and then collapse—or travel. She finished the seven-foot plastiline model of *Telegraphy* in June. Western Union sent her the first payment of four thousand dollars.

But her inability to recover physical stamina brought on the blues. She confided to Daniel French, who wrote her:

> July 15 1915
> Dear Evelyn B
> The sound of your dispirited little voice has been in my ears ever since I talked with you the other day and I have in vain tried to devise some plan or to think of something to say to you that would give you fresh courage. I haven't much to offer now, but I can tell you what a distinguished physician said this morning. Dr. And Mrs. Lambert are here and this morning he inquired particularly about you and then said some very pretty things about you,—as he should. Then I told him how discouraged you were over the frequent ill-turns that you had been subject to, when you had expected to be in better health than ever, after the operation. He told me to tell you that you should not be troubled about that, except for the present discomfort,—that, in normal cases, the patient usually did not entirely recover for a year, and that these attacks that you had been having were to be expected for a while. He has been operated on for that same thing and did not entirely recover for a year or more, but he says he is now in better health than for years before the operation. He attributes much of the subsequent illnesses to the nervous shock that any operation as serious as this is to the system. It would, of course, be better if you could have absolute rest for a couple of months, but, as that is not feasible, he intimated that you must consider yourself in a sensitive state and save yourself as much as possible,- and particularly that you are not to be blue if you don't feel up to par. That will come in due course. There! Don't you feel better?—or have I made you worse as well intentioned folk are apt to do?

> I wish you were up here where we could take care of you, and I had it in mind to entreat you to come up, if only for a day, to give me some points on the "Brooklyn" which is practically finished, but it is evident that "one-night-stands" are not for you, and I would not let you come if you wanted to, unless you could stay a week. Don't forget that there is always a place for you under this roof for as long as you can occupy it at any time.
>
> Always affectionately,
>
> Dan. C. French[30]

By August, she had finished the seven-foot plaster model of *Telegraphy* and had it delivered to John Burdick, a sculptor and plaster molder who would create the pieces of the twenty-four-foot plaster model. Then, it being August, she headed out of town—first to the Bancrofts on Shelter Island, then to Des Moines, Iowa, where she consulted about the future site of the *Allison Memorial.* In early September, Longman and her brother Claude visited Winchester, Ohio, which they called "at first." They found their father's old cider press, a water well, and a cornfield where a house once stood. Then they traveled to Canada for a family reunion, where Longman and her three sisters posed together in front of barns and a wooden rail fence—Longman, the youngest, in the center, in a simple dress, relaxed and smiling, her arm draped across the lap of her oldest sister, Vally.

On her way back, she stopped in Chicago to visit Logan Square. In late September, she made another visit to Des Moines, then traveled with Henry Bacon to Buffalo, New York, where photographs indicate they enjoyed Niagara Falls, both smiling, decked out in hooded ponchos for a wet ride on the *Maid of the Mist*. In October, she made a trip to the Lincoln Memorial and then vacationed at Claude's cottage in Lakeside, Michigan.

At Burdick's later in October, she worked on the supersized plaster pieces of *Telegraphy*—two wings; legs and winding cables; torso, head, arms, and lightning bolts; globe with toes attached—tweaking them so they could be sent to Roman Bronze Works. It had been a trying year. With the steady lights of the constellation of friends in her tiny orbit, she had recovered enough to get *Telegraphy* ready for the foundry, her job finished.

She and the Burdick team took photos of each other with *Telegraphy*'s towering legs and one of Longman sitting on a ladder, her head resting on "Joe's" massive plaster shoulder. Then, as was her custom, they toasted their accomplishment with raised glasses of milk and slices of pie.

Turns out, Longman couldn't mark *Telegraphy* off her high-priority to-do list. When she requested her final payment, she was reminded of her contract—that she wasn't finished until she had seen to it that *The Spirit of Telegraphy* was installed; until the plaster pieces were put together in one massive bronze piece and the colossal figure was raised to stand on tiptoe atop the tower, 434 feet above the street.

NOTES

1. See https://www.ncpedia.org/biography/bacon-henry-jr.
2. Holzer, 267.
3. Ibid.
4. HB to EBL, undated, Loomis Chaffee.
5. HB to William Howard Taft, May 28, 1922, Wesleyan University Archives.
6. Longman scrapbook, Loomis Chaffee.
7. Charles Grafly to General Grenville M. Dodge, March 10, 1915, Loomis Chaffee.
8. James S. Clarkson to E. R. Harlan, March 19, 1915, Loomis Chaffee.
9. W. A. Clark to General E. M. Dodge, March 22, 1915, Loomis Chaffee.
10. "To Operate on McAdoo," *New York Times*, March 12, 1915, 1.
11. DCF to EBL, March 12, 1915, EBL note at bottom of letter, Loomis Chaffee.
12. DCF to EBL, March 13, 1915, EBL note at bottom of letter, Loomis Chaffee.
13. DCF to EBL, March 12, 1915, Loomis Chaffee.
14. DCF to EBL, March 13, 1915, Loomis Chaffee.
15. DCF to EBL, March 18, 1915, Loomis Chaffee.
16. HB to EBL, probably March 16, 1915, Loomis Chaffee.
17. HB to Margaret Bancroft, March 15, 1915, Milton Bancroft Collection, Manuscript Group 133, Indiana University of Pennsylvania (IUP), Special Collections and University Archives.
18. Margaret Bancroft to Milton Bancroft, March 15, 1915, Milton Bancroft Collection, Manuscript Group 133, Indiana University of Pennsylvania (IUP), Special Collections and University Archives.
19. Margaret Bancroft to Milton Bancroft, March 13, 1915, Milton Bancroft Collection, Manuscript Group 133, Indiana University of Pennsylvania (IUP), Special Collections and University Archives.
20. Margaret Bancroft to Milton Bancroft, March 15, 1915.
21. Margaret Bancroft to Milton Bancroft, March 22, 1915, Milton Bancroft Collection, Manuscript Group 133, Indiana University of Pennsylvania (IUP), Special Collections and University Archives.
22. Margaret Bancroft to Milton Bancroft, March 23, 1915, Milton Bancroft Collection, Manuscript Group 133, Indiana University of Pennsylvania (IUP), Special Collections and University Archives.
23. Margaret Bancroft to Milton Bancroft, March 29, 1915, Milton Bancroft Collection, Manuscript Group 133, Indiana University of Pennsylvania (IUP), Special Collections and University Archives.
24. Longman scrapbook, Loomis Chaffee.
25. Margaret Bancroft to Milton Bancroft, April 22, 1915, Milton Bancroft Collection, Manuscript Group 133, Indiana University of Pennsylvania (IUP), Special Collections and University Archives.
26. Longman scrapbook, Loomis Chaffee.

27. Margaret Bancroft to Milton Bancroft, April 27, 1915, Milton Bancroft Collection, Manuscript Group 133, Indiana University of Pennsylvania (IUP), Special Collections and University Archives.

28. Margaret Bancroft to Milton Bancroft, April 30, 1915, Milton Bancroft Collection, Manuscript Group 133, Indiana University of Pennsylvania (IUP), Special Collections and University Archives.

29. Margaret Bancroft to Milton Bancroft, May 4, 1915, Milton Bancroft Collection, Manuscript Group 133, Indiana University of Pennsylvania (IUP), Special Collections and University Archives.

30. DCF to EBL, July 15, 1915, Loomis Chaffee.

Chapter 15

Still Bizzy

Such praise is not for mere humans.

—Daniel Chester French

In June 1916, Daniel Chester French, in a panic, wrote to Longman: "Listen to me— I need you and I want you, not because (this time) you are a charming lady, but because you are a sculptor." Feeling the pressure of creating an important presidential statue for his friend's national monument, he was confounded as he enlarged his model of Lincoln.

"I have sawed Lincoln in two and I have been trying him with different lengths of body and I find I can't decide what is best by myself. . . . I need your critical eye to help me to a decision and the decision must be before Monday when I expect Marcetti to set up the big one. Can't you come up Saturday if we will promise to return you, in better order than you came, Sunday evening? . . . I am quite aware of how much I am demanding and I know that it may not be practicable for you to come, but I wish you could."[1] Proving his request was strictly business, French enclosed ten dollars for expenses.

Bizzy-izzy-she-was, working on projects in various stages of completion: *Telegraphy* for New York City; the *Allison* for Des Moines, Iowa; *Illinois Centennial*, for Chicago's Logan Square—and she hadn't ignored her ideal pieces: on a worktable was *The Future*.

But the *Lincoln*, as well as her beloved friends, were at the top of her list. She did travel to Chesterwood to look at French's *Lincoln* puzzle two days later, as he had requested, on Saturday. French finished the seven-foot model by October—about the same time Longman finished modeling her pieces for the Lincoln Memorial: the ornamentation of the inscribed Lincoln speeches.

Bacon planned two "memorials" inside the monument: Lincoln's Gettysburg Address on the south wall and his Second Inaugural Address on the north wall. He designed the lettering himself, and Longman designed the wreaths—double wreaths—and eagles below each speech.[2] In conversation with Bacon and French from the start, and being "the last word in ornament," as French referred to her, Longman seemed the obvious choice.[3] Honored to contribute to the national project, and knowing the undertaking was well over budget, she did her work without compensation.

Her ornamentation reflected Bacon's elegant design. Beneath eagles at each end of the speeches, she constructed simple laurel-leaf wreaths with berries—a Grecian symbol of triumph. The double wreaths in the center of the tablets are alternating boughs with laurel berries and pine branches with cones, historically related to human enlightenment. At the ends, royal eagles sit, their sharp talons poised, stunning wings spread, heads with prominent beaks turned to face each other, eyes closed, as if they are at peace and ready to defend Lincoln's words.

Her wreaths were delivered to Washington, D.C., in the winter of 1916. After they were installed in the memorial, Longman would finish them on-site.

With many works in progress, nevertheless, Longman had started the year with an extended holiday. In January, she accompanied Henry Bacon to Southport, North Carolina, where his family had lived when he was a child. She photographed Main Street with its wide village green; facing the green, the Windley School, which Bacon attended from age ten to fourteen; his two-story family home (Henry was the oldest of seven children); and its wraparound screened porch. In nearby Wilmington, where the family had moved next, Longman photographed Parsley House, which Bacon, in 1912, had built for a local lumberman. It was unique in that Bacon designed few houses, and this one was octagonal, built with coquina—oyster shells mixed into concrete—for walls.

By June, Longman's sketch models of the *Illinois Centennial* bas-reliefs were complete and she wrote to the museum director that they were ready for inspection in her New York studio—as photographs are "always unsatisfactory and would be particularly so in this case where there would be distortion owing to the circular character of the monument."[4] Carpenter asked Bacon and French to look at them (which they probably already had, while she worked on them) and said he also would try to get some trustees to inspect them. But a couple of weeks later, he asked for photographs and a description instead. She consented and had photographs made, though she protested a bit—perhaps a bit sarcastically, not one to be dismissed: "I regret that it was not found practicable to inspect these models here in my studio, but I realize that it is difficult for busy men to make the trip."[5]

Again, she had set herself a challenging task, as with *Ceres*: a circular bas-relief. With the photos, she sent a detailed description of the figures in relief, including inscriptions festooned with fruits and wreaths of laurel. The standing figures would be about seven feet tall; *Illinois*, somewhat taller. Her work reflected the thinking of the predominant view of history at that time, one that may make us wince, or have a stronger reaction, in our time. The detail spoke to her research, symbolism, her own understanding of the culture, and her amazing ability to create stunning bas-reliefs. In this case, as she described to the trustees, "The modelling, while strong in relief, has been kept very flat in character in order to preserve the integrity of the silhouette of the drum." She endeavored, she wrote, "to make a simple and direct arrangement, to harmonize with the dignity and simplicity of the architecture."

> To the right of this tablet stands an Indian, representing the earliest history of Illinois. Wearing the splendid war-bonnet of his race, but otherwise almost nude, he stands with folded arms turning his back upon the civilization which is to come. Behind is his squaw and child, the attitude indicating the usual feminine curiosity and also deeper interest in religion as expressed by the symbol of Christianity upheld to her wondering eyes by Pere Marquette. The priest, perhaps the noblest character of early Illinois history, wears the long robe of the Jesuit order. One hand holds forth the cross while the other bestows the apostolic blessing. The next figure is that of Robert de La Salle, the intrepid French explorer, clad in the costume of the 17th century half soldier and half coureur de bois-leather coat, half-armor and coon-skin cap, his weapon the flint-lock rifle. Finally comes the aristocratic and handsome figure of the Virginian, Gen. Geo. Rogers Clark, who, almost without troops and with no government support, conquered and retained Illinois against the English and their Indian allies in the war of the Revolution. He carries the Stars and Stripes having been, it is said, the first to unfurl the new flag in Illinois. All of the foregoing figures are representative of the history of Illinois before her admission to statehood. The three last mentioned characters will, in the finished work, be portraits as far as obtainable data will permit.
>
> This brings us to the South side of the monument where Illinois sits enthroned in sovereign state. Her crown [indecipherable word] the life-giving grain and her sceptre the distaff, symbol of industry. In her right hand she holds the scroll of the law. Her capacious lap overflows with the fruits and flowers of the earth. Her throne is decorated with conventional eagle-wings, heads of the American lion, and fasces, the latter symbolic of executive power. On the lunette of the back of the throne appears the state motto: "State Sovereignty—National Union."
>
> Continuing to the right, the following ideal figures represent the advancement of Illinois during the past century. First, both historically and in importance, is

> Agriculture, a female figure carrying the corn, wheat and sickle. Then comes Manufactures represented by a powerful iron-worker clothed in overalls and leathern apron and carrying the sledge-hammer. Next in natural sequence follows Transportation—Mercury with the winged cap and sandals, symbolic of speed, in his outstretched hand a model of a locomotive and in the other hand that of a steam-ship. The next figure is that of Education—an old man in Greek garb, holding aloft a geographic globe. At his knee stands a young boy holding an open book. Last comes the Fine Arts, the culmination of civilization—a laurel-crowned female figure carrying the painter's palette, the architect's triangle, the violin and the sculptor's mallet, her attitude expressing both the will and power for further advancement.
>
> This brings the beholder again to the North side of the monument, and it will be noticed that the tablet bearing the inscription is flanked on either side by the antipodes of civilization in Illinois—the Fine Arts and the Aborigine.[6]

In early August, she received a response. Various trustees had viewed the photographs and reportedly seemed well-pleased with the design. Henry Bacon had recommended the work "very highly." However, instead of approving her design from the photos of her clay sketches, they requested a plaster model as well.

Longman replied from Chesterwood, where she would remain for a few days more and then, per their request, have casts made of the sketches. Casts were shipped to Chicago by the end of the month, after a short delay due to the fact that glue for the plaster couldn't be used during Manhattan's hottest days. When her design finally was approved sometime that fall, she had a year, until October 1, 1917, to complete the clay model of both the bas-reliefs on the drum base and the eagle atop Bacon's seventy-foot Doric column.

The *Allison* was close to being finished. Sculptor John Burdick assisted Longman with plasticine models of the remaining life-sized figures. Some of the models and the bas-relief of William Boyd Allison were already at the bronze foundry. *Republic*, which would sit atop the monument, had been carved in marble at the Piccirillis' studio in the Bronx.

The Piccirilli brothers were six, all Italian stone-carvers like their father; renowned sculptors themselves. Longman was a frequent client, as was Daniel French. The brothers also would carve her base for the *Illinois Centennial*, and, famously, French's *Lincoln*. Often on summer Saturday mornings, Henry Bacon arrived at Longman's studio, viewed her week's work, and together they went to the Piccirillis for lunch in the big kitchen with an iron stove, where Attilio tended tomato sauce. Sculptors and well-known New Yorkers gathered around a large, rectangular, marble-topped table. A tumble of giant chunks of marble littered the backyard, visible through the kitchen door. Lively chatter mounted as guests drank homemade wine from pottery crocks and feasted on Attilio's spaghetti.[7]

Figure 15.1 Longman used a pneumatic sculpting tool in the Piccirillis' studio to finish the marble of Republic, which would crown the Allison Memorial. Source/Credit: Photograph from the collection of the Loomis Chaffee Archives, Loomis Chaffee School, Windsor, Connecticut USA.

In a stunning photo, the Piccirilli kitchen table is covered in white cloths and dishes. Small U.S. and Italian flags fly from a ceiling fixture overhead. Along with Horatio, Masanielo, Furio, Getulio, Attilio Piccirilli, and an unidentified man, a relaxed Longman, her legs extended, her feet crossed under the table, artfully drapes her right hand around her brother Claude's shoulder; her left hand holds the hand of Henry Bacon, standing behind her.

After lunch with the Piccirillis, Bacon, who had been a pitcher as a student at the University of Illinois, and Longman often went to a big-league baseball game. Once, while visiting her brother Claude, she told the *Evansville Journal-News*, "I'm a real fan and I seldom miss a big-league game on Saturday afternoons when my weeks-end holiday commences."[8]

Committed to finishing marble pieces herself, in July she worked in the courtyard at the Piccirillis', tweaking the giant marble *Republic*, sometimes with an air chisel. For the photo this time when she finished, she sat on *Republic*'s generous lap.

Figure 15.2 At table with the Piccirilli brothers, a relaxed Longman artfully draped her right hand around her brother Claude's shoulder; her left hand held the hand of Henry Bacon, standing behind her. Also: (L-R) Masanielo, Furio, Getulio, and Attilio Piccirilli. Two unknown figures in the back. Source/Credit: Photograph from the collection of the Loomis Chaffee Archives, Loomis Chaffee School, Windsor, Connecticut USA.

Escaping the city's late-summer heat and responding to another request from French, Longman stayed two weeks in the Berkshires at Chesterwood. Often, at the lively home of the Frenches, she joined others for tennis and dancing, but she always also spent time conferring about Dan's work. This time it was not her advice that French sought, but sittings.

There is no documentation about his portrait of Longman; probably it was meant to speak for itself, and so it raises questions. The statue is of her head only, her hair softly draped in front and braided in the back. Most notably, her eyes are closed, prompting considerable conjecture among curators about why he chose to sculpt her with eyes shut.

Perhaps he meant it to be an ideal piece rather than an actual representation of his friend, though it clearly is a portrait of her. Perhaps it's a private amusement that he didn't portray her "dangerous" eyes, the ones Mary French observed captured her husband from day one. Or perhaps he meant to indicate she was so talented she could do anything with her eyes closed. Or maybe he made a mask of her face, requiring her eyes to be closed, and liked it so much, he sculpted it.

Also confounding is why French placed an Egyptian symbol at the top of the marble plinth upon which his sculpture sits. It is the Egyptian sun disc "flanked by the outspread wings of Horus, the sky god with rearing cobras in the center." Maybe this was his way of referencing her *Spirit of Telegraphy*, which she soon planned to triumphantly raise into the sky above Manhattan. For the Egyptians, rearing cobras symbolized protection for the king and his

Figure 15.3 Daniel Chester French's portrait of Longman, in marble, 1920. Source/Credit: Davis Museum at Wellesley College, Wellesley, MA, Gift of Nathaniel H. Batchelder Jr. in memory of his beloved wife, Elizabeth Burnquist Batchelder (Class of 1939).

power, and they were often used in funeral pieces—the icon an offering for continued life. So maybe her eyes were closed as she received a sort of blessing from her teacher/colleague/beloved friend.[9]

In early winter, Longman spent another two weeks at Chesterwood, perhaps as French finished his model. The result is a beauty, a moment forever kept, stunning, later carved in marble. Longman looks very much alive, safe and serene.

Edgar Harlan, curator of the Iowa State Historical Department, learned of French's head of Longman when he and French corresponded about a list of American sculptures. Harlan had come to know and admire Longman as they worked together siting the *Allison*. In one letter, while Longman was at Chesterwood, Harlan wrote:

> I am glad to know Miss Longman is resting with you at Glendale. The wish of my life is that I could have a home suitable for the rest and recreation of such as she. There is not a soul on this earth with which I have come in contact which

> excels her in its quality of conscientious work, and it seems to me that every person and influence with which she comes in contact owes to her.

French offered Harlan a plaster model of his head of Longman for the state art collection in Iowa. In response, Harlan gushed:

> I never had much respect for Herodias' daughter until this moment. You should have seen me dance at the offer of Miss Longman's head, *sans* the charger, and when I imparted your suggestion to the others of the twenty-four people on my staff, there was . . . delight.
>
> Miss Longman is thought of among us as a real, genuine, human creature with more than a spark of genius in her, and to have her head, modeled by you, as your choice of your work to be deposited here with us while we live and those after us forever, arouses in us an enthusiasm I cannot possibly over-state.[10]

On December 19, French wrote to Harlan informing him that the head of Longman was on its way by railway express. "I trust it will reach you in safety, and although I cannot hope that it will meet properly your exalted view of Miss Longman's personality, I do hope that it will at least remind you of her and that you will consider that it properly represents me in your archives.

"I have not yet had an opportunity to show Miss Longman your letter—and I am not sure that it would be good for her soul to do so. Such praise is not for mere humans."[11]

French, who did send the letter to Longman, wrote by hand, after the last paragraph, "Why, why! DCF."

When French's plaster arrived in Des Moines, Harlan's rhapsodies continued to ring out:

> If I was extravagant before, I would if I gave full expression to my feelings now, make myself absurd in your opinion. I just do not see how it is possible to so nearly take the place of a living person as you have made this head take the place of that of Miss Longman.
>
> I feel it should be draped with Indian tresses as the only thing needed to make the upper part of the head her own. Then there ought to be a lurking tremor about the temples and lower parts of the cheek where it joins the chin, then if the eyes were to open I would expect "What!" in utterance from the lips to throw up a lump from the throat, then the whole face to break into a smile and into the full day of good humor.[12]

A month later, Longman wrote to Harlan, with a tease and a scolding. She had evidently sent him a study of the head of the *Republic* for the *Allison*, for which she had not received notice of its arrival in Des Moines.

> Mr. French showed me the letters he received from you apropos of his bust of me. I appreciate very much the nice things you said about me in them—but why

> do you never acknowledge anything I send until I prod you! If the small "study" of the head of the Republic on the Allison Mt. which I sent some months ago was not received I will forgive you. While of course I could not be expected to be quite as lovely as a bust of me by Mr. French, it still seemed most appropriate to send,—and if you do not think so I can certainly use it myself!
>
> Now that I have scolded you I will wish you and Mrs. Harlan a "Happy New Year"—though one twelfth of it has already gone.[13]

Somewhere in a busy year, she found time to create a silver document box for her friend Jacob Schmidlapp in honor of his family, to be given to his son as a Christmas gift. The box, unlike anything else she made, was an exquisite riot of ornamentation, every panel of figures was bordered in a repeating leaf pattern. On the top panel within a ribboned border was a double bust medallion labeled *Jacob Godfrey Schmidlapp 1849–* (his death date—*1919*—was filled in later) and *Emilie Balke Schmidlapp 1858–1900*. Four medallions flanked them to honor every member of the family. The box interior was lined in wood and green velvet. The left end also had the inner ribboned border and the inscription: "Made as a token of friendship for Jacob Godfrey Schmidlapp by Evelyn Beatrice Longman in the year 1916." On the right end, the inscription, "Presented as an heirloom to Carl Jacob Schmidlapp by his father Christmas 1916."

Not only had she somehow, amidst deadlines for the monumental pieces, managed to create the beautiful box for her friend, she had also helped secure a job for another friend, model Hettie Anderson. In April 1916, Longman wrote to Robert de Forest, president of the Metropolitan Museum of Art, promoting Anderson to be employed there.

Her effort to assist friends and family in financial difficulty was a thread throughout her life, from her time as a warehouse clerk, when she gave all her college savings to a friend in need. The series of events in which Longman tried to help Anderson also illustrate her ability to understand people, an empathy born of childhood chaos and close observation as a portraitist.

When de Forest gave Longman's letter requesting employment for Anderson to Daniel French to read, French replied that Longman's letter was "pretty nearly a masterpiece of expression." As Longman had said in the letter, no longer extant, her reason for thinking of the Museum as a place for Anderson to work, now that modeling had ended for her, was that she felt Anderson would "feel lost without some connection with art matters."[14]

Her ability to see deeply into the people she portrayed in sculpture was not only evident in the sculpture, but also in her relationships. More and more, as her resources increased, she showered friends and others with generosity and compassion. And yet, those moments would come when she was thoroughly judgmental and dismissive.

Figure 15.4 Longman sat atop a ladder to rest her head on plaster *Genius of Electricity's* shoulder. Source/Credit: Photograph from the collection of the Loomis Chaffee Archives, Loomis Chaffee School, Windsor, Connecticut USA.

As big a project as ever, there remained *Telegraphy*. Architect Bosworth and Longman had viewed the giant finished pieces of plaster in November 1915 at Roman Bronze Works. Seemingly, her most challenging work was done. As Samu wrote, the pointing up process "is a potentially risky one for the sculpture: as a work is enlarged in not two but three dimensions, the slightest errors in proportions made on the part of the sculptor, while not visible in smaller models, are exaggerated exponentially. Longman's Telegraphy was enlarged by almost three and one-half times without revealing any flows in proportion."[15]

Having delivered the plaster to the foundry, Longman thought her contract was accomplished and requested her second payment, of two thousand dollars. Though she received the second payment a week later, she was reminded that the third and final installment would not be paid until the figure was installed. "Your contract provides that you shall personally supervise and criticize the execution of the bronze statue to be made from your model and consequently your Contract will not be completed until this part of the work is done."[16]

As expected from the start, her design created technical challenges for the foundry. There was concern about the possibility of lightning strikes hitting what would be the second-tallest point in New York City. Massive wings in the wind-swept skyline could be another problem, and the elegant swirl of cables, long and looping, were a casting nightmare; the foundry made the mold for the cable out of wood rather than plaster. The complex figure was cast in twenty-four pieces.

Since *Telegraphy* would be attached to its base only by its toes, Roman Bronze Works planned to anchor the figure to its base "using steel pins six inches in diameter that went up as far as its mid-calf . . . the wings were attached by roman joints, a technique similar to dovetailing in carpentry," Margaret Samu wrote. "Roman joints are reinforced by bolts and blind pins, making them remarkably strong attachments that are still able to move in the wind without weakening the structure. Packing the joints with soft lead gave the surface an appearance of seamlessness."[17]

The *Genius of Telegraphy*, as it was called until the moment it was installed on the tower, then owned by AT&T, it became *Genius of Electricity*; later, in the 1930s, *The Spirit of Communications*; finally, simply *Electricity*, or *Golden Boy*, was ready for installation in October 1916.

Longman saw him all put together at Roman Bronze Works in Greenpoint, Brooklyn, before he was crated. It took a week to box up the twenty-four-foot, ten-ton statue and slowly transport him from Brooklyn to Manhattan's financial district.

The morning of October 24, *Telegraphy* was removed from its crate, still bound by ropes and lying face-down on a narrow slab of wood. Workers

Figure 15.5 Hundreds watched from nearby office windows as Longman's 24-foot, 10-ton figure was slowly raised to the second highest point in Manhattan. Source/Credit: Photograph from the collection of the Loomis Chaffee Archives, Loomis Chaffee School, Windsor, Connecticut USA.

attached him to a crane for the last leg of the slow climb to his final reveal above the Manhattan skyline. Office workers watched from windows. Men were stationed on the building's cornices to push *Telegraphy* away in case he came too close.

Longman's view was from the roof, where she watched the giant wings of her Zeus come closer and closer until, after an hour and a half, he cleared the last cornice and was lifted onto a scaffolding next to the tower. There he was released from his ropes, and a crane raised him vertically and set him on the tower, at home in the sky now. In the coming days, *Electricity*, as he was now called, would be dressed in a skintight layer of gold, inspiring the name he would best and longest be known by, *Golden Boy*.

Bosworth, the building's architect, wrote to French:

> I am delighted with your letter of appreciation of Miss Longman's splendid work on the figure on the tower. Her problem was certainly a difficult one and to make a figure both living in spirit and decorative in effect in this place is indeed a triumph. I saw it yesterday without scaffolding for the first time and immediately telephoned her my heartiest congratulations.[18]

Two months later, in the chill of an Iowa winter, Longman and Henry Bacon oversaw the installation of the *Allison*. Installed first, Henry's fountain base; then the massive base that would hold all Longman's figures, then *Republic* atop the base, the bas-relief of Allison in front, and finally, the six figures along the sides. Dedication was tentatively scheduled for June 1918, but there is no account of it ever happening, perhaps due to World War I or the Spanish Flu pandemic.

Of all her monumental public statues, *Electricity* had the most exposure, and it became her most iconic, beloved, and well-known work (even if, as it often was with public sculptures in that time, most people didn't know who sculpted it). He stood atop the AT&T tower for sixty-five years. A smaller copy was made to top the company's pavilion at the 1939 World's Fair in New York. A drawing of *Golden Boy* decorated the cover of AT&T's East Coast phone books for thirty years. An indication of how much Longman's elegant figure became a part of civic life is a cartoon drawn by a University of Texas student for its satirical magazine, *Texas Ranger*. *Electricity* stands at the door of a woman who came to answer the doorbell and upon seeing him announces, "It's that man from the telephone office."[19]

Every time AT&T moved offices, *Golden Boy* was taken down, sometimes reconditioned, and moved as well. The first move was in 1983; there have been four more. Thayer Tolles, in her article about Longman in *American Sculpture in The Metropolitan Museum of Art*, wrote that *Telegraphy* is "an icon of technological progress and capitalism."[20] Marc Roussel, who twice restored *Telegraphy*, told Margaret Samu that Longman's statue is a "technical *tour de force* unmatched anywhere in the country."[21]

At one point, during a move, the National Museum of Women in the Arts offered to purchase *Electricity* to install atop its building in downtown Washington, D.C. Legend has it that AT&T employees protested that they wanted to keep their "Golden Boy," and so AT&T did. Since 1980, it has been on the ground rather than atop a building—which Longman would have protested with all her mighty aesthetic fervency.

Currently, it stands on a plaza at street level outside the AT&T headquarters in downtown Dallas, giving viewers a chance to see it not as it was intended, four hundred feet in the sky, but up close, where, in fresh, smooth gilding, Joe's muscled arms, chiseled face, and feathered wings can actually be seen. An attentive security guard watched over, and when I visited, he told me that employees of AT&T are very fond and protective of their Golden Boy.

The guard isn't the only sentinel watching over the statue. As I stepped close to take a photograph of Longman's signature on the bottom of the Sol's tiptoed-feet, a voice from out of nowhere bellowed soberly, scaring me half to death: "Step back from the statue."

Though millions came to know, and many—to this day—feel sentimental toward *Golden Boy*, it was not Longman's favorite, and it was far from her last hurrah.

NOTES

1. DCF to EBL, June 22, 1916, Loomis Chaffee; Holzer, 272. Marcetti helped French with the life-sized plastiline.

2. Batchelder to Frances D. Whittemore, April 29, 1930, Loomis Chaffee. Whittemore lived in Topeka, Kansas, and had written to Longman about the lettering on the Lincoln Memorial. Horton Batchelder answered for Longman. Because this letter is the definitive document on the question of who did what, I include the pertinent parts: "Mrs. Batchelder did the decorations—the wreaths and eagles, about the two inscriptions at the Lincoln Memorial. The letters were designed by Henry Bacon and, as you say, are very beautiful. They weren't Mrs. Batchelder's, though the ornament is. . . . If you mention Mrs. Batchelder, will you please try to be quite specific, as errors have often been made. She did only the wreaths and eagles that I have mentioned, nothing on the outside of the building and nothing else inside."

3. Jonathon Rawson, "Evelyn Beatrice Longman," *International Studio*, Volume 45, Numbers 177 to 180, 1911–1912, 456.

4. EBL to N. H. Carpenter, June 2, 1916, Loomis Chaffee.

5. EBL to N. H. Carpenter, June 30, 1916, Loomis Chaffee.

6. EBL, "Description of the Sculpture for the Centennial Monument, Logan Square, Chicago, Ill.," Loomis Chaffee.

7. NHB notes for Lois Patchett's presentation, Loomis Chaffee.

8. A. J. Lorenz, *Evansville Journal-News*, April 19, 1919.

9. With thanks for their learned conjectures to Dana Pilson, Donna Hassler, of Chesterwood; Thayer Tolles, Janis Kamrin, at the Metropolitan Museum of Art.

10. Edgar R. Harlan to DCF, December 5, 1917, Chesterwood.

11. DCF to Harlan, December 19, 1917, Chesterwood.

12. Harlan to DCF, January 14, 1918, Correspondence File 25B, Part 3, Group 3, Iowa Historical Department.

13. EBL to Harlan, February 4, 1918, Correspondence File 25B, Part 3, Group 3, Iowa Historical Department.

14. DCF to Robert deForest, April 19, 1916, Chesterwood Archives; Chapin Library, Williams College.

15. Samu, 60.

16. Marc Eidlitz & Son to EBL, November 16, 1915, AT&T Archives and History Center, Warren NJ, Box 127, 10 01 01.

17. Samu, 60.

18. Bosworth to DCF, November 15, 1916, Chesterwood Archives; Chapin Library, Williams College.

19. The undated cartoon is signed "John Frazer/Texas Ranger." *Texas Ranger* was a student satirical magazine at the University of Texas from 1923 to 1972.

20. Lauretta Dimmick and Donna J. Hassler, *American Sculpture in the Metropolitan Museum of Art: A catalogue of works by artists born between 1865 and 1885* (United Kingdom, The Museum, 1999).

21. Samu, 61.

Chapter 16

Lincoln

I am awfully sorry you were disappointed and I can see why but . . . you don't want to win all the prizes at once; there would be nothing left to live for!

—Daniel Chester French

Wrapped in heavy winter coats and hats, Henry Bacon, Dan French, his daughter Margaret, and Longman stood on frozen mud one February morning in 1917 at the construction site of the Lincoln Memorial in Washington, D.C. The upper portion of the forty-five- to sixty-five-foot-deep foundation had yet to be covered. Wooden scaffolding rose to the roof between two Doric columns. Cables stretched here and there. Workers toiled on temporary platforms. Just as ancient Greeks might have looked upon the construction of the Parthenon, which had inspired Bacon's design, the group listened to the architect explain progress on the massive project. Margaret snapped a photo of her elders.

Inside, the four made their way to the spot where French's rendition of Lincoln would be set. Though the original plan was for a twelve-foot statue on a raised pedestal, even from the beginning Bacon and French had concerns about the size of the statue in such an expansive room. This day, they got a look when French set up his seven-foot plaster model.[1]

Their suspicions were realized: the statue looked puny. French and Bacon took a photograph of the model and had eighteen-foot and twenty-foot solar images made. Workers moved the giant photos, backed by beaver board and mounted on two-by-fours, closer, then farther out from the wall in the atrium.[2] After long consideration, and no firm decision about the sculpture's size, the four made their way to Union Station. Sitting with the others in a

Figure 16.1 Daniel Chester French, Henry Bacon, and Longman at the Lincoln Memorial during its construction. Source/Credit: Photograph by Margaret French. Chesterwood Archives; Chapin Library, Williams College, Gift of the National Trust for Historic Preservation / Chesterwood, a National Trust Historic Site, Stockbridge, Massachusetts.

mahogany-paneled carriage on B&O Railroad's Royal Blue Line passenger train, Longman fervently made the case for a larger statue—all the way back to New York City.[3]

It was easier for her to be impassioned—not that Bacon and French disagreed, but they were up against an over-budget project and the bureaucracy of a federal commission. Though the original plan for the statue had been either bronze or marble, the budget had been for bronze, considerably less than the cost of marble. The architect and sculptor had already insisted that the Commission approve marble instead—better against the buff-colored stone walls.

Longman's reported insistence was not in vain: French requested approval of a nineteen-foot statue with a ten-foot pedestal. Additional steel struts would have to be added to the floor to support the weight of the larger, marble statue. Within months, the Commission granted permission for the change. With the Piccirilli brothers on board to carve the marble for twenty-five thousand dollars, the budget for creating the statue rose from fifty thousand to seventy-five thousand dollars; its actual cost turned out to be around eighty-eight thousand dollars (about $2.2 million today).[4]

On the next trip to Washington, D.C., Mary French went along with her husband, Longman, and Bacon. It turned out to be a momentous day—April 2, 1917. In the margins of a photo of the two couples at the Lincoln Monument, Longman made note: "On this day President's message to Congress—about declaration of war with Germany."[5]

Longman's Lincoln wreaths would be installed and ready for her finishing around the first of October. She had promised to complete the bas-relief model for the *Illinois Centennial Monument* by the same date. A spring and summer's work ahead of her, on May 6 she was hospitalized again, this time with diphtheria.

Admitted to isolation at the Minturn Pavilion, a women's ward at Mount Sinai Hospital in New York City, she remained there until June 7. During visits, Henry Bacon and Longman each donned white hazmat suits that covered them from toe to head. In one of the photos Longman later pasted into her scrapbook, they stood on a balcony at the hospital overlooking a courtyard. It's hard to see how protected from disease Henry really was, with one arm around Longman's back, his other hand in hers, sharing ebullient smiles through the openings in their wimple-like head coverings.

When graduated from the protective gear, Longman sat outside in the courtyard visiting with staff as they worked in flowerbeds. Eventually she was released in time to take a train to Toledo to be with family for her niece Clara Tewksbury's wedding. Bacon met her there to attend the celebration, and the two returned together to New York City, where she was behind on the *Illinois Centennial* work. It was becoming a pattern—work, illness, work harder. She labored long days through the summer and, as always, finished before the deadline.

In early August, she wrote to the director of the Chicago Art Institute, who was overseeing the *Illinois Centennial* project, advising him that the working model was four-fifths finished and that $3,500 had been due her when the model was half-finished. Once again, she entreated him to have someone designated by the trustees to inspect her work in person at her studio. "Even when completed it cannot be justly judged from photographs owing to the fact that photographs of a large cylindrical object taken at so close a range as is necessary in my studio must be unavoidably distorted to a great degree."[6]

A week later, she wrote to the Art Institute's business manager that she would have the model ready for the molder by October 1. She made it clear she was keeping to her contract in spite of considerable obstacles and that she wanted them to inspect the model without the delays she experienced with her sketch model.

> The terms of my contract allowed me just one year in which to complete this work, four months of which time was taken from me by the Trustees . . . for the consideration of my sketch; another two months, May and June, were lost to me by reason of a protracted case of diphtheria. You will thus see that my time on this work has been cut exactly in half through no fault of my own. Since my return from the hospital I have been working extremely hard and for long hours in an effort to make up for this loss so that the monument may be erected on time, and I hope that the Trustees will second these efforts by having the final inspection of the work made promptly, before October first. Any time during the last two weeks of September will be agreeable to me, and I write you thus early that there may not be a day's delay in delivering the model to the moulder when it is ready.[7]

Carpenter sent the names of three trustees who would inspect Longman's models. On September 13, she wrote to Carpenter that she finished the *Illinois* earlier than she anticipated and that she hoped the visits from the "three gentlemen can be expedited."

> As soon as this work is given to the moulder I must go to Washington and do some marble-cutting in an open unheated marble structure, and am very anxious to get this done before the weather gets cold.
>
> I shall appreciate it very much if you will make an effort to get the gentlemen here as soon as possible. Mr. French saw the work a day or so ago.[8]

A week later, she sent a telegram to one of the trustees asking him to make the inspection early the following week. Carpenter sent her a letter the same day telling her that none of the three men would be able to inspect her work and that if French gave a favorable opinion, as Bacon had given to Carpenter earlier that day, that would be sufficient.

That was that. Soon after, Carpenter wrote that Bacon and French had given a "very satisfactory statement" of her work. While she never managed to get anyone from Chicago to come look at the model (as opposed to the Iowans who came, saw, and were enraptured), Carpenter authorized her to proceed with the casting.

Longman was off to D.C. The next day, she and Bacon were at the tidal basin near the Lincoln, fishing. On October 1, the eve of the auspicious day of her sculpting at the monument, she joined her brother Claude and Bacon at Luray, in Virginia's Shenandoah Valley. It was probably Claude who took a memorable photo of Longman and Bacon, capturing their closeness as they were wrapped in coats and warming in the sun. Bacon sits on a stone wall, cigarette in hand—almost another permanent appendage. Longman is perched on a stone a little higher, beside him; they smile at each other as if they are the only ones in the world.[9]

There is a quiet somberness about the following day. Dressed in the work apron that fully covers her dress, Longman sits calmly on a bench outside the wooden construction shack, as if backstage for a premiere performance. Striking are photos of her in "priestess" poses. In one she stands next to a

Figure 16.2 Henry Bacon and Longman shared a private moment at Front Royal, VA, the day before her finishing work on the wreaths at the Lincoln Memorial, Washington, D.C. Source/Credit: Photograph from the collection of the Loomis Chaffee Archives, Loomis Chaffee School, Windsor, Connecticut USA.

column at the top of the wooden stairs at the front of the Memorial looking out toward the Washington Monument. In another she stands in silhouette next to a Doric column in a patch of sunlight, her head raised.

At work on the wreaths, she leans into them, making finishing touches with a small chisel. She carves her initials discreetly, "EBL," on top of a pine cone on the double wreath below the Gettysburg Address.

For her work on the *Lincoln*, Bacon gave Longman an extravagant, breath-taking token of his appreciation: a golden wreath of leaves and pine cones evocative of Longman's *Lincoln* wreaths, for her hair. Her favorite stone, a topaz (the same kind of jewel he had given her in 1914 in San Francisco at the Japanese tea garden), is set in the heart of a green-enameled flower at the center of the piece. Created by popular New York City jeweler Edward Caldwell, the adjustable hairpiece contains two and a half ounces of gold. It is inscribed: "To Evelyn Beatrice Longman, given to her by Henry Bacon. 1917, July 21. A token for her work that she did on the Lincoln Memorial."[10]

Though their work together was as yet far from complete, Bacon also had made for Evelyn and for French small, gold replicas of the eleven-foot tripods on buttresses flanking the steps leading up to the monument.

Figure 16.3 The only woman who worked on the Lincoln Memorial, Longman finished her marble wreaths on site. Source/Credit: Photograph from the collection of the Loomis Chaffee Archives, Loomis Chaffee School, Windsor, Connecticut USA.

A month after the United States entered World War I, several delegations of Allies came to New York City, where they were greeted and celebrated with much fanfare. First to visit were the French and British war commissioners. Soon after, Daniel French signed a contract to create a medal commemorating that visit. He designed the front of the coin, the obverse, and Longman modeled the reverse side.

French designed a head of Victory for the coin; her helmet decorated with lilies of France, oak leaves of Great Britain, and the pine of the United States. Longman modeled three figures on the reverse: Joan of Arc, a knight, and Liberty in armor and a star-studded cape, carrying a sword in her left hand. The figures extend their right hands in the center.

In a momentous year, Longman created her next "ideal" piece, *The Future*. First had been love—*L'amour*, or *Consecration* as she finally titled it. Now she created *The Future* and began work on *Nature*, which she wouldn't complete for another five years. Longman would describe *Nature* when she sent the plaster to the Chicago Art Institute to be included in an alumni exhibition: "A female figure has been used as representing the element in nature most intimately connected with the propagation of life. Calm, relaxed but powerful, she contemplates intensely, lovingly, a trifle sadly the mystery of life embodied in an egg which she holds carefully and lovingly in her and, shielding it the while from the eye of the careless observer. She rests upon a seat of rocks and earth covered with oak branches and ivy—the latter symbols of the masculine and feminine elements in nature. At the rear, partly imbedded in earth, is a ram's skull, suggesting the eternal sacrifice—nature turning her back upon death and engrossed in the new life."[11]

Destiny would come later.

Writer Adeline Adams described Longman's ideal pieces as expressions of "her own vision of life and art. . . . Midway between her more monumental creations and her portraits is an imposing body of ideal figures, in which, unaided by architectural tradition and unhampered by the family of the sitter, she has expressed her own vision of life and art."[12]

As with all her ideal pieces, in contrast to her commissions, they are all in marble and mostly devoid of any other symbolism besides the figures themselves. *The Future* is a simple marble piece, with scant ornamentation—a single vine around a low, flat oval base. A young female nude rests her weight on her right leg, her left leg bent. She holds her left hand lightly on her chest; her right hand, palm down, fingers slightly spread, reaches out. Her face is framed by two long curls on each side (similar to those she modeled on *Frances*), accentuating her youthfulness. Her gaze is intense, curious, cautious. Adams described *The Future* as a "young girl, slim, reticent, commanding."[13]

The Future won the Julia A. Shaw Memorial Prize for best woman artist in the 1918 National Academy of Design's annual exhibition. Longman was not happy; she complained to French, who was on the Awards Committee, that she won the woman prize rather than the best overall award. French tried to soothe:

> Dec. 7, 1918
> Dear Evelyn B.
> With the desire to pay Miss Longman, sculptor, the highest honor possible, the Committee on Awards seem to have somehow slipped up. There was no dissenting voice from the verdict that your statue (The "Future," E. B. L.) was the pre-dominant piece of sculpture in the exhibition. The award of Shaw prize came about in this way.
>
> This prize is "For the most meritorious work of art in the Exhibition produced by an American woman." . . . Your statue was marked with an "S" showing that you intended to compete for it and, as the jury considered that your work met the requirements, it was our duty to award the prize to you. The Watrous Medal might also have been given you, and, in fact, this was suggested, but it was decided that it would be better to distribute the honors and it was given to Grafly.
>
> If both prizes had gone to you, I fear the cry of favoritism would have been raised, in view of the composition of the jury, that would have spoiled any pleasure you might have taken in the victory!
>
> I am awfully sorry you were disappointed and I can see why, but other years are coming and you don't want to win all the prizes at once; there would be nothing left to live for! The statue is well placed and, judging from the interest and admiration it excited among the jury-men it is going to win you universal applause. It looks fine!
>
> I am sorry you have been troubled in spirit; so have I.
> Always affectionately,
> D.F. (Whatever that stands for.)[14]

Longman's *Future* would win the W.M.R. French Gold Medal of the Art Institute of Chicago in 1920 and the Widener Gold Medal of the Pennsylvania Academy of the Fine Arts in 1921. French, in his role on The Met's sculpture purchasing committee, recommended the Museum acquire the work in 1925; it didn't. However, the civic-minded women of the Centennial Club of Nashville purchased *The Future* that year and gave it to the city's Parthenon "as a tribute to the centennial ladies of 1897." They envisioned the girl as "at once eager and hesitant, tentatively looking ahead but not yet in the act of moving forward."[15]

Unlike for *Consecration*, Longman left no words describing the values she expressed in this ideal sculpture. Viewers who know her background might wonder if in making the piece she harkened back to her own youth. Her nudity, her hand on her chest, as if in a gesture of self-protection, could portray vulnerability. Even so, her open gaze, her arm stretched forward, her fingers slightly spread open, she dares to reach for the future, as did her creator. And what are we to make of the fact that she characterized the future as female?

As it turned out, *The Future* prefigured a moment in her own way forward. Soon there would come the opportunity for an unimagined swivel in trajectory that, when she was age forty-three, enjoying another summit in her career as a sculptor of monumental public work, raised unanswerable questions about the future of that career.

Gwendolen Sedgwick Mead, a descendant of a signer of the Declaration of Independence, met Nathaniel Horton Batchelder, a recent graduate of Harvard University, at a tennis tournament in Newport, Rhode Island, which he was covering as a stringer for the Associated Press.

Also tutoring for a family in Philadelphia, he then signed on as a faculty member at the Hackley School, in Tarrytown, New York, where he began his teaching career in earnest. He and Gwendolen were planning to marry when he moved to the Hotchkiss School in Lakeville, Connecticut, to become the head of the English Department. As required by the school at the time, Batchelder requested approval to marry. While administrators at Hotchkiss granted permission, Gwendolen's mother was not so approving of the marriage. And she wasn't the only one who found teaching an inadequate calling. Batchelder's father, a banker from Salem, Massachusetts, told him, "Horton, there's no money in teaching"—though he never tried to stop him.[16]

The couple eloped to Boston and were married on Thanksgiving Day, November 24, 1910. Theodore Chickering Williams, a Unitarian pastor who had been the Hackley School's first headmaster, officiated. Two years later, Batchelder took a position as the first headmaster of a boys' school—yet-unbuilt—in Windsor, Connecticut. The newlyweds thrived in their new environment as they created—physically, academically, and culturally—the Loomis Institute. When the school opened in September 1914, Horton and Gwendolen endeavored to create a friendly, family-like atmosphere for the boys.

"Small groups of boarding students helped Gwendolen Batchelder prepare Sunday night suppers at the house (the Headmaster's House was one of the first buildings finished on the campus) and then gathered to eat popcorn and hear Mr. B read aloud from novels such as the *Prisoner of Zenda*. Mrs. B hosted holiday celebrations for the boys on Thanksgiving, Halloween and Washington's birthday." Sick and injured boys bunked in at the house. The Batchelders estimated in a 1915 letter to board chair John M. Taylor that during the school's first year, they had had at their home "not far from 150 overnight guests, and served approximately 500 meals in addition to teas etc. for teams."[17]

The entire student body and faculty were excited about the birth of the couple's first child, on February 9, 1917. Two weeks after the birth, Horton Batchelder received the phone call he and the Loomis community had been waiting for: Gwendolen and the baby boy were ready to come home from the hospital. Batchelder immediately drove the twelve miles to Hartford to fetch them. When he arrived, he was given tragic news: Gwendolen had died, probably of an embolism.

Batchelder, the faculty, and the students were devastated. What Batchelder described as Gwendolen's "buoyant and overflowing spirit" was suddenly gone.[18] He now not only had a new school to operate; he also was grieving the loss of his partner, and instantly was responsible for the care of an infant son, a role for which he was not prepared. The elder Batchelders cared for baby Nathaniel Horton Batchelder II in Salem, his father traveling there often for visits. Many years later, "Skip," as he came to be known, told of his father's "agony" during that time.

The school newspaper reported Gwendolen's memorial service, held in the Loomis chapel:

> Mr. Howe spoke briefly, emphasizing her lovable qualities, and intense interest in the school, the fellows, and everything connected with it. She had a great love for every part of the school life, and her interest was surpassed only by her zeal in promoting the common welfare. And though she is now absent from us in body, her spirit still moves among us, and her influence will be felt in the school for many years to come.[19]

A few months later, on Loomis' first graduation day, in June 1917, students gathered early in Founders Chapel to witness the baptism of baby Batchelder. That year, Gwendolen's annual end-of-the-year prize, for "industry, loyalty, and manliness," took on special significance.

To create their memorial for Gwendolen, students designed a circular garden with a flagpole in the middle to be built outside Founders Chapel. When the flagpole arrived at the train station in Windsor, forty boys lifted it to their shoulders and carried it the mile up the road, across the Farmington River Bridge, and to the school for a dedication ceremony. In the circle at the base are the words: "Gwendolen Sedgwick Batchelder. Inspirer of our gracious customs."

For their memorial, Loomis trustees named the new infirmary, still being built, Gwendolen Hall—fitting, since she had welcomed sick students into her home. They planned a portrait of her to be placed into a vaulted alcove in the new building; Batchelder was charged with finding a sculptor to create the piece. He enlisted the help of Velma Williams, the wife of his friend and colleague Theodore Williams, who was also his son's godfather. Velma

Williams's cousin had a friend who knew Daniel Chester French, who recommended three sculptors, including Evelyn Beatrice Evelyn.

Batchelder and Velma Williams viewed a plaster version of Longman's *Consecration* in an installation at the Metropolitan Museum of Art.[20] Here was a beautifully rendered sculpture of a couple in an embrace. Batchelder looked at no other work. The family story is that when someone pointed out that the sculptor was a woman, Batchelder is said to have blustered something like: "I asked for the name of the sculptor, not the gender."

The Museum helped Batchelder contact Longman. And in May 1918, they began corresponding about a Gwendolen memorial. Batchelder would soon discover he was dealing not with the submissiveness of the woman in *Consecration*, but with a self-assured, assertive, gifted, charming woman who seemed oblivious to his growing personal interest in her, as she was focused on getting to know the woman he'd loved.

NOTES

1. Holzer, 273–74.
2. Margaret French, 273–74.
3. Batchelder manuscript, Loomis Chaffee.
4. Holzer, 275, 287.
5. Longman scrapbook, Loomis Chaffee.
6. EBL to George William Eggers, August 8, 1917, Centennial File, Art Institute of Chicago.
7. EBL to N. H. Carpenter, August 16, 1917, Logan Square File, Art Institute of Chicago.
8. EBL to Carpenter, September 13, 1917, Logan Square File, Art Institute of Chicago.
9. Longman scrapbook, Loomis Chaffee.
10. See https://www.pbs.org/wgbh/roadshow/season/9/portland-or/appraisals/1917-caldwell-hair-ornament--200405A15/.
11. EBL to Robert B. Harshe, December 8, 1922, Art Institute of Chicago Archives.
12. Adeline Adams, "Evelyn Beatrice Longman," *American Magazine of Art*, Volume XIX, Number 5, May 1928, 237.
13. Adams, 249.
14. EBL to DCF, December 7, 1918, Loomis Chaffee.
15. Description of work, the Parthenon, Nashville, Tennessee.
16. Nathaniel Horton (Skip) Batchelder II, unpublished manuscript, Loomis Chaffee.
17. Karen Parsons and John Ratte, *Cherished Hopes and Honorable Ambition. A Centennial History of the Loomis Chaffee School* (Windsor, CT: The Loomis Institute, 2014), 14.

18. Batchelder to EBL, November 1, 1918, Loomis Chaffee.
19. *Loomis Log*, February 28, 1917, Loomis Chaffee.
20. "Exhibition of American Sculpture," The Metropolitan Museum of Art, March 17, 1918 (until 1926).

Chapter 17

Parnassus

I'm so glad you're an academician—and so unspoiled by your honor! You're an inspired genius and a wholly adorable person!

—Nathaniel Horton Batchelder

While the Piccirillis carved the marble *Illinois Centennial* drum, Longman modeled a bust of Bacon: thin, mustached, dimpled chin; hair combed higher on the right side, right eyebrow raised a bit, right eye wider; serious gaze—or perhaps on the verge of a slight smile.

He and Longman were collaborating on another memorial, a World War I monument for Naugatuck, an industrial town along the Naugatuck River in southern Connecticut. Early in Bacon's career, when he was an assistant to Charles McKim, the firm had been hired to design several buildings and a town green. Bacon designed three of them, including the railroad station. Later, in 1910, when he was on his own, Bacon was hired to design a memorial bridge over the river.

Back again, his and Longman's one-hundred-foot-tall flagstaff would rise above a limestone structure in the shape of a sarcophagus: On the east side, two figures, representing war and peace. A draped male, dressed in helmet, breast, and shin plates, kneels and leans against a shield. Cannonballs are piled beside him. A nude female figure gathers drapery in one hand and kneels beside a stack of fruit and books. The two figures face each other; she holds a long branch that crosses atop the sword he grips. In the center, a laurel wreath encompasses the words, "Victory is Consecrated by a Righteous Peace."

On the west side, Longman lettered the names of the townsmen who served in the war. On the north and south ends, garlands of fruit are draped from rams' heads. Below, the inscription: "Armed and Resolute Might Triumphs Through Unselfish Valor." And, on the other side, "In time of Peril the State is Fortified by Discipline Learned in Peace."

The Naugatuck project would be Bacon and Longman's last collaboration.

In April, when the Piccirillis were ready for Longman's finishing work on the *Illinois*, she began chiseling in their studio, and continued to do so off and on through July. In mid-May she wrote to Horton Batchelder with her vision for the Gwendolen Batchelder bas-relief.

> The uplift, physical and spiritual, which I mentally see in the portrait, with the Easter lily, symbolic of resurrection, at the breast, and the baby seraph's head below, also upraised, but seen in front view.
>
> The space demands some decoration other than the tablet, and, on account of Mrs. Batchelder's love for them, I think nothing could be holier than two beautiful festoons of flowers.[1]

The design was the easiest part. For a year, they corresponded in detail about the price, material, accompanying festoons, words for an inscription, and coordination with the building architect. In the process, as others had, Horton Batchelder became smitten. On intermittent business trips to New York City, he made arrangements to visit Longman to discuss the memorial. One day he watched her work at the Piccirillis, using air chisel, hand chisel, and mallet. He was fascinated, and impressed. Later he would tell a reporter, "She'd been working for months with the pneumatic tool on the huge drum of the *Illinois Centennial Monument*. She would often spend all day taking off a teaspoon of marble."[2]

When Batchelder learned Longman and Bacon soon would be visiting nearby Waterbury, he offered to drive over and take them to Loomis in Windsor, so that Longman could see the site for the *Gwendolen*. Around the 20th of July, in Bacon's company, Longman made her first trip to Loomis School and Batchelder's home.

Back in New York City, Longman wrote to the headmaster: "I wish to thank you again for the hospitality shown Mr. Bacon and myself; we both enjoyed very much the little glimpse of your charming home and fine school."[3]

While in the area, she and Bacon also visited Wesleyan University in Middletown, where he had designed the master plan for the campus and several of the buildings. They took photos of each other—Longman, in summer white long-sleeved blouse, long skirt, and flower-bedecked hat; standing next to the cornerstone of a building inscribed "1917"; Bacon, in a light-colored summer suit, standing next to a white column, straw hat in hand.

Wesleyan's Olin Library, which he designed, would become the repository for his papers and other items, including Longman's *Athena*—the head of the *Allison's Republic*, which she had renamed after the Greek goddess of wisdom and given to Bacon. Also in the Olin Library is the first casting of her bronze bust of him.

On August 7, the Loomis trustees approved Longman as sculptor of the *Gwendolen* and agreed to pay her $3,900. In mid-August, Longman and Bacon traveled to Chicago, to Logan Square, where the *Centennial* would be erected. On that trip, they also visited Garfield Park, where a bronze casting of Dan French's *Corn Maiden* had been placed. Bacon photographed Longman sitting on the stone base looking at the great oxen and the female figure that she, at nineteen, had first seen at the World's Columbian Exposition, when she boldly declared she could do that. Indeed, she had, and now she was in Chicago to see to the installation of the massive public monument she had created for the centennial of the state of Illinois.

Following Longman and Bacon's yearly outing with her family at Claude's lakeside bungalow in Michigan, Longman returned to her studio, and Horton Batchelder continued visits to New York, allegedly to watch her process making the bas-relief.

In September, Longman and Bacon joined the Piccirilli brothers at Logan Square, where they smoothed out the joints of the *Illinois* drum, Longman delicately removing marble dust. On the final finishing day, she, Bacon, and the Piccirillis were photographed in the completion ritual: handshakes and smiles, toasting with milk and pie.

The dedication of the monument was part of a weeklong series of events in Illinois to celebrate the state centennial. At 3 p.m. on Sunday, October 13, 1918, ten thousand people gathered for music, a pageant, and an address by Governor Frank O. Lowden at the unveiling of the statue.[4] While history was the centerpiece of the week, the present moment could not be ignored, and Lowden reminded the throng of a recent memo from Berlin, that "the war is not over"; he urged that the populace not accept a "premature peace" and allow General Pershing and the troops to continue to do their jobs. Longman and Bacon attended the extravaganza; Longman saved photos of herself standing next to Governor Lowden.[5]

Two days later, she received a letter from the Art Institute of Chicago with a bonus check for $1,500. It was the first and only time she was paid more than was in her contract. Astonished, she made a note at the bottom of the accompanying letter: not only did she receive more than she'd bargained for during a process that was especially irritating, but it came from businessmen. She wrote that Daniel French had only once received more than his contract

Figure 17.1 As was her custom when finishing a monument, Longman and the Piccirillis toasted their work on the Illinois Centennial with milk and pie. Source/Credit: Photograph from the collection of the Loomis Chaffee Archives, Loomis Chaffee School, Windsor, Connecticut USA.

called for, but that was a contract with personal friends. This, she emphasized, was from a committee of "business men."[6]

While "overjoyed" that the committee had showed their satisfaction with her work in this way, she felt badly for the Piccirillis. She and Bacon felt the carvers were losing money on the project, and they had tried to get more payment for them. So, when she got the bonus, she offered to share it with the Piccirillis. They, and the committee, refused her offer.[7]

In October, Batchelder, in a dilemma over the *Gwendolen* inscription, wrote to Longman requesting a visit with her in New York. "Can't I come down and discuss this with you—writing is not very satisfactory? I'm quite busy, but could take a late afternoon train any day, reaching New York at 8:10 & come back on the 11:15. If that is not a good time I will make it possible to find another. I want you to let me be behind the scenes in this work & know it at all stages."[8]

Longman replied that there was no need; the inscription was something he had to decide upon himself. Horton eventually decided there would be no inscription, only Gwendolen's name. And eventually Longman welcomed all his visits to her studio.

Longman and Margaret Bancroft had continued to exchange letters over the years, Margaret sending photos of both Milton and John, in Europe, in their wartime uniforms. Margaret had also sent Longman some of Milton's letters describing his experiences working as an illustrator in Europe for the Red Cross. Longman shared them with Bacon before returning them to Margaret.

On November 7, hearing that an Armistice had been signed, Longman wrote:

> Dear Margaret,
> The great news has just come and I must write a word of joy to you!
> How happy you must be! Happy that both of your dear ones went while there was danger and so very happy that that danger is now mostly past. I had a very bad attack with my neck today, but I got an old New Year's horn and tooted it out of the window all by my lonesome while the joy bells and whistles were making their din!
> Oodles of love to you all from
> Evelyn B.[9]

That was the false armistice, when all of New York City and many other U.S. cities celebrated wildly before the actual armistice four days later.

Longman's series of illnesses seemed never-ending. At that point, she was dealing with osteoarthritis. On November 18, in a letter to Margaret, she wrote: "The osteoarthritis is all over my body now—especially my feet—also hands. I am having an osteopath twice a week. The neck is better now."[10]

Daniel French tried to console her:

Dec 13, 1918
Dear Beatrice
I cannot pass over in silence the veiled reference to your health in your note to me. It is impossible for any of us to associate you in our minds with anything but perfect health, you were so evidently made to order, so to speak, with every physical perfection, and all the ills that have assailed you seem somehow not of you, but as something outside and apart and utterly incongruous.

I still believe that all these annoying symptoms will soon pass away and that you will emerge better than ever. I do not wonder that you become discouraged, brave and buoyant as you are, but you must not ever feel that there is anything serious the matter with you. There is going to be a time and to spare for you to climb to the top of the ladder—you are near the top now,—and to garner all the medals in sight on the way. Don't think anything else for an instant,—and please don't make us catch our breath with the shock of your hinting at anything else.

I wish you had somebody to take care of you,—even Henry or poor old me!
Affectionately,
D.C.F.[11]

In spite of her pains and stiffness, she finished the sketch model of Gwendolen by early December. Batchelder responded: "My dear Miss Longman: I'm delighted that the sketch model is ready so soon. Will it be convenient if I run down on Thursday morning as I did before, reaching your studio about ten? Very sincerely, Horton Batchelder."[12]

The *Gwendolen*, the *Illinois Centennial*, the *Henry Bacon* bust were all finished, to happy acclaim. Longman went into her post-success, give-the-body-a-rest funk.

Horton Batchelder would say he fell in love with Longman through her art. Longman said she was first impressed by Horton's interpretation of the character and personality of his wife, Gwendolen, and his devotion to her memory and to their son.[13]

Close to a year after they started work on the *Gwendolen* memorial, Horton wrote:

March 9, 1919
Dear Miss Longman:

You said you should be happy all day because your work had pleased me. I've already been happy for longer than that for the same reason. For months I've lived more for that portrait than you can well imagine. It was true that I had had no doubts of your success, but to see one's dearest hopes so beautifully realized gives one a positively spiritual exaltation. And, your dear thoughts for my boy touched me beyond words. I owe you much that I can never repay. What a great gift you have, this to enrich the lives of others! I'm impatient for the next visit.

Very gratefully yours,
Horton Batchelder[14]

Loomis trustees sent Longman a check on March 20 for $2,730, 70 percent of the total price for the monument. A month later, she wrote to Horton that the *Gwendolen* plaster was ready for him to see. After his inspection, Batchelder wrote:

April 28, 1919
Dear Miss Longman:
Neither words nor roses nor, I fear anything else can ever really tell you my gratitude. But because you are a great artist you can feel another's mood and need not be told. I've felt positively exalted ever since my visit.

I'm so glad you're an academician—and so unspoiled by your honor! You're an inspired genius and a wholly adorable person![15]

Faithfully yours,
Horton Batchelder

Longman responded, noting changes that Batchelder had evidently suggested:

April 30, 1919
Dear Dr. Batchelder:
I cannot sufficiently thank you for your beautiful letter received this morning. Such things are, next to doing the work itself, the greatest joy an artist knows.

I have made some infinitesimal changes in the mouth, made the hair project less over the forehead and worked on both shoulders;—all very slight changes, but which have improved the effect very much.[16]

Longman was there, on April 17, 1919, when a committee from D.C. arrived at the Piccirillis' to inspect French's *Lincoln*. Photos show "Mssrs. Fulton, Northrop, Kimball, and Smith" posing with Longman and Bacon around Lincoln's head and around his leg. Another shows Longman sitting on Lincoln's arm.[17]

Horton's last letter about the creation of the *Gwendolen* mentioned his continued involvement in what he spoke of as their co-creation—and a growing familiarity with the artist.

Figure 17.2 As Daniel Chester French and Henry Bacon had relied on Longman's opinions from the start, she was in the (back of the) room when the Lincoln Memorial committee met with Henry Bacon (seated) at Piccirillis, to view the progress of French's Lincoln. Source/Credit: Photograph from the collection of the Loomis Chaffee Archives, Loomis Chaffee School, Windsor, Connecticut USA.

> May 1, 1919
> Dear Miss Longman:
> There!—I haven't taken a deep breath all day. It's near midnight and I'm still surrounded by litter, with a gorged waste basket spilling over onto the floor, but I'm going to have a quiet moment with you about the tablet. I'm glad you feel that the effect is improved by the slight changes I suggested. Most critics would have considered it already perfect. . . .
> It's been a gray and rainy May Day. I wish I might have been at hand to hang a gay basket on your door knob, but I've been too stupid even to think of sending one.
> Faithfully,
> Horton Batchelder[18]

At this point, it seems that visits replaced letters. Dilemma was on Longman's horizon. With *Electricity/The Spirit of Communication* atop New York City and displayed widely as AT&T's corporate logo; *Future* recently awarded the Shaw Prize; her contribution to the Lincoln monument ready for its dedication; monumental pieces—the *Illinois Centennial* and the *Allison Memorial*—now installed in states farther west, she was at the peak of her career.

Seeing to it that her talent was acknowledged, Daniel French nominated her to be a full member of the prestigious National Academy of Design. He asked twenty-six men, including Bacon, to add Longman to their nomination lists. Among those he asked to honor a "deserving" Longman were Herbert

Adams, Alexander Stirling Calder, Cass Gilbert, Childe Hassam, Isidor Konti, Paul Manship, Edward Potter, Louis C. Tiffany, and Harry Watrous.[19]

No female sculptor was a full member of the National Academy of Design. Emma Stebbins had been named an associate member in 1842. A sculptor of public sculptures, as well, Stebbins's best-known work was the *Bethesda Fountain* in New York City's Central Park. She was the first female sculptor nominated for full membership, but there was an issue around her membership procedures. It was a setback for her, but she was living in Paris by that time, and her name was never resubmitted for full membership.[20]

Longman, who had been an associate member for ten years, was admitted as a full member in 1919. The. First. Woman. Sculptor. Her standing was indisputable. She had reached the top, officially. To what heights did she have her mind fixed next?

NOTES

1. EBL to NHB, May 19, 1918, Loomis Chaffee.
2. Fran Blake, "Woman, 78, Completes Edison Bust," *Boston Globe*, December 14, 1952, 113.
3. EBL to NHB, August 4, 1918, Loomis Chaffee.
4. "Let Pershing Decide Peace, Lowden Urges," *Chicago Tribune*, October 14, 1918, 3.
5. Longman scrapbook, Loomis Chaffee.
6. William F. Tuttle to EBL, October 15, 1918, Loomis Chaffee.
7. EBL handwritten note in margins of letter from Tuttle, Loomis Chaffee.
8. NHB to EBL, October 9, 1918, Loomis Chaffee.
9. EBL to Margaret Bancroft, November 7, 1918, Milton Bancroft Collection, Manuscript Group 133, Indiana University of Pennsylvania (IUP), Special Collections and University Archives.
10. EBL to Margaret Bancroft, November 18, 1918, Milton Bancroft Collection, Manuscript Group 133, Indiana University of Pennsylvania (IUP), Special Collections and University Archives.
11. DCF to EBL, November 13, 1918, Loomis Chaffee.
12. NHB to EBL, December 3, 1918, Loomis Chaffee.
13. Lois Palches with NHB notes. Nine-page biographical outline, Loomis Chaffee. Lois Palches was a friend in Oyster Harbors, Massachusetts.
14. NHB to EBL, March 9, 1919, Loomis Chaffee.
15. NHB to EBL, April 28, 1919, Loomis Chaffee. Batchelder also wrote: "I haven't written [indecipherable word] Schmidlapp yet, but I have written to the President of the Trustees to see if he has any objection to a copy of the panel going to Cincinnati. I've thought all the time of this work as belonging to you and me. As a spiritual possession it does, but from a worldly point of view it is paid for by the Trustees, and I suppose they have some right to be consulted, though I've no doubt of

the answer. For myself I think it would be selfish not to share such beauty with any who really desire it."

16. EBL to NHB, April 30, 1919, Loomis Chaffee.
17. Longman scrapbook, Loomis Chaffee.
18. NHB to EBL, May 1, 1919, Loomis Chaffee.
19. Evelyn Beatrice Longman file at The Metropolitan Museum of Art Archives.
20. Elizabeth Milroy, "The Public Career of Emma Stebbins: Work in Marble." https://digitalcollections.wesleyan.edu/object/artfp-16.

Chapter 18

In the Glade

Go on your brave and splendid way dear Beatrice.

—Henry Bacon

While Horton Batchelder would one day admit to lacking self-confidence as a young man, it was not a characteristic obvious to others by the time he was a headmaster. Tall, handsome, charming, smart, and self-assured, he was a planner, a builder, a man with a vision—and a commanding presence. When the Loomis trustees, in their search for a "rare man . . . so many-sided a man," after considering twenty-six applicants, hired Batchelder in June 1912, his ability to get his way soon became obvious.

The trustees had brought in a professor of architecture from the University of Pennsylvania, Warren P. Laird, to consult with them in choosing an architecture firm from the eleven that had submitted designs for the new campus. Laird recommended one firm's proposal, but Batchelder preferred the Colonial Revival design by another firm, Murphy & Dana. He said at the time that the unified colonnaded quadrangle of Murphy & Dana's design fit his vision of the school as a place for "the American ideal of democracy, a community made up of many men of different kinds, each respecting the ideals of the others and working for the common good."[1]

Murphy & Dana got the contract. "On long debate," was all that was reported about how the trustees chose Batchelder's choice rather than that of their architectural consultant.[2]

Neither would Batchelder's vision be thwarted by the unexpected personal challenge of crushing sadness after the loss of his partner following the birth of their child. He relied on his parents in Salem to help him care for his infant son; set about honoring his wife, Gwendolen; and continued managing, coaching, and teaching at the new boys' school.

At the time Longman met him, Batchelder was freshly widowed, a new single parent, the first headmaster of a prep school; she was at the peak of her career. Self-assured of her talent and direct in her business dealings, she was charming and determined—born of her childhood perseverance out of poverty, her tenacity as a woman producing monumental public art, and her internal fortitude through physical vulnerability.

Horton Batchelder was unlike other men in her life. Though French and Bacon and Schmidlapp were, in their own ways, forces to be reckoned with, and Batchelder, like them, was becoming a man of stature respected in his field, he was neither quiet, nor artistic, nor reliably sensitive.

The question of marriage began to stew.

Most married women sculptors of Longman's time created smaller, more domestic statuary. While her portraits and ideal images were acclaimed in the art world, her commissions had been mostly for monumental public works, the work she'd set her heart on as a young woman. Would commissions stop if she were to marry?

Too, she must have considered her bohemian life in New York City. Her studio was there; her connections; her friends. What would it be like to venture into the daily routine of a prep school? Could she relocate to Connecticut and still get work? Was she capable of fulfilling the obligatory duties of the wife of a headmaster? Would she want to? She was forty-four years old in the summer of 1919 and didn't expect to be a mother; now she was faced with becoming a parent of a toddler. While she had once proclaimed that parenting made a person whole, jumping into it at this point in her life must have been sobering. The question at hand—worst-case scenario—loomed: If to marry Nathaniel Horton Batchelder and take on all that came with him meant she would have to give up her career, was she willing to do that?

Longman consulted her teacher and colleague and dear friend, who would certainly understand the dilemma she felt she was facing, even if it wasn't exactly the one he himself had had to make. Not surprisingly, Dan French encouraged her to marry. As much as he admired and promoted her career, her gift for creating beautiful and meaningful sculpture, he also loved her, felt protective of her, and had always hoped there would be someone to take care of her, especially in those times, which were often, when she was ill.

Coincidentally, perhaps fortuitously, Longman's situation had much in common with an Alice Freeman, whose portrait bust she had been commissioned to create. A person of determination, Freeman had taught herself to read at age three and had become a college president—the first woman in the nation—at the age of twenty-seven.[3] Similar to Longman's predilections,

Freeman's tireless work ethic had created health issues, and at a high point in her career, she was also faced with the decision of whether or not to marry.

In preparation to make the bust, Longman read her biography, *The Life of Alice Freeman*, written by her husband, Harvard philosophy professor George Herbert Palmer. She must have been compelled by Freeman's story, recognizing the similarities with her own: childhood poverty, determination in the face of a patriarchal culture, success in a career where she broke ground for women, frequent illness, and the dilemma around marriage and career.

Alice Freeman had been the oldest of five children in a family that struggled financially; it fell to her to help care for her four siblings. Her mother, Elizabeth, was an advocate for children and for women's rights; her father, a farmer, graduated from medical school when Alice was six, which made it possible for her to attend a co-educational academy in Windsor, New York. Alice won awards for her compositions and her oratory performances. At seventeen, she was ready for college, but that was almost unheard of in 1872. Her parents allowed Alice to enter the University of Michigan only after she promised not to marry until she had paid her parents back for not only her own education, but also her brothers'.

When her father's financial situation worsened and he asked her to return home, Alice acquired a teaching position in Illinois as she continued her studies, speaking at her commencement in 1876. Taking a job as the principal of a high school in East Saginaw, Michigan, Alice moved her family to that city when her father declared bankruptcy in 1877. Although she began to experience health issues, she would continue to be self-supporting the rest of her life.

The president of the University of Michigan recommended Freeman to Henry and Pauline Durant as they were planning the opening of Wellesley College, with its all-female faculty. Feeling the need to stay close to her family, she refused the Durants' first two offers to join the faculty, but in 1897, she accepted the offer to head the history department. Two years later, she became the president of Wellesley.

As its leader, she was instrumental in moving the curriculum from a Christian school of domestic sciences to a rigorous academic institution. As a model of the "New Woman," Freeman showed doubters that higher education for women was valuable and that women could be both attractive and intellectual. Out of a conviction born of her experience, she believed that higher education is "life insurance for a girl."

Freeman established feeder schools for Wellesley and a system on campus where students and faculty lived together in cottages. A brilliant and tireless administrator, she also was in demand as a national public speaker and often was featured in magazine stories. She founded what would become the American Association of University Women. But she suffered from "weak lungs" (her sister had died of tuberculosis), and at one point in her presidency, she was told she only had six months to live.

Harvard philosophy professor George Herbert Palmer, who was widowed with two children, proposed marriage to Freeman in 1886. And he insisted she resign from the presidency of Wellesley. It was a dilemma for Freeman that must have resonated with Longman—though, it turned out, neither George Palmer nor Horton Batchelder expected the women to give up their careers entirely.

Palmer supported Freeman's work and believed she already had achieved her most important service to Wellesley. Too, he was deeply concerned for her health, as she was exhausted and showing signs of tuberculosis. Freeman spent several months deliberating the decision, and when her resignation from Wellesley and her engagement were announced simultaneously, a debate ensued: feminists were appalled, and anti-feminists claimed their views were justified.

Unknown by either contingency was the arrangement that Freeman and Palmer had made: unconventional for the time, it was a "marriage of comradeship." Following a period of health restoration, Freeman continued her work, lecturing, consulting, writing articles, and serving on boards, including the Massachusetts State Board of Education. She resigned as a trustee of one college after learning a young African American woman had been refused admission because of the color of her skin. Palmer became the first dean of women at the University of Chicago, where she was required to be in residence several months every year. George Palmer managed their home in Cambridge as Alice worked and traveled. When she died at forty-seven, in 1902, she had indeed modeled the life of a "new woman," as an academic leader, builder, writer, and wife.[4]

In 1909, Daniel Chester French had been commissioned to create a memorial for Palmer. Installed in the Houghton Chapel at Wellesley, French's portrait in relief captured the spirit of education/the spirit of Alice Freeman Palmer, guiding a young woman scholar toward the future.

Now Longman was tasked with creating a bust of her for the Hall of Fame for Great Americans at New York University's uptown campus. As well as reading Palmer's biography of his wife, Longman read and reread all of Alice Palmer's poetry. And she had several conversations with George Palmer himself. When she showed him the bust of Palmer, which she had modeled in the woman's maturity, George Palmer told Longman he preferred his wife be presented as youthful and vivacious. Longman altered the work, almost completely redoing it.[5]

The bust is simple without ornamentation. Palmer's blouse has a modest ruffle at the collar, and drapery evoking a scholar's robe hangs over her bust in a ragged edge. Her wavy hair is pulled to the back of her head so that her face dominates the piece. Longman has captured intelligence, warmth, earnestness, and a settled weariness in her young features. Though vivaciousness is not explicitly evident, Palmer was pleased with Longman's second version. He kept a slightly tinted plaster cast of the bust in his home and later had a replica of the bronze made and placed in the Wellesley library, in the room where his collection of rare editions of ancient and modern poets was housed.[6]

Perhaps the Freeman-Palmer marriage inspired Longman to explore with Batchelder how they could maintain their separate, demanding careers while sharing life together. At some point, he told her he would build a studio for her at Loomis. A studio in Windsor might not guarantee that she would still receive small commissions, or commissions for monumental works, but it expressed Batchelder's unwavering support for her career in sculpture, the very thing that had brought them together.

In April, Longman was addressing letters to "Dr. Batchelder." By July, she had decided to marry him.

"After much soul searching, good advice from Daniel Chester French, to take the step, she thought she was severing her professional connections and would have few, if any commissions," Batchelder wrote.[7]

A reporter for a Connecticut newspaper said that at the time Batchelder became enamored with Longman, "Her work was enough for her and she was perfectly happy with it—so completely contented, her friends used to say—that her marriage came as a surprise to them."[8]

Some years later, Longman explained to a reporter, making light of her arduous decision: "Mr. Batchelder came to get me to make a portrait of his first wife. I had to stay here [at Loomis] a week on the job, and that was fatal! You'd know why if you ever saw Mr. Batchelder."[9]

In many photographs over the years, Longman was pictured in front of hotels where she and Henry Bacon stayed during trips for work and vacation. One photograph in her photo album is in keeping with this pattern, though differences are striking. Instead of a hotel, it is a private, vine-covered home, and neither she nor Henry Bacon is standing in front. It is in Annapolis, fifty miles from Washington, D.C., where they often worked and visited.

Longman's simple caption under the photograph tells as much of the story as we probably will ever know.

"Annapolis" July 4, 1919 — H.B. & E.B.L.

A momentous, vine-covered time together on Independence Day seemed to indicate a certain, perhaps bittersweet, ending/beginning.

Figure 18.1 Longman's bas-relief of Gwendolen Sedgwick Batchelder and, symbolically in the cherub, the birth of her son. Source/Credit: Photograph by A. B. Bogart. From the collection of the Loomis Chaffee Archives, Loomis Chaffee School, Windsor, Connecticut USA.

There is no indication that Longman was present on September 18, 1919, at the Loomis's Founders Chapel for the dedication of her bas-relief of Gwendolen Sedgwick Batchelder, when Batchelder described the vitality of his wife's life: She had grown up on a small island off the Massachusetts coast, sailing and swimming the mile across the harbor. At Loomis, she gardened and had a fond connection with animals. "Every place where she dwelt for even a short time spoke her direct, vigorous, beauty-loving half masculine and wholly feminine touch," Batchelder explained.

During the ordeal of building the campus in Connecticut's cold and snowy winters, Gwendolen "was the piper who kept our spirits up," said Batchelder, recounting the story of how she went to visit the workers and ended waist-deep in a snowdrift; the story of how her boot caught in the mud and she had to step out of it.

"With her own intensely active temperament that gave itself too freely for her own good to any cause she embraced, and shrank at no sacrifice or hardship, she could understand neither laziness, nor disloyalty, nor cowardice," Batchelder said.

"We come not to mourn a spirit departed, but to rejoice at a spirit still with us; to consecrate ourselves to the continuance of a work nobly begun; to dedicate a building to a precious memory; to unveil a portrait the surpassing loveliness of which shall serve to keep alive for all time a gracious and inspiring personality."[10]

The chapel service was followed by a smaller ceremony in the new infirmary, Gwendolen Hall, in a space Batchelder referred to with Longman as "our little sacred spot." Longman's portrait was unveiled by the four student winners of the Gwendolen Sedgwick Batchelder Prize for Industry, Loyalty, and Manliness. In profile, waves of hair frame Gwendolen's pretty, young face and are swept into a bun at the nape of her neck. She emits strength, dignity, softness. A lily decorates her bodice. There is no inscription; rather, only her name: *Gwendolen Sedgwick Batchelder*. Beneath the tablet, an exquisite fat-cheeked, winged cherub recalls the birth of her child, and to each side, there were festoons of flowers.

Longman and Batchelder first announced their engagement to Daniel French. He told Mary, but they kept the news from Margaret until Longman and Batchelder's surprise visit to Chesterwood:

> Oct. 4, 1919
> Dear Beatrice.
> Mary was as excited over the news that I brought home to her as I expected and so far we have kept the secret from Margaret and all the household. I feel as if my bottle might not stand the pressure, however, till next Thursday and that it might burst at any moment!
>
> This is only to tell you what is a matter of course,—that we shall be waiting with open arms for the advent of yourself and your "gentleman friend" sometime Thursday afternoon. How long can you stay and how long can Mr. Batchelder? It will be the event of the season, almost of our lives.
>
> With even more affection than usual,
> Dan. C French[11]

Responses to the news from Batchelder's parents and brother Osgood were wholeheartedly congratulatory, as well:

> Salem Oct. 12-1919
> My dear Son Horton,
> I am greatly surprised at your news and equally pleased. I don't know of anything that has made me so happy in a long time. When you told me of that informal supper in your kitchen the thought flitted through my mind that maybe

something more would follow, but I don't remember that I ever gave it a thought after that.

I want very much to see my daughter-to-be and hope you will be able to bring her here before a great while. I shall not try to send her anything but my love just yet. I want to know a little more about what she likes first and flowers are sure to wilt on the road.

It will be very nice indeed if Evelyn can be in Windsor when we come for our fall trip.

. . . Your father says he wants to add a word so I leave space for him and send a great deal of love.

As ever,
Mother

This is just what we have always wished. We shall welcome a new daughter most cordially, and I know we shall like her very much. We are anxious to see you together as soon as possible.

Sincerely,
Father[12]

Horton's brother Osgood wrote from Chicago:

October 14, 1919.
Dear Horton,
I approve most heartily and send you sincere congratulations but I decline to be surprised, inasmuch as I thought the idea a good one the latter part of August. Surely you did not think advancing years had robbed me of powers of observation. I thought I could see a little unusual interest there and now I know it. However, not being given to telling all I think, have kept my own counsel, but I will admit to being strongly impressed and equally strongly hoping that events might turn out as they have. The question of art also arose in my mind. Of course that must be taken care of. What a wonderful atmosphere you will be in.

And you are sensible too, to take the step, you need a wife so much where you are, and your choice certainly meets my complete approval, how could it be otherwise?

My best to you
Osgood[13]

Osgood, in his letter welcoming Longman to the family, cast his vision of the couple's new life:

Chicago, October 14, 1919
Dear Evelyn,
I extend to you a most sincere welcome as a prospective member of the family, in fact I am going to leave the word "prospective" out right from the start and insist that you are a member from now.

I can hardly express my delight in greeting you again, even at this distance . . . as Horton's fiancé.

We brothers have been singularly close to each other, even for brothers, and that means that Horton's happiness comes very near to me and that I am very happy in his good fortune.

I know you will be very happy with him and that you will add very much to the charm of Windsor by your presence, that you will be a further inspiration to him in his splendid work in the education of youth, and I know also that he will give you his affection and admiration in continuance of your own splendid achievements.

I can't imagine a . . . more enchanting environment in which to live than that which you two can make in the midst of the school life.

I am glad that I had the opportunity of seeing you at Windsor last summer and having liked you so well.

I hope you will like your new relatives as well as I know they will like you.

Sincerely yours

William Osgood Batchelder[14]

Osgood would be Horton's best man. Horton gave him a small version of Longman's *Victory* as a thank-you gift. Osgood's teasing of Longman at Batchelder family gatherings would become a family tradition. One can imagine that she responded in kind.

Longman's letters to her family were high-spirited:

October 14, 1919

Dearest Betty & Cecil.

Hold your breath—hard! I am engaged to be married—needless to say, to the finest man in all the world! He is 39 years old and is head-master at the Loomis Institute, Windsor. Conn., (six miles from Hartford) a boys' preparatory school, and it is there, of course, that I shall live.

You'll both think he is splendid and he is!

I am visiting here at the Frenches' for a few days. He motored me up from New Haven last Thursday, and drove over again yesterday to see me—and all the Frenches and their guests are "crazy" about him. His name is Nathaniel Horton Batchelder—and he uses Horton for the "first" name. We shall announce our engagement very soon, and be married in the late spring or early summer—as soon as my work will permit.

He has a little boy 2 1/2 years old—and I met him through making a tablet to his wife, who was a wonderful and beautiful woman in whose memory they had just erected a memorial infirmary.

Lovingly,

Evelyn[15]

Longman's brother Claude accepted her request that he walk her down the aisle:

Dearest Evelyn
Your letter came last night and I am writing at once for fear someone else will get my job. You bet I will give you away. Don't get scared. I mean no harm, but will be happy to give you away in the right way. . . . I had hoped for some simple honors in the declining years of my life but did not look for any up to this high standard. . . .

And by the way you and Horton are coming to Lakeside for part or all of your Honeymoon. Wasn't that the promise you gave me when I consented to the engagement?

Where and how is Hal? I have not seen him nor heard from him for four months. I have heard he might not be well. He is my dearest friend and I cannot bear to think of him as ill or in any trouble. I may write him today.

Best love to you sister dear
Claudius
Friday[16]

Claude's letter to Horton:

Oct. 29, 1919
Dear Mr. Batchelder
. . . Frankly I will say the first news which came in a sweet unassuming woman befitting the character of my beloved sister made me feel something as a parent might feel whose only child is about to leave the homestead . . . a feeling at first half sad then happy then finer than either as the real meaning of it all was realized. Except of course I am only a brother, and there was really no homestead. I know that the thought of making a home for herself is very dear to Evelyn.

I am jealous for her happiness and have a deep faith that the sort of man who has won her love can and will make her happy. It is the best proof of his good qualities that such a woman . . . finds in him the man she can love and is willing to make her life companion. Especially in this time I think in a woman who has lived a larger broader life than most women and whose lot as fallen among many of the choicest spirits in the idealistic world of art.

In a sense therefore I already know you because I know in some degree the kind of man who would appeal to her, though I shall be happy to know you for yourself.

Evelyn means much to me—a sister of sisters, a companion of a life time, a woman of women. I hope I may not seem prejudiced in her favor when I say that I believe you are a man honored among men by her love. . . .

Sincerely yours,
G.C. Longman[17]

One particular letter to Batchelder upon the announcement of his engagement to Longman is evidence of a rarity: that Longman had a female friend outside her circle. In her letter, Katharine Corbin Parsons, the daughter of General

Henry Clark Corbin, whose portrait Longman had created, speaks to Longman's character and to their friendship.

> 667 Madison Ave.
> New York City.
> My dear Mr. Batchelder—
> Evelyn has told me of her happiness and I am so glad for her—and am writing to tell you how glad I am for you—I know so well her loveliness of character, her optimistic vision, her delightful companionship, and can imagine nothing more satisfactory than having her always near. I think it is wonderful that she will have just the kind of interests I know you can give her—In the home life and all it brings. I do not know when a piece of news has given me such satisfaction for Evelyn is very dear to me. Hoping to soon have an opportunity of meeting you.
> I am very sincerely yours
> Katharine Corbin Parsons
> Mrs. William Usher Parsons[18]

The Frenches were thrilled with Batchelder. Margaret French, writing to William Penn Cresson, who would one day be her husband, reported that Batchelder was "a thoroughly splendid person" and "he really seems pure gold" and "she has found a jewel."[19]

Of Longman she wrote: "She is so happy . . . and her enthusiasm is contagious; it is such fun suggesting and planning the details of her wedding."[20]

In an undated letter, Henry Bacon wrote:

> Beloved Beatrice—
> Indeed you are beloved, and so beloved by all who know you that your old Cousin Hal wishes that he could do something splendid for the world in thanks for his share of your dear friendship—I will too! Bless your dear heart a thousand times—
>
> Go on your brave and splendid way dear Beatrice and count always on the hearty help and willing hands of your loving Cousin Hal who sees you surrounded always with everything that is best in life—
>
> My wish for you dear Beatrice is all of beauty & radiance—May happiness fill your heart to overflowing
> Always your loving Cousin
> Hal—[21]

The wedding would be scheduled around work deadlines of three commissions: the *World War I Monument* in Naugatuck; the bust of Alice Palmer Freeman, and a fountain, *Youth Eternal*, at Hecksher Museum on Long Island.

Youth Eternal was commissioned by industrialist August Hecksher, who was opening an art museum in Huntington, Long Island. Hecksher's philanthropic work in New York City had been focused on improving the lives of children. The marble water fountain is a tribute to childhood. Bas-reliefs of storybook-like figures decorate the basin: a pelican and a monkey face off, with their children playing together at their feet; a giant cat is nose to nose with a bumblebee; a mouse gets a lift from a lizard; a giant grasshopper is slowed behind a snail; a duck in a hat spreads its wings; a giant mouse with umbrella and briefcase sets off to work with his little mice scampering along. There's a giant lobster, rabbit, and sea dragon.

Three children are perched atop the fountain, delighting in a bronze frog on the ledge below spouting water from its mouth. Modeled by Hecksher's grandchildren, the youngest stands in the middle, looking apprehensive, his hands folded across his chest, while an older brother, resting on his knees, encircles his brother reassuredly in his arms. A sister crouched beside her little brother holds him close.

The inscription around the rim reads: "Forever will thou love and they be fair."

With his payment, Hecksher wrote to Longman, "It has rarely afforded me greater satisfaction to pay a bill which I have owed."[22]

Longman was fond of the fountain and later had another cast, in concrete and bronze, which she installed outside her studio.

By Christmas 1919, French's *Lincoln* was installed at Bacon's Lincoln Memorial, though French, standing on a scaffold, would continue to sand its seamlines through the spring of 1920.

Longman took her fiancé to the Frenchs' annual Christmas party in Daniel's New York City studio. There is no record of the toastings that year. One suspects there was no mention of "husbands."

In June 1920, Mary and Daniel French sent engraved invitations to Longman's June 28 wedding, to be held at Chesterwood. Margaret French would be maid of honor. She wrote to Cresson in May, describing Longman's sheer delight:

> I had such an amusing time at Beatrice Longman's the other night; she got out all her trousseaux, all her pretty lingerie and things, and tried everything on. If anyone could have seen us capering around in pink silk pajamas and yellow crepe de chine chemises they would have thought we'd gone mad.[23]

And Margaret recorded one of those sentimental moments that Loomis boys experienced from their headmaster only now and then:

> Beatrice's fiancé is bursting into print in this month's Atlantic you will see an article called "Democracy and Education," by Nathaniel Horton Batchelder. . . . He was so excited about this article that he had his check for it $70, changed into gold pieces, which he brought to Beatrice, wasn't that sweet? She says he has so much sentiment and never misses a trick.[24]

Figure 18.2 Longman-Batchelder wedding party in the glen at Chesterwood: (L-R) brother of the bride, Claude Longman; Maid of Honor, Margaret French; Evelyn and Horton; Best Man, Osgood Batchelder; the Reverend Alfred Manchester. Source/Credit: Photograph by EHT. From the collection of the Loomis Chaffee Archives, Loomis Chaffee School, Windsor, Connecticut USA.

The ceremony was held in the glade in the Chesterwood Studio Garden. Dan French decorated his friend's wedding space with oriental carpets and a drapery backdrop in front of a flowered and draped "altar" with blooming arbor vitae on either side. Garlands of laurel festooned a green-curtained canopy.[25] Set prettily at the end of the vine-covered pergola on the front porch, three women—the Eastman String Trio of New York, on cello, harp, and violin—played Wagner's "Bridal Chorus," then provided music during the reception. Budding opera singer and French and Longman friend and model Rosalie Miller sang.

One hundred guests made their way to the glade for the 4 p.m. ceremony. Batchelder's pastor, the Reverend Alfred Manchester, of the Second Unitarian Church at Salem, led the service. The *New York Times* reported: "The bride wore a medieval costume of deep cream satin with gold and pearl embroidery. A veil of gold net was held in place by a coronet of gold leaves with pearl ornaments. She carried white and yellow columbine.

"Miss Margaret French was her only attendant. She wore orchid colored organdy with cream colored lace and a yellow sash."[26]

The guest list included three-year-old Nathaniel Horton "Skip" Batchelder II; Longman's sister Louise Tewksbury from Toledo; and Batchelder's brothers and their wives.

Other guests were friends from Boston, New York City, and Stockbridge, Massachusetts, including art patrons, like William August Marburg of Baltimore; friends Velma Williams (who had helped Batchelder find a sculptor for the Gwendolen portrait) and Nina Larrey Duenya, also from Boston and Stockbridge, a famous writer and celebrated World War I relief worker whose father founded the YMCA.

French family friends who had become Longman's Chesterwood friends included Will French's widow, Alice, who, at Longman's request, later created a pastel of the Glade. Some guests had historical vitae, including the grandson of Harriet Beecher Stowe, who lived in Stockbridge. Gwendolen's uncle Robert Sedgwick was in attendance. Henry and Laura Bacon were not reported to be guests.

It must have been a momentous day for Daniel French, to see his beloved friend marry—and at his home. He wrote to a friend, "She was married in the little glade in the woods where the stone steps are, just off the garden, and it was the prettiest thing that ever was."[27]

For his wedding gift, French gave the couple a Carrara marble of the bust he made of closed-eyed/ideal Longman, set on a Sienna marble base with the Egyptian sun god ornamentation in gold.[28]

Batchelder would say of French, "I always felt Mr. French was my father-in-law."[29]

Batchelder gave Longman a yellow sapphire pin, filigreed in grape leaves and grapes, which Longman had designed.[30]

On their wedding night, Batchelder would later recall, "a tremendous thunderstorm came up and she [Longman] stood at the window reveling in it. To her it was an omen of a dynamic life on which we were entering."[31]

Nothing was more certain than that life—as a headmaster's wife in a prep school—would be "dynamic." Yet to be determined was what would become of what had been her heart's first desire: a career in monumental public sculpture.

NOTES

1. Karen Parsons and John Ratte, *Cherished Hopes and Honorable Ambition. A Centennial History of The Loomis Chaffee School* (Windsor, CT: Loomis Institute, 2014), 11.
2. Ibid.

3. Palmer actually followed Ada Howard, who had been the college's first president, but in name only, as Wellesley College founder, Henry Fowle Durant, made the decisions.

4. Info about Alice Freeman Palmer is from online sources, accessed June 2, 2021. https://www.massmoments.org/moment-details/alice-freeman-and-george-palmer-marry.html; https://archive.org/details/alicefreemanpalm00amer/page/n20/mode/1up?view=theater.

5. NHB letter to Emily Norman, NYU alumnus, of February 21, 1928, explaining how EBL gathered material for preparing the Palmer bust, Loomis Chaffee.

6. Ibid.

7. Batchelder unpublished memoir, Loomis Chaffee.

8. Bob Vickery, "World Famous World Sculptor Works Hard in Studio," unspecified Connecticut newspaper, March 20, 1921, Longman scrapbook, Loomis Chaffee.

9. Ibid.

10. Memorial for Gwendolen file, Loomis Chaffee.

11. DCF to EBL, December 4, 1919, Engagement Letters file, Loomis Chaffee.

12. Henry Morrill Batchelder to NHB, October 12, 1919, Engagement Letters file, Loomis Chaffee.

13. Osgood Batchelder to NHB, October 14, 1919, Engagement Letters file, Loomis Chaffee.

14. Ibid.

15. EBL to Cecil and Betty Longman, October 14, 1919, Engagement Letters file, Loomis Chaffee.

16. Claude Longman to EBL, undated. Engagement Letters file, Loomis Chaffee.

17. Claude Longman to NHB, October 29, 1919, Engagement Letters file, Loomis Chaffee.

18. Katharine Corbin Parsons to NHB, undated, Engagement Letters file, Loomis Chaffee.

19. Margaret French to William Penn Cresson, October 10 and 15, 1919, Daniel Chester French Papers, Library of Congress, Margaret French Cresson Correspondence, Boxes 63–66.

20. Ibid.

21. Henry Bacon to EBL, undated, Loomis Chaffee.

22. August Hecksher to EBL, October 1920, Loomis Chaffee.

23. Margaret French to William Penn Cresson, May 8, 1920, Daniel Chester French Papers, Library of Congress, Margaret French Cresson Correspondence, Boxes 63–66.

24. Ibid.

25. *Hartford Daily Courant*, June 29, 1920, 11.

26. "Evelyn B. Longman, Sculptor, Marries; Bride of Nathaniel H. Batchelder at Daniel C. French's Estate in Stockbridge, Mass.," *New York Times*, June 29, 1920, 10.

27. DCF to Robert Underwood Johnson, November 12, 1920, Chesterwood Archives.

28. Skip would eventually give it to the Davis collection at Wellesley, in honor of his wife, Betty, an alumnus.
29. NHB unpublished manuscript, Loomis Chaffee.
30. Ibid.
31. Ibid.

Chapter 19

The Island

Those beautiful sensitive fingers played that she was modeling my face.

—Nathaniel Horton "Skip" Batchelder II

In 1913, the infamous "Armory Show" (the International Exhibition of Modern Art) had exposed North Americans to abstract art for the first time—shocking, even angering art enthusiasts, and outraging classical artists. They feared their realistic art would have to move in the direction of the abstractions of the exhibiting Europeans: Picasso, van Gogh, Gauguin, Cézanne, Duchamp, and Matisse. Even twenty years later, near the end of his life, when he was sculpting *Andromeda*, his most provocative sculpture—softly beautiful, erotic, classical allegory—Daniel French, after seeing an exhibit of Matisse sculptures, wrote to Longman: "I think that altogether it is the greatest insult to human intelligence that I have ever met. I have seen isolated specimens of his enormities, but not such a mess as this. How long is this going to last? Longer than I shall, I fear."[1] Indeed, French would die eight months later; though, like Longman's—and Matisse's—his work lives on.

In 1930, even as NYC boasted Longman's golden, "modern" Zeus, the second-highest point in town, the trend toward the avant garde threatened to undercut her future work. As she transitioned from her old life in the city to her new life as mother and wife of a prep school headmaster in Connecticut, she still planned to create beauty in the way she had first envisioned it. Her new, state-of-the-art studio, à la Chesterwood, with its railroad track and high ceilings, made it possible to continue sculpting monumental public art, her first love.

As ever, she would challenge herself—creating a couple of her ideal works in colossal proportions and expanding her skill and vision for portraiture and allegory in bas-relief—always within the bounds of the classical preference for expressing beauty.

Determined to create beauty her way, Longman would experience—and overcome—the fallout as the culture did, indeed, move toward the avant garde. With changing tastes, placing her colossal works (her self-described "masterpiece" among them) would require every last ounce of Longman's legendary tenacity.

The village of Windsor, Connecticut, is a sweet place, set just west of the parallel Farmington and Connecticut Rivers. A block from the village green is the nineteenth-century train station, with mansard roof, dormers, and carved cornices. Longman arrived and departed this station as she made her way between the hustle of the city, with its galleries, foundries, stone cutters, friends, and wealthy clients, and the deceptively bucolic prep school, where, by early 1921, she worked in a new studio befitting a renowned sculptor.

Named "Chiselhurst-on-Farmington," the studio was modeled on Daniel French's at Chesterwood. With Horton's commitment to fund it, Loomis trustees gave permission to erect the studio on campus, a short walk from the Headmaster's House. A wide front porch facing east was furnished with inviting wicker chairs; bas-reliefs of the dancing maidens on Longman's Panama Pacific *Fountain of Ceres* decorated the porch walls. A cozy reception room opened into the huge main room of the studio, which faced west with two-story, floor-to-ceiling paned windows. Mantels held some of her earlier, smaller creations. With high hopes, she designed the soaring workspace so that she could climb tall ladders and work on monumental pieces.

In addition to the spacious studio, there were smaller rooms: the models' room, the handyman's room, a drawing studio; the modeling room, with a drain in the floor.[2] As with French's Chesterwood studio, railroad tracks were installed beneath the floor so the monumental works could be rolled out and viewed in daylight.

Though it is referred to as "the Island," the land where the Loomis Institute was built is not technically an island. However, driving or walking from the train station across the Willow Road bridge over the Farmington River toward the Loomis enclave gives one the sense of crossing to an island—and it becomes one when the rivers flood.

Native river tribes, including the Poquonocks and Podunks, hunted the area and dwelled along the riverbanks until the Dutch purchased land and in 1633 established a trading post a few miles south, at what is now Hartford. Settlers from Plymouth Colony then established a trading post where the Tunis (Farmington) River joins the Quinnectuckut (Connecticut) River at the south end of Windsor, which claims to be "the first English settlement," Connecticut's "oldest town."

The first house on the land was built by people from the Plymouth Colony in the so-called Plymouth Meadow. After a smallpox epidemic destroyed tribes along the river valley, trading came to a halt, and settlers from the Massachusetts Bay Colony moved into Plymouth Meadow. James Loomis, his wife, and eight children came in the autumn of 1639, and in 1640 Loomis was granted ownership of that land, twenty-one acres on the south bank of the Farmington River.

Eight generations of Loomises lived in the colonial-style homestead on a bluff overlooking the rivers. In the seventh generation, Colonel James Loomis and Abigail Sherwood Chaffee Loomis owned the general store in the village of Windsor. They farmed as well, and James served in the first regiment of the Connecticut militia and then in the state legislature. Education of their five children was a high priority. Two sons graduated from Yale, in 1827 and 1835.

The five siblings had eight children among them, all of whom died at young ages. The last, James Chaffee Loomis's son Jimmy, was a senior at Yale in 1867, when he succumbed to typhoid fever, leaving the Loomis siblings without heirs to their considerable estates. To honor their children, in 1874 the Loomises chartered the Loomis Institute, to be built on their homestead land along the rivers. Hezekiah wrote the "Family Testimony," April 29, 1878: "a sentiment, born of the strong natural love and sympathy between us, and intensified by the loss of all our children, crystallized into a desire to leave some memento of our lives, failing the natural one of succession; and this finally took the form of a free educational establishment, called the Loomis Institute."[3]

Their dream would be realized forty years after its inception—the delay due to their agreement to provide for each other through their retirements, since they had no heirs to do so. The Loomis family's plan for the Loomis Institute included free education—and so it was for four decades, though there were fees: four hundred dollars for residential students (in 1914) and one dollar a week for day students' lunches. Osbert, who incidentally was an artist, envisioned a "family system," in which faculty and their families lived in residence halls with Loomis students. That is still the case. When all the Loomises had died—the last in 1910—the Institute was ready to hire its first headmaster.

As the first headmaster, a position he would hold for thirty-seven years, Nathaniel Horton Batchelder had a great deal of influence on developing the curriculum, culture, and climate of the new school. Loomis opened with three courses of study for boys—college preparation, agriculture, and business. For the girls—day students in separate classrooms from the boys—there were courses for college preparation and domestic science.

Batchelder, influenced by Charles William Eliot, who was president of Harvard while Batchelder attended the university, included practical application as part of a Loomis student's education. Business students ran the school's book and stationery store. As they advanced in their studies, students kept accounts for the dining hall, power plant, laundry, and farm. Agriculture students raised market gardens and field crops, tended the poultry flock and dairy herd, and kept business records for their projects. All students did chores as if in a family, cleaning common spaces in dorms and classrooms and waiting tables in the dining room.

From the beginning, Batchelder had envisioned a school that did not "set its seal" upon a boy. "If the time comes when you can recognize a Loomis boy by his speech, by his clothes, or still more fatally, by a standard attitude of mind, on that day we shall have failed," faculty member John Edmund Barss summarized Batchelder's philosophy. "It is the plan of Loomis that each boy shall continue to be himself, but that that shall be his best self, developed in surroundings friendly to such growth.[4]

"The rubber-stamp personality is anathema, and . . . a boy shall be encouraged to go on with his real interests. If he wants to experiment with radio, he may do so; . . . if he loves birds, he may wander afield with a binocular without being regarded as a freak; a vigorous athlete may grow flowers on his window-sill and excite no amazed comments; . . . the unpardonable sin is to have no interest, scholastic, sporting, or scientific."[5]

Today the co-ed school aims for the goal Batchelder articulated: "Inspiring a commitment to the best self and the common good."

The Loomis Institute had been open six years when Longman moved to "the Island." In the fall of 1920, there were 162 boy students (118 residents; 44 day students) and 12 girls (all day students).[6] Longman came as the new wife of the headmaster, as well as bringing fresh excitement as a nationally acclaimed sculptor. Her home then was the headmaster's house, affectionately referred to as the Head's House. It was unlike any place she had lived—neither the cramped Chicago rooms nor the farmhouse garret of her youth in Canada nor the top floor studio/living quarters of New York City apartment buildings. It was a grand, two-story brick house with fourteen rooms, including a conservatory, five baths, attic, basement; four fireplaces and three verandas. Windows had shutters, the hipped roof was slate; library walls were covered in grass cloth, and the floors were oak and Georgia pine. There were built-in cupboards and cabinets, a dumbwaiter, and an incinerator.[6] The large formal garden next to the house with its dense plantings of roses, hedges, and perennials had been designed by Boston landscape architect Sheffield Arnold, who mapped plantings for the Loomis campus.

Not only was the house Longman's new home, the home of a family, it was also at the heart of the school's hospitality operations. Guests were often invited to stay overnight, and some school events were traditionally held at the Head's House. Too, it was the childhood home of young Batchelder, "Skip," as he would come to be known.

When Gwendolen died, Batchelder had enlisted the help of his parents in Salem, who in turn had enlisted the help of a nanny, who would pin baby Horton to the bed at naptime to keep him quiet.[7] Though he would also have caregivers at Loomis, it must have been a happy turn of events, at the age of three, to settle into a new family, with both a father and a mother.

New to parenthood, Longman's playful style emerged. She read to Skip in the evenings, sessions that included tickling and back-scratching and swatting imaginary flies that were really moles on his back; chasing make-believe mice that scampered over him—surely precipitated by the experience of real mice during her own childhood in Canada.

She incorporated what she knew—modeling clay—into her games with Skip. He later recalled the "immense joy" of laying his head in his new mother's lap while "those beautiful sensitive fingers played that she was modeling my face, taking an imaginary lump of plastiline . . . then working out the eye and the nose, the mouth and the ears and working the hair and so on."[8]

In the garden, Longman turned loathsome tasks into games that delighted Skip. When bugs invaded rosebushes, they picked insects off the leaves, threw them on the walkway, squashing them while chanting "Loo-miss" (squash, squash). "Loo-miss" (squash, squash).[9]

At the age of forty-six, though she had spent time with her siblings and their families, the Frenches at Chesterwood, and the Bancrofts at Shelter Island, Longman had lived most of her life without any semblance of her own family. While life at a prep school in the head's family was atypical, it was indeed family life, and she embraced it with devotion. A daily rhythm developed. At 5 a.m., Longman made the three-minute walk from the house, through the garden, and across the lawn to her new studio. Batchelder's before-breakfast routine included taking one of the seven straight razors—labeled Monday, Tuesday, Wednesday, etc.—from a box, then honing it on a leather strop for his daily shave. Longman, Batchelder, and Skip shared breakfast at 7:30 a.m., and then Longman returned to her studio and Batchelder left for the chapel service at eight, always seated at his place in the front left pew. Afterward he sometimes visited Longman in her studio, but more often he went to his office at the end of the quadrangle, where two-story paned windows afforded him a full view of the campus over which he governed.[10]

School lunch was at one, then Longman and Batchelder were back in studio and office. They often also ate dinner at the school and dropped by a faculty member's home afterward, Batchelder discussing business while Longman talked with his wife. This wasn't always pleasant for the women, as Longman's aesthetic tastes would take over her better judgment. She was known to tell faculty wives how to rearrange their furniture and otherwise decorate their homes.

Too, though she performed the more mundane duties expected of the headmaster's wife, she wasn't always simpatico with Loomis wives. One story describes Longman's response when a faculty wife called her to say she couldn't take her turn arranging flowers in the chapel because she had a 102-degree temperature. "That's no excuse," Longman reportedly snapped, then hung up the phone.

Here was a woman who had made her way through poverty and frequent illness as she developed a successful career in a man's world; a woman who was now trying to sustain that career in a setting where such an attempt was unique, juggling it with her Loomis life (including taking her turn at serving tea and arranging flowers) and her family life, with husband, son—and 162 or so other boys. She had little patience for what she perceived as mere complaints.

Perhaps there was no excuse for her snippiness, but Skip wrote that fever would not have been a sufficient excuse to his mother: "Mother had tremendous force of character and of course she had overcome all kinds of difficulties in her own life and she was not terribly patient with other people who had obstacles that she considered insignificant.

"I have known her to go to official functions with a temperature of 102 even though she had to come back and collapse in bed for the next two days. There was an immense sense of noblesse oblige in both my parents. The show went on and if you didn't feel well, it was too bad, but the show went on anyway."[11]

Faculty meetings were held in a different home each Monday night, where couples shared coffee and then husbands sat for a business meeting. Sunday chapel was at noon. Batchelder, in his black graduation robe, often delivered the sermon. On Easter, he and Longman dressed up: Batchelder in striped trousers, morning coat, gray ascot, and top hat. Longman, in her finest, carried a parasol. They walked arm in arm from the chapel, down the "Senior Path" to lunch in the school dining hall.

Sunday night supper especially was a family time, when household staff had the night off and Batchelder cooked. "My father loved to cook Sunday night supper himself for Mother and me at Loomis," wrote Skip, ". . . [beginning] with one-quarter pound pure butter, eight eggs and a half pint or more of thick cream, courtesy of the Loomis dairy farm."[12]

Some Sunday nights the family welcomed students in the library. After a skit, which a faculty member was called on spontaneously to create, Batchelder would read aloud. One memorable evening, French instructor René Cherny amused the gathering by eating cereal and milk using a slotted spoon.

Family life included time in Longman's studio as well. Skip played there at times, with clay and toy soldiers and props and costumes Longman used for modeling. Sometimes it was Batchelder who piled the plastiline on a shellacked board for Longman's next model.[13]

To get away, Batchelder and Longman regularly climbed into a green, double-ended rowboat with a rudder. Batchelder rowed while Longman steered their way up the Farmington River to a favorite quiet spot on the bank where they picnicked on sandwiches, fruit juice, and coffee; watched the sunset; and read poetry. Shunning the foxtrot and other "modern" dances, Batchelder liked to waltz, rather vigorously, and at Loomis school dances, the floor would clear as the headmaster and the sculptor spun gracefully across the gymnasium.[14]

During faculty picnics on the lawn on the river side of the Head's House, people flowed in and out of the dining room, kitchen, and pantry. Following this and other school events at her home, Longman counted the silverware "not because she thought anybody had stolen it but because she was afraid that someone would have dumped it inadvertently into the garbage," Skip wrote later. "And when she couldn't find a spoon or a fork we literally went through garbage, she and Father and I, until we were sure that there was nothing disposed of in it. Mother was nothing if she was not tenacious."[15]

End-of-the-season football breakfasts became legendary. The entire football squad was invited for Sunday morning breakfast at the Head's House. It was an eating contest—this year's team trying to eat more than last year's team. Longman kept records: six dozen eggs, eight loaves of bread, twelve quarts of juice, etc. "If one could eat at least one more egg than the previous season's group," wrote Skip, "then you had the record and there were great shouts."[16]

Batchelder loved football and coached at Loomis in the early years. Later, when administrative duties prevented him from coaching, one of his summer pastimes was to strategize plays on paper and then corral Longman, Skip, the cook, the housekeeper, and whoever were houseguests at the time out in the driveway to take positions and run the plays to see if they would work.

Holiday traditions were memorable at Loomis. For Thanksgiving dinner in the early days before the boys could go home conveniently, the dining room was set up in round tables for twelve: ten boys and a teacher and his wife or eleven boys and a song master. Student waiters for each table gathered in the pantry and then, carrying large platters of turkey, processed around the dining hall to cheers and clapping. As a bird was brought to each table, a carving contest ensued. Batchelder was the carver supreme, delicately cutting off wings and legs, slicing the breast. He served light or dark meat to each guest, per their preference, and then spooned out the stuffing. When all were served at a table, the diners applauded. No one was supposed to out-carve the head. One year, a new teacher ignored the tradition and won the carving contest. Batchelder's retort: "I carved a bird. He merely dismembered it."[17]

At Christmastime, the night before the boys went home for the holiday break, they gathered in the school library, where two easy chairs with great bronze chandeliers on each side were set in front of the big fireplace. A festive procession began when the smallest boy in the school, dressed as a jester in a green and red suit with bells, tumbled and jingled toward the fireplace. Student Council members, with red sashes set across their torsos (Longman had laid out the sashes for them in Batchelder's office), processed toward the fireplace. Then a football player dressed as a woodsman carried a Yule log with an ax in it to be placed in the fire. Finally, Batchelder, in blue suit, and Longman, in long green gown, came forward and took their places in the chairs.

With lights out, sitting in front of the glowing, flickering fire, Batchelder read from Dickens's *A Christmas Carol*, pausing after each ghost, when lights were turned back on and the gathered stood and sang a couple of Christmas carols before the darkness descended and Batchelder read again. Afterward, they shared cookies and, Batchelder's favorite, ice cream.[18]

Even while she was living her new life—engaged with Skip, Batchelder, and people in the school—Longman sometimes experienced it as surreal. This is not surprising, as her new life contrasted markedly with her earlier life—living alone and thoroughly immersed in the art world of New York City with Bancroft, French, and Bacon, each very different from her new husband. Undaunted of course, she persevered into her new life until it became more

Figure 19.1 The state-of-the-art sculpture studio Batchelder had built for Longman, at Loomis Institute. Their home, "the Head's House," is in the background. Source/Credit: Photograph by White Studio, NY. From the collection of the Loomis Chaffee Archives, Loomis Chaffee School, Windsor, Connecticut USA.

normal. It took a while. More than a dozen years after her wedding, in 1933, while away to model a bust, she wrote to Batchelder: "It is a long time since I have had that disconcerting feeling of the first few years after our marriage, when I'd look at you and suddenly feel that I was living with a stranger! A shocking thought!! But I knew that we had been legally married and that the certificate was in my possession."[19]

A 1916 graduate described Batchelder as "primarily a builder. When he started out to build a building (or character in a boy), he did just that. He dominated his faculty and his student body. Right or wrong, he never looked back for praise or blame."[20]

In a speech to the Newcomen Society in 1964, Frank Grubbs, who succeeded Batchelder as Loomis headmaster, said that his predecessor was "versatile, creative, a lover of the outdoors, apostle of physical fitness and tireless in the performance of daily duties. Having complete confidence in his ability to find the right solution to any problem, he tolerated little objection to his ideas and even less to his program."[21]

> Right or wrong, he was a man of conviction. He was always ready to stand up and be counted. He made enemies and friends with equal speed. Few people ever felt indifferent about Horton Batchelder. They either loved and admired him immensely, in spite of an awareness that he was not always right, or they disliked him intensely. The latter group of antagonists was much smaller than the "aficionados" and "Mr. B," as he was called by his students and the younger faculty members ("Batch" to his intimates) was able to enlist a loyal following who helped him build one of the great New England schools . . . great and in many respects unique, which is a very significant . . . adjective to use here.

Grubbs notes that Batchelder was "passionately anxious to make Loomis great but different from the conventional preparatory schools. He knew that this was what the founders wanted when they established the 'free and gratuitous' clause in the charter, and it was his belief that character and habits of vigor were the chief goals that Loomis should seek to instill in its students. College preparation would be taken in stride if that was what the boy needed, but it should never be the chief goal."[22]

Nevertheless, Grubbs also reported that while the vocational courses were central to Batchelder's vision of Loomis, the majority of academic students went on to Harvard and Yale, and they were successful there. "The saying was, 'If Mr. B will recommend you, Harvard or Yale will accept you.'"[23]

And so it was that Batchelder's shadow loomed. The little things: He wouldn't tolerate candy or gum wrappers or, God forbid, cigarette butts littering the campus. There was no smoking in buildings on campus, except on the third floor of Founders Hall. Batchelder smoked a church warden's pipe at home if he smoked at all; rarely at the office unless he was alone late at night reading faculty reports. Some faculty members went for coffee and a cigarette in Windsor during their free periods, a practice that befuddled headmaster, who couldn't understand why they'd go so far for a cup of coffee.

The big things: the moments his notorious anger was about to explode—the "launching of Olympian thunderbolts," as Skip described his father's outbursts—were heralded by his eyebrows, which everyone watched carefully.

Many years after his graduation from Loomis, alum Bill Lese told this story:

> You remember how Mr. B regarded daily compulsory chapel and how he particularly was fond of finding someone "dickin" . . . in chapel. Well, one day when the B was thundering down at us, I kept staring at him—sort of hypnotically, trying to draw his beetle brows to mine. Somehow I succeeded, although no one was ever ready for that B stare from the pulpit!! The time came for one of the B's long impassioned prayers. The custom was for everyone to bow their head in reverence and pray—God would we ever pray—while thunder, fire, and brimstone rained down upon us interspersed with biblical quotations, a little Frost, some Socrates, but mostly B. Whether I was hypnotized or not I'll never know—sort of a case of the hypnotizer being hypnotized but I did not bow my head in the customary fashion but kept staring at the bushy eyebrows and lion mane of silver.
>
> Suddenly the bell sounded simultaneously with the final Amen and everyone rushed for class. I wasn't fast enough, for a huge B paw clamped upon my shoulder and the B demanded—"Lese, when we pray you don't seem to bend your head and pray like everyone else. Don't you believe in God?" "Well sir," I timidly replied, "when I pray sir, I like to look God right in the eye, sir." "Hurmpf and guffaw" and the B stomped off to his office.
>
> A few days later the B stopped me in Founders and asked of me, "Say Lese, I am going to deliver the sermon at Kent next Sunday and would you mind if I repeated your reply, 'when I pray I like to look God right in the eye'?" "Why yes sir, I mean no sir—thank you sir—God bless you sir."[24]

A 1923 Loomis alum wrote of Batchelder as exceedingly confident and idealistic. There was "no ounce of apathy or cool disposition in this dynamic man. . . . He loved to win and was not a philosophical loser."[25]

Once, during a football game with Kent School, its headmaster, Father Frederick Sill, and Batchelder, both with "magnificent" tempers, argued with a referee over a play and almost came to blows until students on each team escorted Sill and Batchelder back to their benches.

While the threatening eyebrows warned of imminent anger and "held his official position," as Skip wrote, there was sometimes a twinkle in his father's eye that evidenced another side to the formidable head. Batchelder is known to have stayed with sick students in the infirmary when a nurse was unavailable; often students stayed in the Head's House during their recovery. When one senior broke a serious rule and was put on probation, reclassifying him to "group four," which meant no graduation, he behaved extremely well from then on and eventually mustered the courage to go see Batchelder about his graduation status. The headmaster told the student, "Well, if all goes well and you continue in your present vein then automatically as you walk down the aisle to get your diploma your classification will change from group four to group three and you will then be eligible for a diploma."[26] Rules were important, but as in this case, he found ways to bend them, said Skip; it was the spirit rather than the letter of the law that mattered.

"Your father had a rare and wonderful talent for making friends," Val Gendron wrote to Skip in 1956. "He used to climb aboard my Bookmobile every Monday and sit and pass the time of day for an hour or so, and it was always a time of laughter and good cheer. It was something I looked forward to every week."[27]

The eyebrows or the twinkle: it could be either, in the blink of those eyes. Skip wrote:

> Father was the preacher at the Sunday chapel and did so in his usual long black baccalaureate gown and hood. I don't remember the service exactly but I do remember that he and Mother walked out afterwards and were standing on the porch of Founders that faces the dining hall about in the middle of the Senior Path and some of the boys and their girls came out to be there, too, seniors I expect, and Father said to one of the young ladies, "I'll race you to the other end of the campus and the dining hall." And she said, "Alright, but I'll have to take my shoes off first." She had high heels, of course. And Father said, "Well, if you can take your shoes off I ought to be able to take my shoes off." So she kicked her shoes off and gave them to her date and Daddy took his shoes off and gave them to Mother and "Ready, set go." They raced down the Senior Path to the Dining Hall. At the far end each with appropriate shoes, they walked into the dining hall, everyone assembled, and Father said grace. He could flip between the ceremonial occasion and the joyous celebration of life without the slightest hesitation, handling each perfectly naturally.[28]

The artist cast an exotic aura at Loomis. She wore peasant-style dresses, wrapped her hair in a turban, and donned a long sculptor's apron while working.

Longman's impact on "the head" was astonishing to friends and associates. Neither her buoyant spirit, warmth, and charm—nor her fierce confidence—were diminished by marrying the man with the larger-than-life persona. In fact, Longman seems to have had the same effect on Batchelder that she had on others. As Henry Bacon before him, Batchelder was eager not only to companion Longman, but also to assist her in any way possible. In no way did his tendency to dominate apply to Longman. Rather, he became devoted to her and her career, managing the business side of her work.

In addition to running a prep school, he learned the many technical intricacies of creating and transporting sculpture, and he soon began communicating Longman's detailed requests and demands to foundries, galleries, truckers, and others involved in creating, moving, and displaying her works. His many tasks were made easier by what he called his "jack-rabbit mind, always leaping from topic to topic"; made easier as well by his obvious enjoyment of her companionship. His "avocation," as he put it, was "sharing in the reflected glory of Mrs. Batchelder's work."[29]

Without commissions, and with new loves to model, Longman's first works in Chiselhurst were a round bas-relief of Skip and a bust of Batchelder. On the medallion of Horton Junior Aged Five, a smiling Skip is encircled by storybook characters—ducks, flowers, hatted cricket, rabbit . . . and a mouse.

Longman began her portrait of Batchelder's head during their honeymoon period and worked on it for the next two years, he sitting many times as Longman crafted his face and character to her liking. The inscription at the nape of his neck: "Nathaniel Horton Batchelder First Headmaster of Loomis Institute Made by His Wife Evelyn Beatrice Longman In the Years 1920–1922." His thick, wavy hair, parted down the middle, is a distinguishing feature of the piece. And the eyebrows? Longman portrays his bushy eyebrows without a hint of the infamous threatening temper students often witnessed in those animated brows. Rather, her characterization of her husband is strength, dignity, pride, and—there, in the eyes, as he looks directly at the artist, and the viewer—kindness.

Longman would keep her model of Batchelder's head in her studio for years. It would not be shown publicly until she gifted Loomis with a bronze in 1949 on the occasion of his retirement, when it found a permanent home in the foyer of Founders Hall.

But she wasn't finished with his portrait. She had an idea for an ideal piece—a two-person group—this time in monumental size, to elicit an emotional response as well as portray a value she held—that of service and compassion. The person embodying that value for her—whose face is on a kneeling, winged angel offering water and solace to an ailing man lying on the ground—was her husband.

Visitors to her studio were often struck by the small-scale version of the piece and expressed their fascination with *The Good Samaritan*, which she considered the model for the monumental sculpture. For now, she was glad simply to keep the small version of "the angel" near.

NOTES

1. DCF to EBL, February 1, 1931, Chesterwood Archives; Chapin Library, Williams College.
2. Vickrey, Connecticut newspaper, March 20, 1921.
3. Fowles, 22.
4. Grubbs, 14.
5. Ibid.
6. *Hartford Courant*, September 16, 1920, 11.
7. NHBII (Skip), unpublished memoir, Loomis Chaffee.
8. Ibid.
9. Ibid.
10. Ibid.
11. Ibid.
12. Ibid.
13. Ibid.
14. Ibid.
15. Ibid.
16. NHBII (Skip), unpublished memoir, Loomis Chaffee.
17. Ibid.
18. Ibid.
19. EBL to NHB, February 10, 1933, Loomis Chaffee.
20. Parsons and Ratte, 14.
21. Grubbs, 14.
22. Ibid.
23. Ibid., 18.
24. *Loomis Chaffee Alumni Bulletin*, October 1978.
25. NHBII (Skip), unpublished memoir, Loomis Chaffee.
26. Ibid.
27. Val Gendron letter to Skip, January 27, 1956, Loomis Chaffee.
28. NHBII (Skip), unpublished memoir, Loomis Chaffee.
29. NHB's "five-year retrospective," Loomis Chaffee.

Chapter 20

Reliefs

Her capacity for doing bas-relief in a realistic way is far above anyone else. . . . It's extraordinary how she handles depth.

—Marilyn Rabetz

Longman's relationship with Daniel Chester French seemed to take on a different flavor following her marriage and relocation to Windsor. If they had relished life in the zesty Big Apple, they now savored a somewhat more mellow existence in small-town Connecticut and Massachusetts during the months French was at Chesterwood. Their visits continued in their respective country studios, seventy miles apart. Longman's unlikely living situation turned out to be a welcome convenience for the Frenches, who could stay over at Loomis on their travels between New York City and Chesterwood.

He first visited her studio in May 1921 and declared it "a great success, the best I ever saw, and I am sure you are going to find great satisfaction in it. I think mine is as wide as yours, come to look at it, but it isn't as complete as yours. I wish I were nearer to you so that I could make believe to help you out with the aesthetic details that remain to be done."[1]

After the first visit Dan and Mary made to Windsor, he wrote to Longman: "I hope you and the Hortons will run over here soon. It's so easy!"[2]

> Dear, Dearer, Dearest Beatrice,
> What a good time I did have! It was all delightful,—the time (of year) the place (an enchanting environment) and the loved ones together! We really did have fun in the studio, with your statue and my Musica didn't we? I shall live it all over often in retrospect and, among other things, rejoice in the happiness that has come to you.[3]

Longman noted on the letter that *Musica* was a "humorous (modern) head which he did here for fun" and had cast "secretly."

Longman's work in her studio built upon the success of *Gwendolen*, expanding and honing her gift for creating bas-relief. Marilyn Rabetz, who taught drawing in Longman's studio at Loomis Chaffee School for years following the Batchelders' retirement to Cape Cod, spoke of the cherub in the *Gwendolen* as an illustration of Longman's skill. "Her capacity for doing bas-relief in a realistic way is far above anyone else . . . including Daniel French," said Rabetz, who wrote a biographical essay about the sculptor for a 1993 Longman exhibition at Loomis Chaffee.[4] "The way things fade out in her bas-reliefs—unbelievable. . . . It's extraordinary how she handles depth."[5]

The first two commissions in her new studio were reliefs. French was involved in both—and was the subject of her most ambitious relief since the giant door days. In 1923, she proposed a portrait of him that would include some of his works. Protesting appropriately, he agreed to sit for their favorite photographer, A. B. Bogart, later that year. Longman chose a nail-studded, heavy leather–covered wooden chair for the sittings. Meanwhile, she created a medallion to celebrate the fiftieth wedding anniversary of Emily and Robert de Forest and a memorial to Theodore Chickering Williams.

Emily Johnson became engaged to Robert de Forest the day The Metropolitan Museum of Art was founded, in 1870. This was fitting because Emily's father, John Taylor Johnson, president of the Central Railroad of New Jersey, was one of the museum's founders and its first president. Having grown up surrounded by her father's collection of American works (Frederic Edwin Church, Thomas Cole, Asher Brown Durand, John Frederick Kensett, Winslow Homer), Emily developed her own interests—furniture and decorative art, including Mexican *maiolica* and Pennsylvania Dutch.[6]

Her husband, Robert, general counsel for the Central Railroad of New Jersey, began serving on The Met's board in 1889 and was named president in 1913, a position he held until 1931, the year Daniel Chester French's term on The Met's board also ended.

As the couple's fiftieth anniversary approached in 1922, they decided to donate a major expansion to The Metropolitan Museum of Art—the American Wing: sixteen period rooms and three exhibition galleries. There, some of Emily's collection is housed, as well as Longman's reduction of the bronze *Victory*. Robert de Forest spoke with Daniel Chester French about a souvenir for guests at the philanthropists' golden anniversary reception. French, who had talked with Longman about crafting their medallion, wrote to Emily de Forest, recommending his former student: "I wish I could do it myself, although I believe Miss Longman would do it better."[7]

Longman had appeared on Robert de Forest's radar as early as 1906, when she created the bust of John Stewart Kennedy, and de Forest helped arrange for the aging Kennedy's sitting in Longman's fourth-floor studio.[8] Also, de Forest chaired the Red Cross Emergency Relief Committee, which funded the *Monument to the Unknowns of the Triangle Fire*, which Longman had created in 1912. That was also the year The Met first made an acquisition of her works—both *Torso of a Woman* and *Victory*.

For the de Forest medallion, Longman first sculpted a life-sized plaster portrait of the couple, which she then used on the obverse of the medallion. The profiles of Robert (in the foreground) and Emily (beside him), both pleasantly smiling, are circled in dogwood blossoms (symbolizing durability) and the legend: "1872 1922 Robert Weeks de Forest Emily Johnson de Forest."

On the reverse side, Longman fashioned an exquisite oak tree canopy with acorns and the head of a stag in its center—symbols of the de Forest family. Beneath the arms of the oak are more symbols: 1637 and a lily represent Robert's Huguenot ancestry and the year his family came to New York; 1804 and a thistle represent Emily's Scottish ancestors' arrival.

At the base of the tree trunk is a winged spur, emblematic of the Johnson clan. It had been their insignia since the fourteenth century, when the king of Scotland was sent a winged spur as a warning that he should flee to safety. Roots from the tree wind together, to symbolize the couple's marriage, and are clasped at the bottom of the coin with a tiny acorn.

Robert de Forest gave his "enthusiastic approval"[9] of the medallion. "Your plaque has been received and is greatly admired by both Mrs. de Forest and myself," de Forest wrote. "The same is true of the small model."

> The result more than justifies the confidence of our mutual friend Dan French (and I may add my own) in your artistic ability and taste—even to the smallest detail of introducing a little gilding into the wooden frame. In betting parlance, I think it is about one hundred to one against any portraiture giving entire satisfaction. I think with you, judging by this result, the odds are just as strong the other way.
>
> Both Mrs. de Forest and I realize how much thought and care you have given to this particular commission, and the check which I enclose is only a partial recognition of our appreciation.[10]

"It is perfectly beautiful!" Emily de Forest wrote to Longman. "It is most extraordinarily satisfactory in every respect, and even my mouth smiles. The portrait of Mr. de Forest is really excellent, and, after all, that is the most important part.

"One thing that pleases me so much in your letter is the evident pleasure you have had in making it. That of course gives me pleasure also."[11]

For family and friends, the de Forests gave 5 1/2-inch bronze medallions of the portrait side, mounted on wood with gilded detailing. Four hundred copies of two-inch medallions were cast for people attending the de Forests' anniversary reception. A marble of the medallion would be Longman's gift to them. Robert suggested a ten-inch size rather than anything larger, to avoid projecting into the next generation "a family burden or possibly the subject of family difference."[12]

Emily wrote to Longman after receiving the marble in 1924:

> I can assure you that we are perfectly delighted with this beautiful work of art. It really is lovely. Nobody has seen it as yet except our daughter Frances who is, as you probably know, very artistic, and she is perfectly crazy over it.
>
> I can appreciate that this was a labor of love on your part. Nothing short of that would have produced anything so beautiful. The marble is so lovely and the work is so exquisitely done. The size too is wonderfully effective. I did not feel particularly enthusiastic about a marble reproduction, but I assure you that nothing can exceed my enthusiasm at present. . . . I wonder if it is possible for you to appreciate how much pleased we both are.[13]

Emily gave a two-inch souvenir medallion and a five-inch mounted piece to the museum in 1934. Robert and Emily's son Johnstone gave the marble to the Metropolitan Museum of Art in 1946.

Evidently Longman had also created an entirely different bronze medal to honor Emily—perhaps as a result of Emily's comment about her husband's likeness being the most important. As yet, it has not been located. Evidence of its existence is this letter, written by Emily to Longman in September 1923:

> Ain't you a witch! The idea of your remembering all my elaborate details and then putting them into permanent form like this! We had a good laugh over the contents of the parcel when I opened it last night. I think the rear of the medal is more beautiful than the front, but, oh, what an engaging smile I have on my face. I shall have to ask my nephew if my roses were really so large and full blown as those are. The idea of your taking so much trouble and not only modeling it but have it cast in bronze!
>
> I wish you were here so that I could talk it over with you instead of just writing.
>
> With kindest regards for your very nice husband and dear love for your very nice self, I am,
>
> Sincerely your friend,
> Emily J. de Forest[14]

The couples did become friends. Robert wrote to Longman that he would only accept the marble she was making to give to them if Longman would promise that she and Batchelder would visit the woods and lakes at their place in the Adirondacks. "I think it would be an inspiration for both of you. . . . It certainly would be an inspiration for us to have you see them with us."[15]

As the de Forests were about to embark on an "around the world" anniversary trip, Robert advised: "Don't put off your trip around the world until your Golden Wedding. You started too late for that. Take it on the tenth or twelfth."[16]

And, in sharing some wisdom gleaned from his fifty years of marriage, he revealed something of Longman, less than three years into her own union: "Your unwillingness to send Mr. Batchelder's regards because he had gone to Boston and was therefore not present to give the necessary authority when you wrote gives me a delightful insight into the conscientious character of your domestic relations. After you have been married fifty years you will not hesitate to take the responsibility of sending his regards and perhaps even his love. Long before Mrs. de Forest had arrived at this culminating point in her marital career we accustomed ourselves to this degree of mutual responsibility, and even more."[17]

By the end of 1923, French, aged seventy-three, had begun to experience bouts of illness. Longman had the Bogart photographs and French's heavy wooden chair, which she would use for his "in the life" sittings, delivered to Chiselhurst.[18] Then, in early 1924, Longman and Dan French suffered an unexpected, deeply regrettable loss.

Unknown is the last time Longman had seen Henry Bacon. Only one piece of correspondence from Bacon exists in the period following her wedding—from aboard a ship to Europe, dated August 17, 1921.

> Dear Cousin Trix
> I was glad to get your message over the phone yesterday—Here am I bound for France in a fine new & very large steamer—which is now passing the Statue of Liberty—in consequence of which I will soon introduce to my oozygoozlum a fat & large martini cocktail to the health of my friends.
>
> My stay abroad will be short but promises to be most interesting—Will drop you a line from Paris.
>
> Yours Sincerely
> H Bacon
> Remember me to Mr. Batchelder[19]

Though there is no evidence that she attended the Lincoln Memorial dedication in 1922, she evidently did attend an elaborate pageant in Washington, D.C., for Bacon in 1923, when the American Institute of Architects gave him a gold medal, their highest honor. (Henry Bacon wrote to the Bancrofts that

Mrs. Batchelder would be arriving at the Powhatan Hotel, one of D.C.'s fanciest, the morning of May 18, the day of the celebration.[20])

Less than a year later, Bacon quietly went into the hospital for surgery. Prior to his hospitalization, he told Dan French not to tell anyone—that it was not serious, though French had the feeling it was.

Laura Bacon was with her husband when he died on February 16, 1924, following abdominal surgery to remove cancer. He was fifty-seven.

French wrote to Longman the day he got the phone call from Bacon's secretary. The letter is telling: As if he couldn't bring himself to say the words, he began with other news and then, in grief himself, wrote of Bacon's death, acknowledging how it would impact Longman.

> February 16, 1924
> Dear Beatrice,
> The bust of Mrs. Palmer was delivered to the studio a few days ago, and Bogart's Frank was here yesterday and photographed it. Mr. Frazer, one of the three members of the jury, called to see it and naturally was suitably impressed. He said that he felt embarrassed to even be called to look at a work of yours, which of course would certainly be acceptable.
>
> Before this reaches you, you will learn through the papers of the tragedy that has come into our lives. Miss Weisler has just telephoned me of Bacon's death early this morning. I seem to have nothing to say about it that is adequate. I know what a grief it will be to you.
>
> Affectionately,[21]

Bacon's funeral was held in St. George's Episcopal Church, New York City, attended by "throngs," mostly men. There's no indication whether or not Longman was in attendance. Daniel French was one of many pallbearers. Eulogies declared Bacon's greatness of character and that the Lincoln monument was the reason he was put on the planet.

It was said that he put his affairs in order before his surgery; a sketch for a gravestone was found in his desk. The grave marker, simple and elegant, marks his burial in Wilmington, North Carolina. Beneath a stylized scallop shell, perhaps to symbolize the pilgrimage of life, are the words: "The Architect of the Lincoln Memorial at Washington."

Longman pasted stories about Bacon and his funeral in her scrapbook. And she made arrangements to have another bronze casting made of her bust of Bacon. French encouraged The Metropolitan Museum of Art to accept it, a gift from Longman, and they did. It can be viewed by the public in the protected Visual Storage Area at The Met, along with Longman's *Louise*, her two torsos, the de Forest medallions, and the French and British War

Commission Medal she and French created. The *Victory* is on exhibit in The Met's American wing. It was a gift from sculptor Edward Adams in 1912.

Laura Calvert Bacon lived another twenty years. In 1943, Eleanor Roosevelt, in her syndicated column, *My Day*, penned a request for contributions to a fund kept by the Architectural League of New York to help Laura Bacon:

> Like many other artists, Mr. Bacon thought more of his art and less of the material things of this world. When he died, it was found that he had left comparatively little to his wife. For some years friends have been contributing to a fund for her.
>
> It seems only fitting that those of us who have stood before the Lincoln memorial and have been inspired by the figure of Lincoln and his words carved in the stone around the rotunda, should make some slight return in a tangible form to this memorial.
>
> If all the people who have felt gratitude for the truths which this memorial keeps before us would send . . . a small or large sum of money, according to their circumstances, Mrs. Bacon's few remaining years could be made comfortable. We could feel that we had made a slight return for what Mr. Bacon had done during his life for us.[22]

Laura Bacon died two years later and is buried with her husband in North Carolina.

Dan and Mary French; their cousins, the Bushes; and Longman, Batchelder, and Skip frequently traveled together after Longman married. Soon after Bacon's death, they made their way to Bermuda, and the following spring, in 1925, they spent three weeks in the West Indies.

The Caribbean stay helped French recover from an illness, but eight-year-old Skip contracted typhoid, and the last week aboard ship was "horrible," Longman wrote to Margaret Bancroft. Skip spent seven weeks in a New York City hospital, with Longman by his side. Then, as Longman got home and back to work in her studio, Skip enjoyed the "angelic" care of Loomis's head nurse, "Miss Edwards," throughout the summer, until he fully recovered and could go to school. "He is now just as good as ever," Longman wrote to Margaret Bancroft that autumn, "but he had a terrible case, with about all the complications possible and was, I suppose, as ill as it is possible to be and live."[23]

Again, Longman chose a bas-relief for her portrait of Theodore Chickering Williams. Velma Williams, who had helped Batchelder find a sculptor for the *Gwendolen*, commissioned Longman to create a memorial to her husband to be placed in the Unitarian Church of All Souls in New York City, where he had served as pastor from 1883 to 1896.

A Harvard graduate, Theodore Williams also wrote hymns and was Hackley School's first headmaster, when Batchelder was on the faculty. He died in 1915. Longman had never met him, but she certainly knew of him through

Batchelder and, presumably, Velma, who must have also provided photographs. The marble bas-relief Longman finished in 1923 is stunning. The cutline beneath a photograph of it in a newspaper clipping Longman saved offers a brief critique: "Its purity and beauty are strangely stirring."[24]

An angel with magnificently feathered wings hovers around a seated Williams; a long, draping wing nearly embraces him from behind. The angel's other wing spreads across the background of the piece. The angel, her hair knotted at the back of her head, looks down at Williams and holds a lit lamp before him. Seated at a table, holding paper in his left hand and a quill in his right, Williams, in pastoral robes, looks ahead and slightly upward, the trace of an expectant smile on his face. It is as if the angel is ushering him safely from life to death.

As she was working on it, Longman showed the piece to Dan French. He wrote to her, teasingly: "I have thought often of your relief of Mr. Williams. It is sure to be popular,—after you have made the corrections that I demanded!"[25]

Longman exhibited the portrait in the National Academy of Design's annual show in 1923. It won the Elizabeth N. Watrous Gold Medal.

French, in New York for the winter, helped her get it installed. No doubt Longman gave him exacting instructions about installation and lighting. The Piccirillis would set the relief into a wall.

> December 7, 1923
> Dear Beatrice:—
> Mrs. Sidney Smith called at my studio this morning to talk over the placing of the relief and I have made an appointment for Monday morning at nine-thirty to meet her committee at the Church to show the members exactly where the relief is to go and answer any other absurd questions that they may ask. Piccirilli is to begin on Tuesday morning to take down the wall. . . . I impressed upon Mrs. Smith with all my eloquence the necessity of having the electric light exactly right before the relief is shown, in fact, I "butted in" in every way I could think of.
>
> The church is on my way to my studio and I am looking forward to calling frequently while the work of installation is in progress.[26]

Upon seeing the memorial installed, both Emily and Robert de Forest wrote to Longman. Robert: "I am so much interested in receiving a photograph of that very beautiful memorial to Mr. Williams. I think it is very charming, besides being quite original. It seems to me quite to fill the ideal of such a memorial. Moreover, it seems to me the likeness is extraordinarily good, not only as a likeness but as giving a real spiritual impression. I should like to have been one of the committee to award the prize."[27]

Emily: "I think that is the loveliest memorial tablet I have ever seen. You have kept the man's spiritual look without making it too prominent—that is, kind of sickly sentimental. That is what happens very often when a painter or a sculptor tries to make a man or a woman look spiritual.

"I am so glad to know that the tablet was so much appreciated that it received the gold medal."[28]

The memorial to Theodore Chickering Williams remains in the sanctuary of the church, now located on Lexington Avenue.

Longman's idea for French's portrait relief was an ambitious project because of the dynamics of creating a model of a beloved friend, who also happened to be one of the country's most successful sculptors; ambitious, too, because, in addition to his portrait, she envisioned including several of his works. When she explained her idea of a bas-relief that included small renderings of his notable sculptures and asked him to send her a list and photographs of ten of his best, in order of preference, he protested. But in July 1924, he sent the photographs anyway and wrote:

> Dear Beatrice
> Why spend your strength upon rendering me immortal? Keep it for better things. I speedily accede to your request and am sending you a job-lot of photographs of my productions, while I protest against your embarking in so elaborate a scheme with me as the basis.
>
> As to numbering them in the order of my preference, "Who shall decide when all are fair?" The one I am doing now, as usual, is the best, to be superseded by the next! I enclose a list, but who knows so little in regard to the relative merits of his work as the sculptor himself. I think the Minute Man might call for recognition in your relief as being my first-born; don't you?
>
> Some of the best ones haven't much silhouette,—the Milmore, for instance,—and so I am sending you more than the ten you ask for, that you may choose the ones best suited to your purpose. I wish I could walk in upon you in your busy studio. I am glad the Hartford monument is assured. You must be getting rich!
>
> Affectionately
> Daniel
>
> Memory
> Seated Lincoln
> Milmore
> Melvin
> Spirit of Life
> The Sower
> First Division Victory
> Geyser group
> Africa
> Alma Mater, Columbia[29]

When French began sitting in Longman's studio, the task turned out to be sheer pleasure. In profile, French, as usual dressed impeccably in suit, tie, vest, and crisp white shirt, sits with his arms resting on the chair's arms, a carving tool in his right hand, the wisp of an easy smile on his face.

Following sittings during a week in November 1925, French wrote:

> It has been a sudden transition from the peace of your house to the tumult of New York, but it is some relief to be able to recall the charm and the quiet and the home atmosphere which we enjoyed so much for a blessed week. And nothing did I enjoy more than the hours with you in the studio when we had time to get to the bottom of things and settle them for all time!—but more than ever it makes me regret that we are too far apart to commune often.
>
> Mary and I were impressed, as always, by the efficiency and grace with which you preside over your menage and extend your influence so as to take in the whole school. It is really wonderful and that you do it with consummate skill and tact is [undecipherable word] by the attitude of the people toward you. Your husband is a close second, to be sure, but it is easier for a man and, also, he was trained to it!

He let her know his opinion of her work on his portrait:

> I did not half tell you how happy I am about the relief,—except I have compunctions when I think how much time and strength you are putting into it. I am quite ready to go down to posterity on the strength of it and I can't say that about any other portrait that has been made of me. I wish you had a better subject for so fine a thing.
>
> Tell little Batchelder that I gave Mr. Bush the pastels and he was properly impressed.
>
> There is going to be a small exhibition of some of Bacon's works at the Century Club next month and I am going to suggest to the committee that they borrow your bust of him from the Museum. I assume that you will not object.
>
> Give my love to both Batchelders and keep a great deal for yourself.[30]

In December she asked him for more sittings, which he requested be delayed: "I rather hope you can wait a while so that I may come when I really need a rest." By February 1926, he had been to her studio for more modeling sessions. In the letter he wrote her following his return to New York, he made reference to a Washington excursion to correct the lighting of the Lincoln statue. This would take place later that year, in 1926, and again in 1927.

> February 25
> Dear Beatrice
> Here we are home again and already settled into regular habits. Except for clear-cut memories of our visit at Loomis, it is as if we had never been away. Those

memories, however, make a lot of difference and there is besides a general freshened-up feeling wrought by the change of environment and faces. It was just what we needed and I feel quite made over. Now I think I shall live till the Washington excursion. . . .

I certainly did enjoy my hours in your studio,—a combination of peace and quiet and companionship and art atmosphere!—that hardly exists anywhere else. As I told you it troubles me a little to have you spend so much of your time and force on a portrait of me, but I rejoice that you think it worthwhile and in the fact that I am to be "handed down" in this important and dignified way. I think you will get a great deal of praise for it,—in spite of the subject.

Please thank your husband for his practical attentions on our arrival and departure. We are indebted to you both and to Skippy . . . for an ideal visit and an accession of health.

Affectionately
Dan. C. French[31]

She finished her bas-relief of French later that year. He insisted on paying the seven hundred dollars to have it cast in bronze.[32] Adeline Adams wrote of the work in the *American Magazine of Art*: "That portrait is an entirely original evocation of an artist amid his creations; nowhere else has the procession motive been used in just that way."[33]

Longman first exhibited it in 1926 at the Sesquicentennial in Philadelphia.[34] In 1929, Longman sent the French bas-relief to the National Sculpture

Figure 20.1 Longman's portrait of her beloved teacher and friend Daniel Chester French—with some of his key works in the background of the bas-relief. Source/Credit: Photograph from the collection of the Loomis Chaffee Archives, Loomis Chaffee School, Windsor, Connecticut USA.

Society's annual exhibition in San Francisco. In 1936, she gave the French relief to the National Gallery of Art Commission, to be held for a future National Portrait Gallery, which came into existence in 1968.

With exacting detail, Longman executed the brass-studded, leather-embossed wooden chair. Other details differ from the Bogart photo: Rather than his depiction in silhouette, French is slightly angled more toward the viewer. Longman also changed the type of the sculpting tool as well as the position of his right hand. His likeness is impeccable; such a given for a Longman portrait that, after viewing many of her pieces, one almost takes that for granted. Dressed for work in his usual three-piece suit and tie, French is clear-eyed, looking forward, his famous works in place behind him; his expression is relaxed and warm. He seems settled in his accomplishments, but not finished—tool in hand. Above him, left to right, there's the angel of his *Benediction*, seated *Lincoln*, the hooded figure of the *Melvin Memorial*, *Immortal Love*, *Africa*, *Milmore Memorial*, and *Minute Man*.

Longman has inscribed his name in her distinct lettering, dogwood blossoms and leaves on each side, and: "Made by his devoted friend and pupil Evelyn Beatrice Longman, 1926," a pine cone and branch beneath.

Her rendering of French would capture the eye of one of the richest men in the United States. Then George Foster Peabody's admiration of her work would result not only in her creating the medallion for the Pulitzer Prize of Broadcasting—the Peabody Award—but also a series of reliefs installed from Utah to Mexico; and, in a world she had yet to visit: African American schools in the South.

NOTES

1. DCF to EBL, May 15, 1921, Loomis Chaffee.
2. DCF to EBL, May 17, 1926, Loomis Chaffee.
3. Ibid.
4. Marilyn and Walter Rabetz, *Evelyn Beatrice Longman Batchelder* (Windsor, CT: Loomis Chaffee School, 1993).
5. Telephone interview with Marilyn Rabetz, May 10, 2021.
6. See https://research.frick.org/directory/detail/1695.
7. Thayer Tolles, *American Sculpture in the Metropolitan Museum of Art*, Volume 2 (New Haven, CT: Yale University Press, 2001), 581.
8. Robert de Forest to DCF, October 3, 1906, Chesterwood Archives; Chapin Library, Williams College.
9. DCF to EBL, August 29, 1922, Loomis Chaffee.
10. RD to EBL, October 26, 1922, Loomis Chaffee.
11. Emily J. de Forest letter to EBL, November 6, 1922, Loomis Chaffee.
12. Robert W. de Forest to EBL, January 19, 1923, Loomis Chaffee.

13. EJ de Forest to Evelyn Longman Batchelder, April 9, 1924, Loomis Chaffee.

14. EJ de Forest to EBL, September 29, 1923, Loomis Chaffee.

15. RW de Forest to EBL, January 19, 1923, Loomis Chaffee.

16. Ibid.

17. Ibid.

18. EBL note in DCF letter to her, December 7, 1923, Loomis Chaffee.

19. HB to EBL, August 17, 1923, Loomis Chaffee.

20. HB to Milton Bancroft, May 16, 1923, Milton Bancroft Collection, Manuscript Group 133, Indiana University of Pennsylvania (IUP), Special Collections and University Archives.

21. DCF to EBL, February 16, 1924, Box 10, Reels 7–8, Daniel Chester French Papers, Manuscript Division, Library of Congress, Washington, D.C.

22. Eleanor Roosevelt, *My Day*, syndicated column, December 31, 1943. https://erpapers.columbian.gwu.edu/browse-my-day-columns.

23. EBL to Margaret Bancroft, October 13, 1925, Milton Bancroft Collection, Manuscript Group 133, Indiana University of Pennsylvania (IUP), Special Collections and University Archives.

24. Unknown newspaper, clipping in Longman scrapbook, Loomis Chaffee.

25. DCF to EBL, March 12, 1922, Loomis Chaffee.

26. DCF to EBL, December 7, 1923, Loomis Chaffee.

27. RW de Forest to EBL, November 19, 1923, Loomis Chaffee.

28. EJ de Forest to EBL, December 10, 1923, Loomis Chaffee.

29. DCF to EBL, July 9, 1924, Loomis Chaffee.

30. DCF to EBL, November 22, 1925, Loomis Chaffee.

31. DCF to EBL, February 25, unspecified year, Loomis Chaffee.

32. EBL to George Foster Peabody, May 31, 1927, Loomis Chaffee.

33. Adeline Adams, "Evelyn Beatrice Longman," *American Magazine of Art*, Volume xix, May 1928, Number 5, 237.

34. Marilyn and Walter Rabetz, *Evelyn Beatrice Longman Batchelder* (Windsor, CT: Loomis Chaffee School, 1993), 39.

Chapter 21

Loomis Life

She championed the less conventional students, artistic and creative souls who might have had difficulty finding a cordial reception in a typical New England boarding school.

—Nancy Boas

As Longman's life at Loomis increasingly became a team effort, so did her work life. A monumental sculpture to commemorate Connecticut soldiers of the Spanish-American War was case in point. There was Daniel French, who had recommended her to the committee that would choose an artist to create the monument, to be installed in Hartford's Bushnell Park. Longman designed two bas-reliefs for the base of the monument. In one, a sailor kneels, preparing a torpedo, and in the other, a soldier crouches, rifle-ready. But it is a giant, winged, helmeted, armored *Columbia* that dominates the memorial. Atop the prow of a ship, with an eagle figurehead fiercely advancing through stylized waves, she strides valiantly onward, raising torch high, bearing a shield, sword sheathed at her side. This is Longman's way of portraying war without "the horrible features of warfare" (or, as in other monuments, without "any other distressing elements").[1]

Nine-year-old Skip contributed his enthusiasm for the project—especially enjoying playing in his mother's studio with caps of sailors and soldiers; boots and uniforms; a canteen; and a Phyrigian helmet . . . Sword, shield, torch, rifle, and torpedo may have been off-limits.[2]

On Longman's behalf, Batchelder had written to Scovill Manufacturing Company, who made munitions, and buttons, in Waterbury, Connecticut. He inquired about the rifling on the shells used in the Spanish-American War: Was it a single groove or three grooves?

And Dan French was present in her studio at this time as he posed for her portrait of him. Just as Longman's sharp eye could spot problems with French's works in progress, French noticed that *Columbia*'s leg was too short. Already in plaster, it was "a terrible job" fixing it, Longman later noted.[3] She cut away some of the plaster, lowering the prow, which meant reducing the waves beneath, so that *Columbia*'s legs looked two or three inches longer.[4] Gozo Kawamura, a young Japanese sculptor with whom both French and Longman worked, came to Windsor to help her straighten the boat and true the reliefs.[5]

"I hope I didn't discourage you by my radical criticism of the Victory [Columbia]," wrote French. "You would have come to it sooner, or later, I am sure, and it is better to change it soon; isn't it,—so don't blame me too much. I believe it will be all plain sailing, once you get that leg long enough."[6]

Longman wouldn't hold a grudge. French wrote to her: "It was very good of you to reassure me as to my criticism of your Victory."[7]

Turns out, Batchelder learned from Scovill that the copper band around the shell had no rifling. Longman had to fix that as well.[8]

It also came to Batchelder to manage insurance requirements for the monumental piece. The plaster *Spanish-American War Monument* was to be insured before it was transferred for bronze casting at the American Art Foundry in Astoria, New York. Longman wanted to add eight thousand dollars to the two thousand dollars' worth of insurance for trucking the load, and to insure the production at the foundry for ten thousand dollars.

Batchelder juggled as well the complex timing issues around funds coming in and funds going out, in order that Longman could meet her expenses, which were considerable. Out of her twenty-four-thousand-dollar contract, she was required to pay all materials, transportation, insurance, and production costs. Batchelder explained the tricky situation to the secretary of the Spanish-American War Memorial committee:

> Evelyn's contract with the committee is that she is paid "one-tenth upon completion of the sketch, another tenth upon completion of the one-third size models, and three-tenths upon completion of the full-size models." It is customary at that time to have half the total paid, but there was some objection raised, and she consented to the third payment being made two-tenths instead of three. The final payment is due upon the erection and acceptance of the monument. Now it so happens that all the marble is already erected, and Mrs. Batchelder has made a partial payment to the contractor, but what she has so far received makes it impossible for her to pay him in full. It also happens that the bronze casting will probably be finished in February, and the foundry ought certainly to receive something at that time. Under the contract Mrs. Batchelder agreed to have the work completed no later than May 1st, 1927, and as much earlier as possible. I presume you do not want the memorial erected and dedicated in

> February or March, and yet I do not see why a contractor who has completed his work should not receive some payment, in fact, most of his payment, as soon as his work is completed and approved.[9]

Batchelder suggested that the committee issue a formal approval of the marble and make a payment to Longman of whatever amount they saw fit. Longman owed $2,700 more to the contractor than she had paid him and thought it would be sufficient to hold back seven hundred dollars to cover the erection of the bronze. Batchelder also suggested that if there was to be a delay in the installation of the bronze, there should be a payment of four thousand dollars made upon certification by Longman that the cast had been made satisfactorily and that its safe delivery in Hartford was covered by insurance. Longman was not anxious for payments on her account, Batchelder explained, but she liked to pay marble and bronze contractors, who worked on a very thin margin, what they were due, without delay, if satisfactory arrangements could be made.

All issues resolved, on a sunny, breezy Sunday afternoon in May 1927, a parade preceded the monument-dedication ceremony in Bushnell Park, a block from the Connecticut State Capitol. Fifteen thousand people—including Longman's sister Louise, who came from Ohio—watched as two flags were slowly drawn from atop the massive *Spanish-American War Memorial*, when a sudden breeze whipped them off in an unintended, but dramatic final flourish, revealing *Columbia*. There came a "great burst of applause," then a standing ovation for Longman.[10]

French sent a letter registering his approval. "And now let me . . . express my enthusiastic approval of the monument. The statue is splendid, full of spirit and 'go' and power. . . . I will say a lot more when I see you."[11]

At the time of the casting, Longman had a smaller bronze cast made of *Columbia*. She exhibited it in a one-woman show at the Grand Central Art Gallery in New York City in 1930. Later it would come to symbolize the ultimate success of a long-running controversy about educating women students at Loomis.

Even during the interview with the Loomis Institute board of trustees, Batchelder had let it be known that he wanted to develop Loomis as an institution for educating boys, despite the mandate in the school charter to educate both girls and boys. The first three years, classes for a few girls—day students—were held in the west end of the dining room. After the end of the 1922–1923 term, during which fourteen female day students, including two seniors, attended classes at the school, Batchelder and the trustees announced the end of female enrollment. The school was facing a budget crunch, and the girls' day school program was one place they chose to cut expenses. As for the charter's mandate, the trustees explained that since there were no coed boarding schools, they didn't know how to add female boarders.

Windsor residents were outraged. Citizens brought a lawsuit restraining Loomis trustees from closing the girls' program. The Connecticut Supreme Court ruled in the trustees' favor, but on appeal a judge ruled that the school's charter required the trustees to furnish education for girls as well as boys.

When the trustees appealed to the legislature to amend the Institute charter so that a girls' school could be established in a second location rather than on the island, again the townspeople protested, and the state attorney general denied the legislature the right to change the charter. He charged that the school, in closing its classes for girls, had failed the citizens of the state and the people of Windsor.

Already there was class consciousness around New England prep schools. "The way to provide for those for whom the school was intended by its founders," wrote the attorney general, "is to throw out the . . . social climbers. If you do that, there will be ample accommodation for the boys and girls of Windsor."[12]

It's easy to imagine that Batchelder was involved in the response from Loomis, though it officially came from the student council leadership: All forty-three day students at Loomis signed a statement denying any unfair treatment or social discrimination, vowing that they had received the same consideration as boarding students.[13]

The legislature passed an amendment to the charter, and plans began for the second start of the girls' school—in the fall of 1925, in a separate location: a house Loomis owned in Windsor, rather than on the island. Eleven students enrolled. The next year, trustees purchased three houses, including the Chaffee family home, on the east side of the Palisado Green in Windsor, and in the fall of 1927, Chaffee School began operation there.

Chaffee School expanded over the years, so that by 1949, the year Longman and Batchelder retired, a second classroom building was dedicated and Longman donated the smaller *Columbia* to Chaffee School for its new building. For twenty years, *Columbia* stood at the entrance to Sellers Hall, park benches on either side. At some point, she took on the name *Minerva*. "Committee X" dressed *Minerva* for school holidays and special occasions. At graduation in 1963, she was dressed as a senior student, with a skirt, white blouse, sweater, and black-and-white saddle oxford shoes, made of cardboard.

In 1971, long after Longman and Batchelder's reign, Chaffee finally was moved to the island. A new building, Chaffee Hall, was built for the girls, and in the design, there was an alcove created just for *Minerva*. On the day the statue was moved from the old Chaffee campus to the island, she was placed on an open trailer hitched to the school van, and Committee X members, each dressed in a long black dress and carrying a flower, rode beside *Minerva*. They threw chocolate candies to the Chaffee girls walking behind the trailer on the trip from Palisado Green across Windsor to the island. And Loomis Chaffee was born. Finally, as they say, the Loomises could rest in their graves.

Minerva has been moved twice since then to new buildings, both times to an alcove designed especially for her. A statue that began as a symbol of war, portrayed as a grandly helmeted and armored woman striding valiantly toward victory, now stands watch over students sitting beneath her for quiet moments of study. Often wearing a Loomis Chaffee scarf, she also gets fancied-up for special occasions.

At least one Loomis student, David Park, seems to have heartened Longman's artistic existence in her early years at the school. Having graduated eighth grade from Park School in suburban Boston, in the fall of 1924 Park was enrolled at Loomis. He hadn't excelled in academics, but Batchelder, an acquaintance of Park's father, a Unitarian minister at Boston's prestigious First Church, admitted him. "David was the kind of person who was made for Batch [Batchelder]," Elting Morison, Park's friend, said. "He was one of a group that comprised a kind of 'rive gauche' at the school. Some didn't fit in at all socially, some didn't fit in emotionally, some didn't fit in intellectually. But almost all of them had talent and something distinctive about them. . . . Batch planted this group of very unusual people in the midst of these perfectly nice, decent, frightfully conventional middle-class Americans and gave them support. And Mrs. Batchelder gave them support."[14]

Longman "championed the less conventional students, artistic and creative souls who might have had difficulty finding a cordial reception in a typical New England boarding school," wrote Nancy Boas in her biography of Park.[15] In fact, Longman was a major influence on Park, who assisted her and worked on his paintings in her studio. Loomis faculty wife Margaret Newton is quoted in the Boas biography: "Once I said to Mrs. B., 'What a nice boy he is.' Mrs. B opened wide her big brown eyes, and she said, 'He's more than that, my dear. He's a gifted artist, even at his age. That boy is so talented.' Her eyes just shone when she talked about Dave Park. I never heard Mrs. Batchelder go overboard with a compliment that strong. She was quite thrilled to have a boy at the school who was a real artist, not just a talented kid."[16]

Neither did Park excel academically at Loomis. Each year Batchelder discussed Park's lack of progress, and each year Longman advocated keeping him another year. He spent three years as a freshman and was classified as a sophomore his fourth, and final, year. Having had his first commission as a young boy from a neighbor who asked him to paint a picture of her garden (for five dollars), he was exhibiting and selling paintings in Boston before he left Loomis. He moved to California's bay area and worked in abstract expressionism before settling on his own style of figurative art in dark tones. In 2007 his *Standing Male Nude in the Shower* was his first to be sold at an international auction—for more than a million dollars.[17]

Irwin Jones was another Loomis student whom Longman took under her wing. After he graduated Loomis in 1922, he received a note from her that made a great impression on him. In fact, her note seemed brutal at the time. He wrote to her: "It dropped out of such a clear sky, I was so unprepared, so unaware of my own afflictions. It was a definite blow; it stunned, it hurt, and later brought on a state of real depression."

But evidently it had helped Jones eventually come to an understanding of himself: "I prize in you, above all, your belief, your trust in me. It is one of your most loveable and endearing qualities."[18]

> What you have done for me, I am now convinced was one of the sweetest, the finest things you could have done for anybody. I have always loved you for the interest you have taken in us even after our school days were ended and we were far away.
>
> It made a deep impression on me, those occasions when you took the pains, while I was at Loomis, to correct my many feelings. Honestly I am certain there is no one, not even my parents, whose advice would have a better effect on me than yours; you have always been so unbiased, so fair, so clear-sighted. I was deeply touched and affected by your note.[19]

Jones interned with Richard Dana, one of the architects whom Batchelder had selected to design the Loomis campus. When Dana died, Jones became the preferred school architect. In 1937, he moved his office to Hartford, and his residence to the third floor of the Head's House. As well as other projects at the school, he carried out Murphy and Dana's plans for a third residence hall on the quadrangle, named Palmer Hall. Longman created a plaque to celebrate Virginia Palmer and her sister Theodora, who funded the building of Palmer Hall in honor of their father, Frank Loomis Palmer.[20]

Evidence of Longman's profound integration into Loomis's life can also be seen in some of her sculptures during this period. Loomis boys, including Skip's friends, posed for her larger pieces. And in some cases, a student's appearance and character inspired Longman to create a portrait. Ely Norton Buell, a student from Rochester, New York, modeled for her *American Galahad.* An ideal head symbolizing fine American youth, it is Buell's portrait as well. Mounted on wood, *Galahad* was exhibited and sold in Longman's Grand Central Gallery show in 1928.

Stowe Wilder, who graduated from Loomis in 1922, sat for a bas-relief, *Gallant Boyhood*, which became a sportsmanship award for Loomis and five of the school's rivals.

Longman wrote:

> Last year we had at Loomis a senior with a head of such beauty that I could not bear to let him get away without in some way perpetuating it. I therefore asked him to pose for a head in relief and he consented. He happened also to be our quarterback and one day Mr. Batchelder remarked to me, upon seeing my work, that he had "never known Stowe to do a mean thing." I think it was this which germinated my idea of making it a model for "clean athletics."
>
> I started with a football helmet but later discarded that—not wishing to limit it to any one sport, and tried simply to depict youthful beauty and nobility of soul, the Latin inscription, "Non Victor Nisi Virtute" ["Not a conqueror but by virtue"] . . . and laurel leaves, indicating the purpose of the medal.[21]

Ben Hedges, who would be heralded as one of Loomis's "greatest athletes," modeled for Longman's *Song of the Pines*.[22] The sculpture was commissioned by Edith Wickham, who gifted the bronze to her husband, Clarence Horace (an inventor credited with creating the windowed envelope), for their Hartford estate, The Pines. *Song of the Pines*—depicting a young man holding a lyre in his left hand, his right arm artfully stretched as he heartily sings—greeted guests at the entrance of the estate. Longman had a copy cast for herself and exhibited it as well.

As with many others who became friends as Longman produced sculptures for them, so did Abby and John D. Rockefeller Jr. At first, Longman created portraits of two of their sons, John D. Rockefeller III and his older brother David. However, the Rockefeller connection almost didn't happen. Batchelder, who was conflicted about the New England aristocracy of which he was a part, refused John D. Rockefeller Jr.'s request to admit his son John D. III to Loomis.

"There was conflict with Father all the way through life about his family status," Skip wrote.[23] Batchelder, a Harvard graduate, had descended from an early American English-born and Oxford-trained pastor, Reverend Stephen Bachiler, who, to put it mildly, was a "non-conformist minister." In addition to personal behaviors that outraged some, Bachiler believed and preached the separation of church and state, which got him into theological trouble, as well.

Batchelder's father, Henry Morrill Batchelder, captured public attention at an early age when, in 1877, as a correspondent for the *Boston Globe*, he covered a presentation in Salem's Lyceum Hall by Alexander Graham Bell, who lectured about his new patent, the telephone. Speaking into a strange tin and brass instrument, Batchelder called in his news story to the *Globe*. It was the first news dispatch ever sent over the telephone.[24] Later, Batchelder, who had also been working as a bank clerk, became the president of Salem's Merchants National Bank, a position he kept for thirty years.

It seems Horton Batchelder had some of the headstrong Bachilir in his genes. Skip wrote that his father attempted to avoid the class consciousness that thickened his life: "He was not social status–minded, but more independent."[25]

And so, when John D. Rockefeller Jr. inquired about sending John D. Rockefeller III to Loomis, Batchelder replied "that he regretted to have to turn down his son but he did not want to risk changing the character of the school," wrote Frances O. Grubbs, who succeeded Batchelder as headmaster. "He went on to say that if he accepted the boy, it would be unfair discrimination against some other boys who did not have as many privileges as his son."[26] Batchelder also thought that a focus on social status would detract from his work at the egalitarian school, said Skip. A New England prep school could be a challenging place for a headstrong nonconformist.

John D. II himself made a trip to see Batchelder at Loomis and convinced him that it was discriminatory to turn down a boy because his father was wealthy. John D. Rockefeller III and, later, his brother Winthrop, became Loomis students, and the school, for many years, benefited greatly from one of the richest families in the country. Winthrop served as a Loomis trustee (as well as the governor of Arkansas).

John and Abby Rockefeller became friends of the Batchelders. Longman created three sculptures for the Rockefellers around 1925: the bust of David, as a child; the bas-relief of John D. III, while a student at Loomis; and a fountain, *Boy and Fish*, to be installed in the "Playhouse" at John D. Rockefeller's Pocantico Hills estate. It was a favorite of Longman's. She and John Jr. agreed that she would only have two bronze casts made: one for him and one for her, which she promised to keep at Loomis unless he wanted to buy it when she retired. It remains at Loomis in the Headmaster's Garden, as a sculpture, without the fountain. Rockefeller also agreed to have smaller versions cast when people who viewed it at her exhibit at the Grand Central Galleries requested them. "The little Pan will be very cunning in that miniature size and I shall be glad to have other people enjoy him as we do," he wrote.[27]

The nude boy stands on a turtle; its lifted head a water spout. The curly-haired boy with a delighted smile carries a catfish in his right arm and holds an even bigger catfish over his left shoulder.

Following the Batchelders' visit to see the fountain in place, Longman wrote to Rockefeller: "We did enjoy our day at Pocantico, and I love to think of my little boy permanently located in such very happy surroundings."[28]

Rockefeller wrote to Longman, "Every time I see the little boy, I like him better and am delighted to have this charming example of your work in my father's gardens."[29]

Interestingly, it was modern art—Picasso, Matisse, and others—that Abby championed as cofounder of The Museum of Modern Art. But she also favored Longman's work and welcomed her company. When, in 1928, the Rockefellers' second-to-youngest son, Winthrop, transferred from the Lincoln School at Columbia University's Teachers College to Loomis, Abby Rockefeller planned a motor trip to see her son's room. She wrote to Longman, "I am just longing to make you a visit and try my hand at being assistant to a sculptor. I might stand by and hand you pieces of clay and once in awhile try my hand at doing something myself."[30]

In March 1931, she wrote to Longman from their estate in Seal Harbor, Maine, prior to a return to New York City:

> Couldn't you make some excuse for coming down and having a few days of rest with me. . . . You might enjoy seeing the German show which is on at the Museum at this time. I think the Germans have some pretty good sculptors. There are lots of things we might do together and probably there are lots of things you and Mr. Batchelder need to do in New York. Anyway I would love to see you.[31]

Longman gave the Rockefellers the plaster bust of David from which she had made the marble. The Rockefellers kept the marble in New York City, the plaster at Pocantico in the "Playhouse"—which was actually a sprawling Rockefeller residence for those times when the family wanted to be out of the public eye.

Longman wrote in June 1925, as John III was about to graduate: "I hate to think of John leaving us! He has won a real place in my affection."[32]

During spring break in March 1926, the Frenches and Batchelders vacationed in Atlantic City. From there, Longman and Daniel French took a train to D.C. to see about the lighting of French's seated *Abraham Lincoln* in the Lincoln Memorial. It might be the sort of thing artists fret about more than anyone else; for French and Longman, standing before *Lincoln* at certain times of the day was indeed an agonizing experience. Shadows on Lincoln's face painted him ghostly, and the lighting grossly exaggerated his knees.

No one knew an easy way to fix it, and so *Lincoln* had sat off and on in the shadows for the last seven years. With Bacon gone, it fell to French to figure out a solution. He asked Longman to help.

Mary French wrote about this distressing situation in her book *Memories of a Sculptor's Wife*:

> When the Monument was finished and the statue put in place, it was found that the lighting was so bad that for those first few years it was a constant grief to the sculptor and his artist friends . . . with the architect of the building gone, it became a serious problem. . . . I think at the time, Mr. French was so discouraged about it, and for a while so hopeless of any solution of the problem, that he felt that it could never look as it was intended to look.[33]

Margaret French wrote of Longman's role in *Journey into Fame*:

> Dan went down to Washington in March to see the effect of the experiments. He took Beatrice Longman along with him as a sort of champion of Bacon. Beatrice had done some of the ornament on the Memorial and had worked a great deal with Bacon. Dan was afraid that his own enthusiasm for improving the statue might hurt the appearance of the building, and he knew that Beatrice's spirit of fairness to both friends would insist on justice being done to the statue, while not allowing any impairment to the beauty of the Memorial itself.[34]

Late in the process of building the Memorial, Bacon had decided to abandon doors on the building, leaving the statue in perpetual view—the dramatic effect visitors have known since it opened. Doing so changed the lighting, especially considering the stronger light coming in off the reflecting pool, which hadn't been finished at the time of the Memorial's dedication.

Also, Bacon had designed the ceiling to be made of glass, but later used a lightly colored marble instead, which softened the indoor space, but, combined with the effects of daylight, distorted Lincoln. It had been a nagging, back-of-the-burner headache for French and for Longman, and it would take a couple more years to resolve.

Upon Longman's return to Windsor after the March 1926 trip, Batchelder wrote to French that she "feels that the big figure is much improved."[35]

Again, a year later, in March 1927, Longman joined Daniel, and this time Mary French, in D.C., to further try to resolve the problem. Longman developed "a cold in the head" on the train back to New York and insisted on going to the hospital rather than "be a nuisance" to the Frenches in their new, smaller, apartment.[36] French wrote to Batchelder, apologizing for not taking better care of her, but noting that "I think Beatrice enjoyed our brief visit in Washington and her presence meant everything to me in our experiments at the Lincoln Memorial. The results of the artificial lighting surpass my best hopes and I feel very happy about it."[37]

Batchelder wrote to reassure French that Longman was recovering: "As you may know, I ran down to New York twice this week for an hour with Beatrice, and have found her rather better than I had expected. . . . She told me that you had accomplished your purpose in Washington, and I know that she will think a few days' illness a cheap price to pay for the accomplishment of the project of better lighting for the Lincoln. She has had that very much on her mind for years."[38]

French wrote to Longman the same day, March 27, 1927. After apologizing again for letting her go to a hospital and appearing "hard-hearted," he honored her tenacity in a compliment that must have boosted her spirits.

> Although it was a heavy price to pay for it, I hope it will eventually give you some satisfaction to know that you did me so great a service and that your knowledge and your advice and your thoroughness gave me the backing and the brace to get things done right with the Lincoln statue. I am afraid that without you, I should have let things go, short of perfection. I am sure it will be a source of pleasure, too, to have had a hand in saving the life of my statue, for that is about what the new lighting has done for it! I feel very happy about it myself and always, when I think of it, I shall recall your presence and your interest and your sympathy, with gratitude for such a friend as you are to me.[39]

French eventually raised support for funding from Congress to make the changes that finally resolved the Lincoln lighting problem. The Sunlike Illuminating Company of New York created an artificial light using a "reflector with a prismatic arrangement of cobalt oxide mirrors inside" and floodlights were installed on the ceiling.[40] Mary French wrote:

> after months and indeed years of experimenting, a system of artificial lighting was installed which has made it quite as successful as it could be under the best circumstances.[41]

French described himself "as a happier man" by the spring of 1929, when visiting the Lincoln Memorial. The new lighting was "more satisfactory than I could have believed possible."[42]

Determination had won the day. Longman's had been evident from Ohio to Chicago to New York City to Washington, D.C., and now Windsor, Connecticut, where the strong-willed woman inevitably influenced Batchelder and Loomis. And so it was that Loomis was having an influence on Longman—though it seemed her influence was the stronger, and would ever be so.

NOTES

1. NHB to Mary Francis, November 24, 1924, Spanish War Memorial Folder, Longman Collection, Loomis Chaffee.
2. Skip's unpublished memoir, Loomis Chaffee.
3. EBL note on letter from DCF, February 25, unspecified year, Loomis Chaffee.
4. NHB letter to Gozo Kawamuro, February 24, 1926; Note by EBL in DCF letter to Longman, Feb. 25 [year not given], Loomis Chaffee.
5. NHB to Kawamura, March 25, 1926, Loomis Chaffee.
6. DCF to EBL, February 25, unspecified year, Loomis Chaffee.
7. DCF to EBL, March 14, 1926, Loomis Chaffee.
8. NHB to R. S. Sperry, October 15, 1926, Loomis Chaffee.
9. NHB to Chapin on November 29, 1926.
10. "Spanish War Men Honored by Memorial," *Hartford Courant*, May 27, 1927, 1.
11. DCF to EBL, December 22, 1927, Loomis Chaffee.
12. L. W. Fowles, *The Harvest of our Lives* (Windsor, CT: The Loomis Institute 1964), 54.
13. Ibid.
14. Nancy Boas and David Park, *A Painter's Life*. (Berkley: University of California Press, 2012), 11.
15. Ibid.
16. Boas, 13.
17. David Park died in 1960, at the age of forty-nine, of cancer.
18. Irwin Jones to EBL, May 9, 1926, Alumni Letters Folder, Loomis Chaffee.
19. Ibid.
20. The gift was a surprise to Loomis administrators, as the Frank Palmer family had no connection to the school up to that point. Palmer had written a book about the relationship of wealth and labor.
21. EBL to George C. St. John, Choate School, May 14, 1923, Loomis Chaffee.
22. Frank Grubbs, "Mrs. B—Tribute to a Genius," *Loomis Alumni Bulletin*, July 1978, Loomis Chaffee.
23. Skip's unpublished memoir, Loomis Chaffee.
24. "Sender of First News Story by Phone Dies in Salem," *Boston Globe*, January 2, 1931, 25.
25. Skip's unpublished memoir, Loomis Chaffee.
26. Francis O. Grubbs, The Loomis Institute "for better and grander lives" (New York: The Newcomen Society in North America, 1964), 15–16.
27. John D. Rockefeller Jr. to EBL, February 6, 1928, Office of the Messrs. Rockefeller records, Educational Interests, Series G, Rockefeller Archive Center.
28. EBL to JDR Jr., May 21, 1925, Rockefeller Archive Center.
29. JDR Jr. to EBL, May 27, 1925, Rockefeller Archive Center.
30. Abby Rockefeller to EBL, October 6, unspecified year, Office of the Messrs. Rockefeller records, Abby Aldrich Rockefeller, Series AA, Series 1, Box 2, Folder 22, Rockefeller Archive Center.

31. A. Rockefeller to EBL, March 18, 1931, Rockefeller Archive Center.
32. EBL to JDR Jr., June 2, 1925, Rockefeller Archive Center.
33. Mary French, *Memories of a Sculptor's Wife* (Boston and New York: Houghton Mifflin, 1928), 261–62.
34. Margaret French Cresson, *Journey into Fame* (Cambridge, MA: Harvard University Press, 1947), 289.
35. NHB to DCF, March 22, 1926, Loomis Chaffee.
36. EBL handwritten note on letter DCF to NHB, March 23, 1927, Loomis Chaffee.
37. DCF to NHB, March 23, 1927, Loomis Chaffee.
38. NHB to DCF, March 26, 1927, Loomis Chaffee.
39. DCF to EBL, March 27, 1927, Loomis Chaffee.
40. Holzer, 292.
41. Mary French, *Memories*, 262.
42. Holzer, 292.

Chapter 22

Peabody and Company

Moving pictures have taken the place of drama—effects have altogether superseded subtleties and it is a deep joy to find that there are still a few Artists who know that the body of Art must have a soul else it is a dead thing.

—Katrina Trask

The Rockefellers weren't the only super-wealthy people who became friends with the Batchelders and for whom Longman created sculpture. Enter George Foster Peabody.

Peabody, born in Columbus, Georgia, had to quit school when he was fourteen to work in a wholesale dry-goods firm to contribute income to his family. His parents were New Englanders of colonial descent who had moved to Columbus and established a general store that prospered. Young Peabody had attended a private school in Columbus and a few months at Deer Hill Institute in Danbury, Connecticut, before the family's business plummeted during the Civil War.

In 1866, when the family moved from Georgia to Brooklyn, George took the job as a warehouse errand boy. He studied on his own at night in the library of Brooklyn's YMCA, which he later called his "alma mater." Attending a fundraising lecture at his church by General Samuel Armstrong, who was raising money to open Hampton Normal and Agricultural Institute for African Americans, Peabody learned of the need for education of black people. Though he'd grown up with enslaved people in his home, now, informed by Armstrong's presentation, he convinced a group at the church to contribute to Hampton. In fact, supporting education, and especially the education of black people, would become much of his later life's work and would involve Loomis, and Longman.

His own fortunes improved vastly when, also at church, he met a young financier, Spencer Trask, with whom he became friends. Peabody joined Trask's investment firm and there made his millions working especially on financing in electrical engineering (supporting Thomas Edison) and railroads. Peabody's wealth would ultimately be right up there with that of John D. Rockefeller and J. P. Morgan.

He retired at the age of fifty-three, to devote himself hands-on to his philanthropic interests, including the education of black youth in the South. He served on the board of trustees of the American Church Institute for Negroes and boards of all-black schools: Penn Normal Industrial and Agricultural School in St. Helena, South Carolina; the Hampton Institute in Hampton, Virginia; the Tuskegee Institute in Tuskegee, Alabama; and the University of Georgia in Athens.

As young men, Trask and Peabody both fell in love with Katrina Nichols, the daughter of a wealthy couple in Brooklyn. She married Trask, but Peabody's friendship with the couple continued. Fully participating in the lush and exalted society of great wealth that Trask provided, Katrina, an author and playwright, was morally conflicted, which she wrote about in her journal. "Is it right for one person to own vast property whilst another has no where to lay his head?"[1]

Tragically, all four of her children died at young ages. After the first, Spencer built her a refuge in Saratoga Springs, called "Yaddo," named by one of their children who couldn't pronounce "shadow," reportedly referring to the shadow of sadness. When Yaddo later burned to the ground, Spencer rebuilt an even grander home, where the couple hoped to create an artists' retreat. Spencer Trask died in a train crash in 1909. Eleven years later, Katrina Trask married George Foster Peabody, saying that their marriage was "the romantic culmination of a rare triangular friendship."[2] Katrina died eleven months after that. Peabody developed Yaddo into the celebrated artist retreat the Trasks had intended, and so it remains today.

Daniel French had worked with Katrina Trask and Henry Bacon to create a monument to Spencer: a winged angel, *Spirit of Life*, which was dedicated in 1915 at Saratoga Springs. French and Katrina Trask became friends and he eventually served on the board at Yaddo.

In a letter of August 1919, French reported to Longman that Peabody had been pleased to meet her, but the letter does not provide details of the meeting.[3] It's unknown if Trask met Longman then, but she wrote to Longman on January 5 of a year she didn't specify, thanking Longman for sending her a statue of *Consecration*.[4] There is no reference to purchase or gift, size, or medium. Neither does it explain the circumstances under which Longman seems to have turned to Trask for counsel. Considering the possible timing, Trask's marital story, and the fact that Longman's response to this encounter, evidently, was to gift Trask with a statue she valued immensely, of a woman and man embracing, it seems possible their conversation occurred as Longman was deciding on or preparing for her marriage to Batchelder. Trask, a poet and playwright, thoughtfully wrote:

> If you could know the joy and pleasure you have given me, your heart would be glad that you overcame your natural hesitancy in turning to one whom you considered a stranger, showing a large and frank trust in her comprehension and deep sympathy.
>
> I have looked long at this exquisite Statue, so full of purity and passion, so altogether lovely. It makes one think—it makes one feel—and that is the highest art.
>
> It seems to me that modern Art, so called, aims to do exactly the reverse.
>
> Moving pictures have taken the place of drama—effects have altogether superseded subtleties and it is a deep joy to find that there are still a few Artists who know that the body of Art must have a soul else it is a dead thing.
>
> "Consecration" is very powerful and very tender—very strong and lovely. Thank you for sending it to me.
>
> I want to know you. May I hope for that great pleasure sometime?
>
> I am an invalid, as perhaps you know, and am no longer ever in New York but I shall hope that you will sometime come to this North Countr__ {indecipherable letters} and that we may meet. I must know the woman who has made this beautiful thing.
>
> May I?
>
> Peace be with you
>
> Katrina Trask[5]

Whether or not Longman and Trask saw each other after that is unknown. French wrote to Longman in 1924 that Peabody "had his heart set" on a piece of Longman's in an exhibit at the Grand Central Galleries, but somebody bought it before he did.[6] However, by 1931 Peabody owned a tinted plaster of Longman's early work, *Louise.*

Longman and Batchelder would come to know and spend a good deal of time with both George Foster Peabody and his adopted daughter, Marjorie Peabody Waite, visiting them at Yaddo and at Peabody's home in Warm Springs, Georgia. Out of her fondness for Peabody and for Marjorie, in 1925 she created a portrait of Peabody as a gift and took extra care with the plaster cast so there could be replicas, as Waite hoped to have casts made for several schools.[7] Longman was so appreciative of Peabody, she required payment for expenses only. She then agreed to reduce the portrait and design a medal given annually to an African American student in the South who wrote the best essay on world peace. Under Peabody's portrait, Longman scripted the words "Lover of Men." On the obverse of the medal, she designed a flame, the words "Blessed are the Peace Makers," and a banner across the center for the recipient's initials.

Ten years later, Longman adapted the medal design for the University of Georgia's annual award for broadcasting. "The Peabody," a parallel award to the Pulitzer, is still given annually, though the medal's design has been altered slightly: Longman's portrait of Peabody and her signature remain on the prize; "Lover of Men" has been removed.[8]

This was only the beginning of Longman's work with Peabody. When he saw her relief portrait of Dan French, he was inspired to ask Longman to create two more bas-reliefs as tributes to friends: one of William Jackson Palmer, the railroad tycoon of Colorado and Mexico; another of Hollis Burke Frissell, the second principal of the Hampton Institute. In a letter to Longman dated May 26, 1927, Peabody introduced her to Palmer:

> He was one of the youngest of the brigadier Generals in the Civil War; and was known in Europe as well as in America, as the builder of the Denver and Rio Grande Railway system; and also in Mexico as the builder of the Mexican National Railway system.[9]

Longman agreed to create the Palmer relief, for five thousand dollars ($87,600 now), plus trip expenses to Colorado to learn about him, find photographs, and take measurements of the installation site in the Denver train station.

Palmer, born to a Quaker family, grew up in the Germantown section of Philadelphia. As a child, he had been fascinated with steam locomotives. At the age of seventeen, he went to work for the Pennsylvania Railroad Company, which sent him to England and France to study railroad engineering and mining. While in England, he observed that coal was replacing wood for powering locomotives, and when he returned to the United States and became secretary to the Pennsylvania Railroad's president, he told his boss about his observation. The PRR was burning sixty thousand cords of wood per year and stripping trees from rights of way. It became the first company in the United States to switch to coal.

Despite his Quaker roots, Palmer joined the Union Army in his mid-twenties, in support of ending slavery. He helped form the 15th Pennsylvania Calvary; was a scout behind Confederate lines, imprisoned, then released in a prisoner swap; served until the end of the war, receiving the Medal of Honor and, at the age of twenty-nine, the rank of brigadier general. After the war, as many Union officers and soldiers did, he contributed to the education of freed slaves in the South, especially to Hampton Normal School, at the mouth of Chesapeake Bay, in Virginia.

Palmer worked on the Kansas Pacific Railroad, extending the line from Kansas City to Denver, then founded his own company, the Denver and Rio Grande Railroad. He built the narrower three-foot gauge railroad, from Colorado Springs to Trinidad and then through the mountains to Leadville. He established the Rio Grande Western Railway from Denver to Salt Lake City. At Pueblo, he founded the Colorado Coal and Iron Company's steel mill, which merged with another company to become Colorado Fuel and Iron, for decades Colorado's largest employer. He organized and was president of the Mexican National Railway for seven years.

In 1871, he bought ten thousand acres of land and laid out a community, which he named Colorado Springs. He included land and funding for Colorado College and served as a founding trustee. In 1901, when he sold his interest in the Rio Grande Western and became a multimillionaire, he disbursed one million dollars to several hundred employees, the amount depending on their length of service, and established a fund of several thousand dollars for widows and orphans of a coal-mining accident. He gave millions for parks, playgrounds, and roads in Colorado Springs, including funds to pay staff to maintain them.

Besides property in Colorado—including his castle, Glen Eyrie, outside of Colorado Springs—Palmer maintained apartments in London and New York and a castle near Mexico City. He and his wife, Mary Lincoln ("Queen"), had three daughters. Queen experienced health issues, including a heart condition that required her to live at a lower altitude—eventually back in England, where she grew up. She died at the age of forty-four.

Palmer continued to financially support the Hampton Institute, entrusting a gift of securities to Peabody to administer for the school. By June 1929, the school had benefited in the amount of $162,000 (equivalent to more than $2,800,000 today), including $25,000 given for an organ in the chapel.[10]

Longman never met Palmer, but as usual with her commissions, she tried to learn everything she could about him. She and Batchelder traveled by train to Colorado Springs, arriving at 4 p.m. on Sunday, August 28, 1927. She hoped to gather from Palmer's business colleagues, photography studios, and Palmer's personal friends as many photographs as she could—as well as ascertain the character of the man she was to portray.

Peabody suggested an inscription for the Palmer piece. Longman found it "staggering" in length. Batchelder wrote to Peabody: "Mrs. Batchelder is sure that unless it is very much reduced, it will destroy the decorative effect, and also, as a practical matter, she feels that if there is so much to read, most beholders will read nothing at all."[11]

Batchelder said he and Longman would ponder, edit, and send a revision. It seems like Peabody won that round, but Longman found a way to make it work. A lover of lettering, Longman created an elegant inscription, squishing letters (almost every *o* is small) so that the words don't overpower the image of Palmer:

> Union Cavalry General. Pioneer Railroad Builder. Prophet of Colorado's Greatness. He Mapped the Routes of Three Transcontinental Railways. Supervised the Building of The First Road to Denver. Organized and Constructed the Denver and Rio Grande Railroad. Stimulated the State's Industries. Cherished its Beauties. Founded Colorado Springs. Fostered Colorado College. And Served Our Sister Republic of Mexico With Sympathy and Wisdom in Developing Its National Railways.

Beside the lettering, Palmer is seated, knees crossed, in front of a mountain range, including, at Peabody's suggestion, Pikes Peak. A dog standing in front of him peers up at Palmer as the tycoon peers off into the distance. His hair is wavy, combed away from his mustached face. Dressed in suit and vest with a bow tie, he holds maps and a riding crop in his lap, but his right hand is on his leg, as if he has just had a new thought and might be ready to push off and take action.

Still installed in the lower level of the Denver train station, the relief remains a beautiful portrait of one of America's railroad tycoons.

Batchelder wrote to Palmer's oldest daughter, Elsie Myers, in England, on November 21, 1928:

> I can hardly tell you how much pleasure Mrs. Batchelder had in executing this work. She conceived so great an admiration for your father and his accomplishments, and he was such an exceedingly good subject, that she reveled in her opportunities. It was Mr. Peabody's suggestion that Pikes Peak be introduced into the composition. We all feel that this has proved interesting, that it helps the idea of vision and of an active outdoor career. The head of the dog seems appropriate, both as helping the composition and as being characteristic. We had seen a photograph of the General with dogs about him.[12]

In addition to the Palmer in the Denver train station, Peabody eventually had copies made (at a cost of $1,500 each—equivalent to $27,000 in 2024). They were installed in Palmer Hall at Colorado College; the Hampton Institute; the train station in Mexico City; and later, the train depot in Salt Lake City, Utah.

It was a productive relationship for Longman. "It is seldom that sculptors arrange on such a wholesale basis," she wrote a friend years later. What's more, she seemed to feel she had met her challenge. "It was something of a problem to suggest the outdoor man and the pioneer spirit. But, my client, at least, thought I did it well."[13]

With triple responsibilities—parent, wife of a headmaster, and busy sculptor who sometimes modeled two people sitting in relays—Longman was "harassed" by the feeling she was neglecting things she should be doing.[14]

Never mind that; there was one more sculpture to do for Peabody—again in "wholesale" numbers. That challenge would take Longman, and Batchelder, south and result in a series of studies of African Americans that would become portrait busts.

NOTES

1. See https://archives.nypl.org/mss/4795.
2. Ibid.
3. DCF to EBL, August 6, 1919, Loomis Chaffee.
4. Katrina Trask to EBL, January 5 [unspecified year], Loomis Chaffee.
5. Ibid.
6. DCF to EBL, December 10, 1924, Loomis Chaffee.
7. NHB to Marjorie Waite, June 26, 1931, Loomis Chaffee.
8. NHB to Mrs. Nathan Straus Jr., April 26, 1947, Loomis Chaffee.
9. George Foster Peabody to EBL, May 26, 1927, Loomis Chaffee.
10. "Bronze Memorial to Gen. Palmer at Hampton Inst.," *New York Age*, June 8, 1929, 3.
11. NHB to GFP, September 7, 1927, Loomis Chaffee.
12. NHB to Mrs. Leo Myers, November 21, 1928, Loomis Chaffee.
13. EBL to Newcom Carlton, January 3, 1931, Loomis Chaffee.
14. NHB to Mrs. Ama C. Guillet, January 7, 1929, Loomis Chaffee.

Chapter 23

African American Works

Not merely a portrait, but a record of the whole history of Negro education.

—Evelyn Beatrice Longman

The year Longman finished her *William Jackson Palmer* relief, she also held her first one-woman show—in New York City at the extensive Grand Central Art Galleries. It was a tour de force, not only of her sculpture—thirty pieces—but also of her aesthetic sensibilities, her perfectionism, the Loomis teamwork, and her chronic determination.

Near Christmas 1927, as she guided exhibit preparations, she had to take time out for surgery to have a cyst removed from her breast. There was a worrisome limbo until the surgery could be scheduled, but as she discovered, there was no malignancy. Still, recovery required a few days in the hospital, a week's stay in Salem with Batchelder's mother, and then, back in her studio, the discipline to quit working for a midday rest. Though the surgery had been successful, her back was strained.

A trucking company picked up pieces and delivered them to the Grand Central Art Galleries in New York City: from Mrs. John D. Rockefeller, the marble bust of David and the marble relief of John; from Mrs. Marcellus Hartley Dodge, the bronze relief of Hartley; from Mr. Robert W. de Forest, their marble portrait relief mounted on wood; and from Ivan Olinsky, his bronze bust on marble base. Olinsky was one of the artists Longman exchanged works with: for his bust in bronze and small bas-reliefs of his daughters, he painted large, lush, and colorful portraits of Longman and Batchelder to be hung at Loomis.

Loomis carpenter Carl Olson and his staff crated works: *Aenigma*; the bronze bust *Batchelder*; a bas-relief of a Batchelder niece, Eleanor; the bronze relief of French; the relief *Batchelder, Jr.*; *George Parsons*, *Judge Alden P. White*, *Henry Bacon*, and a wall fountain of a baby dancing on a shell; *Peggy* and *Victory*; and *Elisabeth*, *Stowe Wilder*, *Young Pan*, *Louise*, and both *Torsos*. In addition to *Consecration*, two other ideal pieces: *Nature*, listed for twenty thousand dollars, and *Woman Must Weep* (later known as *Destiny*) listed for five thousand dollars. Other works ranged from $150 (*Torso*) to three thousand (*Aenigma*).

In early January 1928, Longman began putting together what gallery manager Erwin S. Barrie said was "one of the finest one man shows ever held in our Galleries."[1]

Loomis art teacher Germaine Rouget Chéruy and artist/student David Park created tapestry-like draperies. Longman remodeled nails used to hang them. To a gallery visitor who inquired about where he could find some of those nails, she wrote: "I'll tell you the secret. There was nothing but the ordinary kind of nail at the Gallery. I couldn't bear their looks, so I took some modeling clay, put it over the nails, gave it that rough cast-iron shape, and daubed it with gold paint."[2]

The show was held over a week. Then she arranged to move the exhibition to Montclair, New Jersey, and after that, Rochester, New York, with some changes, including adding *American Galahad.* As meticulous in arranging those exhibitions as she had been in New York City, she measured the Montclair space, then made a diagram showing where every object would be set. She instructed the trucking company: Wrap all the marbles in white tissue paper and then more substantial covering. To avoid chipping an edge, the works should be lifted straight up off the pedestals and put down the same way.[3]

She placed blue silk cloth over another artist's painting that couldn't be moved from the wall. Her marble ideal *Woman Must Weep/Destiny* was situated at the entrance, so that the first statue people saw when entering the show was of a draped woman, face buried on her arm. At the end of the room, in front of a tapestry, sat *Nature*, a woman reflecting on the egg she's holding.

Following the Rochester show, she spent a week in Salem with Batchelder's mother, to give her back a break.

After an all-consuming winter, Longman made her first trip south in the late spring, to visit George Peabody at the Hampton Institute, where in a few months, one of her *William Jackson Palmer* reliefs would be installed. The Hampton Institute began in 1861, when Union major general Benjamin Butler, at Fort Monroe in Hampton, Virginia, decreed that people escaping enslavement behind Union lines would not be returned to bondage. Many of the people who had been enslaved found their way to a camp set up a few miles from Fort Monroe, and there, under what became known as the "Emancipation Oak," Mary Smith Peake, a free black woman, began teaching refugee children, even though it was illegal. She already had been secretly teaching enslaved and free blacks prior to being hired by the American Missionary Association, which helped fund Hampton.

The Hampton Institute grew from that tree, which still stands on the campus today, with its mission of educating African Americans, first as a normal school, then as a trade school, and finally as a university. In 1878, Hampton also began educating native people, when seventy people were sent from Fort Sill, Oklahoma, where they had been imprisoned by the U.S. government during the Red River War in 1874.

Peabody had asked Longman to create a bas-relief similar to the *French* and the *Palmer* to honor his friend Hollis Burke Frissell, the second principal of the Hampton Institute. Frissell, a white man from New York, was a Presbyterian pastor trained at Yale University and Union Theological Seminary. He went to the Hampton Institute as its chaplain and became principal and president in 1893, serving until his death in 1917.

Frissell and Peabody were friends for forty years. Both worked alongside various organizations involved with the education of African Americans, including as trustees at Penn School on St. Helena Island, South Carolina, and the Tuskegee Institute in Alabama. At the dedication in 1925 of Penn School's Frissell Community House, Peabody had said Frissell was "a man with a rare mind, and a rich and abounding soul."[4] In a letter to Julia Frame Frissell upon the death of her husband, George Peabody wrote:

> I am conscious of the high privilege it has been to know as I have this great soul and count him my dear friend. It means now that I must try to live out in this needy world, which could so little spare him, the real relations of life's sweetness and strength, its breadth, and its height which companionship and service with Hollis B. Frissell have meant. We are all called by his passing on to be more and more what we know men can be.[5]

Dr. Robert Russa Moton, a graduate of Hampton and the commandant of cadets there for twenty-five years, largely under Frissell's leadership, became the principal of the Tuskegee Institute following the death of Tuskegee's founding principal and Hampton graduate, Booker T. Washington. "Dr. Frissell came as near living the life of Christ as anybody I have ever known," Moton said at the Penn dedication. "He never had a small, mean, or trivial thought. He always stood for justice and righteousness."[6] As Frissell had been a national leader in education, letters upon his death came from Theodore Roosevelt and Woodrow Wilson. In 1930, the new library at the Tuskegee Institute was named after him.

Longman had her own connections to the Hampton Institute. Margaret Armstrong, whose father was Hampton's founding principal, Samuel Chapman Armstrong, posed for Longman when she was creating the angel for the Williams Memorial.[7] In 1916, Margaret had married Art Howe, who joined the Loomis faculty that year. A football hero and winning coach at Yale prior to his tenure at Loomis, he then moved on to Taft School in Watertown, Connecticut, where he was a chaplain and a teacher. Art Howe became the president of Hampton College in 1930, the year in which, in November, the *Frissell Memorial* would be dedicated.

Even more compelling a connection for Longman were the people who came to Loomis regularly from Hampton. In programs to elicit financial support, Hampton officials, often including Frissell and/or Moton and a quartet of singers, traveled to schools and other locations in the North. The Hampton Quartet performed folk songs and spirituals, and between sets, Hampton representatives told stories of school activities, alumni occupations, and the successful work of its graduates.

The quartet's bass singer, John Henry Wainwright, must have made a lasting impression on Longman. When Peabody approached her to create a bas-relief of Frissell, Longman suggested a group, to more fully focus on the story of education of African Americans and Native Americans at Hampton. In addition to Frissell, that group would include Wainwright, Moton, a Native American man, and a female Penn student. Peabody concurred.

The preliminary sketch showed Frissell in the center delivering a speech; beside him, Robert Moton; Wainwright on the other side of Frissell; a Native American next to Wainwright; and on Moton's left, a girl from St. Helena Island. After showing the sketch to Moton, Peabody approved it, and in August 1928, Longman contracted for seven thousand dollars to create the Frissell bas-relief for Hampton and replicas for Penn School and Tuskegee—all to be in place by November 25, 1930. She agreed to travel to all three locations to guarantee best sites for the installations.[8]

"The sketch which Mrs. Batchelder prepared almost took Mr. Peabody's breath away," Batchelder later wrote. "It was so much more inclusive and inspiring than anything he had expected. It takes account of coeducation, military, and trade features and the education of Indians."[9]

She studied Native Americans and Frissell from photographs, including one that showed Frissell in profile. As studies for the others, she modeled individual bronze busts of Wainwright, Moton, and a female student from Penn School. In October 1928, the Hampton Quartet was scheduled to perform again at Loomis. Longman arranged a sitting with Wainwright, who agreed to arrive at Loomis prior to the concert and sit for Longman over three days. He requested that it be kept a secret, to surprise his wife, Mary Louise. The Wainwrights had married in 1851 and had four daughters. To keep the secret, Longman kept her work covered while the others from Hampton were on campus.

Longman planned to create a bust and maybe a charcoal sketch of Wainwright. For his image on the bas-relief, Wainwright was dressed in work clothes, which were mailed from Hampton to Loomis. Studio assistant John Burdick's photos, taken during the sitting, show Wainwright standing in a soft, well-worn shirt and trousers, holding a large pipe wrench in his right hand. Batchelder reported that Wainwright was an outstanding model, standing without moving for long periods of time. Excited about the project, he and Longman worked one day from 9 a.m. to 1 p.m., said Batchelder, without either of them realizing how long they had been at it.

A Hampton graduate, Wainwright had toured with the Quartet for forty-one years. Though photos of the Quartet show the men in suits and ties, in the *Frissell* relief, Wainwright is dressed in work clothes (*sans* wrench), evidently to portray the trade aspect of a Hampton education. Longman's bronze head of him celebrates his work in the Quartet. The base is inscribed: "John Henry Wainwright. Forty-One Years of Service with The Hampton Quartette."

Longman's later statement about Wainwright indicates that she found him modest and proud of the work he had been able to contribute to the school; and that in the bust of Wainwright she attempted to express, perhaps influenced by her friend George Peabody, "not merely a portrait, but a record of the whole history of Negro education."[10]

Longman's bust portrays an older Wainwright than the Burdick photos of him. She tilted his head slightly upward; deepened the folds on his face; set a determined jawline, with perhaps a modicum of humor in the mouth. It is a strong image, beautifully wrought.

Wainwright performed and toured with the Quartet another ten years; an auditorium was named for him at Hampton, in Clark Hall, where the first YMCA for black students was housed. The last living member of the Quartet, he died at the age of eighty-seven and was buried in the Hampton University Cemetery.[11]

Two weeks after Wainwright's sittings, Robert Russa Moton sat for Longman at Loomis during three days following a Tuskegee Institute trustees meeting in New York City. Moton had been the president of Tuskegee for more than ten years at that point. In addition to guiding the university and building its curriculum, his influence around the country was significant: serving with wealthy northern whites on boards of philanthropic groups and working with U.S. presidents on issues related to the African American experience.

In World War I, he had been dispatched to Europe, where he visited every army unit with African American troops and confronted unsubstantiated,

Figure 23.1 John Wainwright. Wainwright sang with the Hampton Quartet for fifty years. Source/Credit: Photograph by Dowd, Wyllie & Olson, Incorporated. From the collection of the Loomis Chaffee Archives, Loomis Chaffee School, Windsor, Connecticut USA.

prejudicial charges against black soldiers. It was he who made the keynote address (modified by others) during the dedication of the Lincoln Memorial, then was escorted a block away to the African American seating.

Longman's portrayal is striking in that it seems to convey his approach to advancing the well-being of African Americans. The position of his head is key. Rather than turned or tilted in any way, his head and gaze are forward, as was his approach: look them straight in the eye to face the issues, but without direct confrontation. Longman's portrait is distinctly straightforward and encapsulates Moton's *gravitas*, intelligence, and presence in his movement within and between the black and white communities. Longman teamed up with Abby Rockefeller to give a copy of the Moton portrait to the Tuskegee Institute, with Longman's efforts a gift and Abby paying for the bronze casting.[12]

Over time, aspects of Moton's deferential approach would become controversial. Too, after his death, it was learned that it had been his decision to allow U.S. government syphilis experiments at Tuskegee—without participants' knowledge or medical treatment.

The young woman in the relief was modeled on location at Penn School on the trip Longman and Batchelder made to the South. In March, they took the train; Batchelder had shipped their car by boat to Charleston, South Carolina, for their trip back north.

Before they shipped the car, Longman, ever keenly aware of ornamentation, had a radiator cap she had designed rehabbed for the trip. Radiator caps were "fussy" (her word) miniature copies of sculptures of heads that she made to fit onto cars' radiators. They were sold through the Grand Central Galleries. The unidentified one (perhaps *Peggy/Bacchante*) that was on their car at the time was made of bronze. It was so heavy that it kept falling off, so Longman sent it to Roman Bronze Works to be recast in aluminum. The new one didn't arrive in time for the car's shipment by sea, so was sent to her in South Carolina.

In addition to modeling the Penn School student, the purpose of the trip was to gather data and scope out installation sites for the *Frissell*. From St. Helena Island, the Batchelders met up with George Peabody and Marjorie Waite in Savannah, Georgia, where Peabody was recovering from a heart attack. They traveled then to the Tuskegee Institute in Alabama. Motoring from Alabama to Hampton, Virginia, Longman fell ill, and they stayed a few days at Southern Pines before visiting Hampton. Continuing north, they made stops in Washington, D.C., Baltimore, Philadelphia, and Princeton on their way home to Windsor. It was a 1,500-mile trip, which Batchelder must have driven on his own, as Longman never had learned to drive.[13]

The plaster of the girl arrived at Windsor shortly after they did. Longman's black-patinaed bronze bust became known as *A Girl of St. Helena Island*. Unlike the figures in her busts of Wainwright and Moton, the girl, in smooth, short-cropped hair with bangs, looks away. Her head is tilted a bit, and her large eyes look up. Beautiful, she emits innocence, curiosity, openness, and tentativeness, as well as confidence. In the relief, the girl's hair is curly. In the portrait, her hair is smooth. There is no record of her name.

At center of the large relief, Frissell delivers a speech, his fist making a point across Moton, who looks into the distance. The white fist across Moton seems too dramatic not to be symbolic, perhaps of Frissell's fight for the education of black people. The Native man is at the left of the piece, with a dignified Wainwright and inquiring girl in the background, though plainly seen.

George Foster Peabody was exuberant about the *Frissell Memorial*. He wrote to Longman, expressing how much he valued "what you have done in passing on in such life like fashion the vivid representation of these two notable men. . . . I am honored to have a part in such work by a true and inspiring artist. Again I thank you."[14]

In November 1930, following the dedication of the memorial, which Longman did not attend, Peabody wrote, praising her again:

> We are very happy here in the presence of thy noble and enduring presentation of Doctor Frissell in action. We mourned your absence and that the Batchelders might not also have shared the joy of the . . . appreciation of young and old of this beautifully expressive manifestation of your genius. I am proud in the consciousness of such a fulfillment of my dream and hope—and confidence.
>
> I send you thanks gracious and lovely friend for this privilege of thus sharing a bit in the glory of your thrilling achievement. It means much . . . to have this Spirit of action carried down the generations here to gather—and when Tuskegee and Penn echo forth to thousands more.[15]

Marjorie Waite wrote, "You are a dear lovely and lovable woman as well as a consummate artist!"[16]

In her third one-woman exhibit at the Grand Central Galleries, in January 1932, Longman exhibited the portrait relief of George Foster Peabody, the dark-patinaed bronzes of John Henry Wainwright, and *A Girl of St. Helena Island*. Longman had exhibited *Wainwright* at the National Academy of Design three years earlier. It was eventually sent to Art Howe for permanent display at Hampton; unknown is whether or not this was a gift from the artist.

Longman kept *Girl*. She is in the permanent collection of the Richmond Art Center at Loomis Chaffee Institute.

Loomis, as central as it was to Longman's and Batchelder's life, would not be their forever home. With a view toward retirement, they began exploring Cape Cod to find a place to build a home and studio. They settled on Grand Island, on the south shore near Osterville, at what came to be known as Oyster Harbors, where the waters were warm and the tide fill minimal.[17] The developer's promotional material cast Oyster Harbors as "a congenial community of intellectual people ideal for retirement." In fact, two of Harvard's intellectuals, the infamous economist F. W. Taussig, and the infamous president A. Lawrence Lowell, retired to nearby Cotuit. Longman would create busts of both men.

As "Bayberry au Batch" was being built and in preparation for life on the water, Skip was sent to sailing school at Camp Mashpee. Longman and Batchelder rented a summer cottage close by, but Batchelder removed Skip from the camp after the camp director charged Skip with wearing dirty white socks (Skip held they were clean) to go to Sunday lunch with his parents. Batchelder decided he and Skip could learn to sail with a book and a boat. He purchased a sixteen-foot sloop, a locally made favorite, *Wianno Junior*, named it *Trix* after Longman, and the legendary Batchelder sailing adventures began.

Longman was competitive, it turned out, and she enjoyed being the third crew member racing with Batchelder and Skip: "Dad and I taught each other to sail and later to race and in her we and Mother had many happy hours. Mother never really learned to sail—she was no good at mechanical things. I can recall her frustration when a simple can opener refused to function. Fortunately she never wanted to learn to drive a car.

"There was . . . a race in which I took Mother, who also had a strong competitive spirit, and who, sentimental and emotional as she was, very much wanted us to win. . . . After the race I realized I had failed to round one buoy and so of course we were disqualified."[18]

Batchelder wrote about family times on their next boat, the *Prodigal Pig*: "[Evelyn] learned to sail at 55 and raced, including long distance races to Edgartown and Nantucket, til she was 60. I claimed we were the champion Father, Mother & Son crew of the club—there wasn't any other. I recall one sail back (from which island I don't remember). We left the fleet and came by ourselves. The sky was threatening, the wind strong, and the waves high, pitching the Prodigal Pig about. . . . But Evelyn loved it."[19]

Longman's love of animals, begun in her childhood, had not diminished over time. "We had many picnics in *Trix*," wrote Skip. "Her shallow draft permitted easy beaching. We also fished some, though none of us were really fishermen. I think Mother always felt sorry for the fish. Though she enjoyed eating them."[20]

Batchelder wrote, "She was a pretty good amateur bird woman and might have become expert if there had been time. There was nothing in nature she feared. . . . Once at a school lecture the speaker called forth oh's and ah's by handling snakes. Evelyn walked up and wrapped two of the largest about her neck!"[21]

Longman's compassion for animals was passed along to her son one day in a dramatic moment at their home on the Cape. "I recall an incident when I was a kid, maybe 15. I had a .22 caliber rifle. I'd had instruction . . . at Loomis and shot on the Loomis rifle range. I was eager to shoot outside. One spring vacation Mother and Dad and I were sitting on the bench halfway down the stairs to our beach. . . . A water rat of some sort swam by, perhaps 30 yards away. I took aim, fired, and the rat stopped short, hit or killed. . . . I was shocked at the sudden transformation from life to death. Dad said nothing I can recall but Mother burst into tears. I was not directly reproached—there was no need. . . . I have never shot a living creature since, though I did have great fun plinking bottles and old light bulbs both at the Cape and on the Farmington River."[22]

Learning to sail had been the easy part; life lessons while sailing with his parents continued. The three were in another race, when Longman didn't respond as quickly as Skip felt she should have. He spoke sharply to her. Batchelder stood up, let go of the mainsail, and, no doubt, menacing eyebrows raised, promised to throw Skip overboard if he didn't apologize to his mother immediately.

Perhaps it was the thought of retirement.

Perhaps she got hold of the niggling feeling that there was something she hadn't done that she was supposed to do.

With continuing health issues, at the age of fifty-six, Longman set her mind to fulfilling her desire to create ideal pieces in monumental size. It was probably not the right time, as monumental figurative work was going out of fashion—and there would come a war, preventing, temporarily, the use of bronze, as well as sapping most resources. But it was Longman's time, and soon, in spite of considerable odds and nearly impossible tasks for Batchelder, she would garner the opportunity to create two colossal ideal pieces: one representing genius, and the other, at long last, the angel of compassion.

NOTES

1. Erwin S. Barrie to NHB, December 7, 1931, Loomis Chaffee.
2. EBL to Frederic K. Knowlton, April 18, 1928, Loomis Chaffee.
3. EBL to Frank Kidde, January 24, 1928, Loomis Chaffee.
4. William Anthony Aery, "Hollis Burke Frissell and Penn School," *Southern Workman*, Volume LIV, No. 1, January 1925, 244.
5. Telegram from GF Peabody, *Southern Workman*, Vol. XLVI, No. 1, January 1916, 517.
6. Aery, 244.
7. Anna Slimkus, a cook and wife of a visiting Danish educator, also modeled for Longman's Williams angel. Batchelder's unpublished manuscript, Loomis Chaffee.
8. EBL to GFP, September 10, 1928, Loomis Chaffee.
9. NHB to Edwin Barrie, January 11, 1932, Loomis Chaffee.
10. Statement from the Grand Central Galleries, Wainwright file, Loomis Chaffee.
11. See https://www.findagrave.com/memorial/14230966/john-henry-wainwright.
12. EBL to R. R. Moton, March 1, 1932, Loomis Chaffee.
13. Skip's unpublished memoir, Loomis Chaffee.
14. GFP to EBL, June 11, 1930, Loomis Chaffee.
15. GFP to EBL, November 30, 1930, Loomis Chaffee.
16. MP Waite to EBL, May 25, 1930, Loomis Chaffee.
17. Skip's unpublished memoir, Loomis Chaffee.
18. Ibid.
19. NHB's unpublished memoir, Loomis Chaffee.
20. Skip's unpublished memoir, Loomis Chaffee.
21. NHB's unpublished memoir, Loomis Chaffee.
22. Skip's unpublished memoir, Loomis Chaffee.

Chapter 24

Edison

He is a dear.

—Evelyn Longman

Longman long had been intrigued by Thomas Edison. As she had come to the end of her time working alongside Dan French in his studios in 1904, she entered the National Sculpture Society–sponsored competition for a medal to commemorate Edison's invention of the incandescent light bulb. French was a judge, as well as Saint-Gaudens and John Quincy Adams Ward. Longman's design was one of the top-three finishers. French wrote to Ward: "Don't you think my Miss Longman is pretty smart? Her design was so different from anything that she had ever done before that I did not recognize it at all."[1] James Earle Fraser won the commission.

More than two decades after losing the medal possibility, on March 2, 1930, Longman took a train to Fort Myers, Florida, where Edison's winter home and laboratories were located. She was about to become the only sculptor for whom Edison would sit.[2] Turns out, he didn't mind so much having his face measured with calipers since he liked the science of measuring.[3]

The Association of Edison Illuminating Companies had agreed to gift a portrait bust of Edison to be installed in the Deutsches Museum in Munich, alongside that of German inventor Werner Von Siemens. As a committee of Edison friends gathered a list of names of prospective sculptors, Edward Dean Adams invited Longman to enter her name.

Early in his career, Adams, an engineer and financier, had won a bid to build the first power stations at Niagara Falls. Using Edison competitor Nikola Tesla's alternating-current system, he beat out Edison.[4] Nevertheless, Edison and Adams became friends, Adams eventually serving as a trustee for

Edison's electric companies, as well as in other capacities. Adams was also a trustee of The Metropolitan Museum of Art for forty years. Among many Met committee assignments, he chaired the Finance Committee for more than a decade and was a member of the Committee on Sculpture. He had purchased Longman's *Seated Female Figure* for his private collection before gifting it to The Met in 1927.

There was no requirement to create a model for the competition, only to submit photographs of completed works. Because Adams knew her work so well, she didn't need to send photographs except so that others on the committee could view them. She chose portraits of people whom Adams knew: the bas-relief of Daniel Chester French, the bust of Henry Bacon, the de Forest medallion. She also sent photographs of the bronze Bancroft bust and a more recent marble bust, *Elizabeth*, a model of the daughter of Loomis Latin teacher John Edmund Barss, her eyes closed, her braided hair wrapped around her head.[5]

The committee selected Longman. It was an honor and another fine financial opportunity. Portrait paintings and a full-length sculpture of Edison by James Earle Fraser had been produced, and another was in process. But evidently no sculpture had been done from sittings with Edison. Indeed, Adams suggested Longman begin her modeling from the many photographs of Edison already available and then have Edison sit when he returned to New York in June. Longman argued she would need to take measurements of Edison at the start, and she wanted photos taken showing the details she desired. Furthermore, catching Edison in June in New York in between his work would be harried for him and would extend the sittings into the summer. She proposed she go to Florida during the first two weeks of March to model him there.

"Much of it can be done from photographs that I will have taken on the spot, and the sittings need not be long," she wrote to Adams. "In the course of two weeks we should finish the entire work, as far as the modeling is concerned, though, of course, marble cutting will take considerably more."[6]

Adams underscored that although Edison's family and friends appreciated the honor offered Edison by the Deutsches Museum, they were concerned about his health: "Mr. Edison is advanced in years and infirm in condition. His friends, while still impressed with flashes of his former vigor, realize that his life is precarious and we therefore desire to proceed as readily as possible with his portrait bust."[7]

Mina Edison was not eager for her husband to sit for Longman. She preferred Longman use only photographs to create the bust: "It is impossible for me to promise that he would ever sit for two hours a day for two weeks. I am sure that he will not consent to it, and I would not want him to do so as he is not well enough, and whoever does the bust will have to take him as they can."[8] She did agree that Florida was the better place to see Edison.

The persistent Longman finally got her way. Concurring that the major part of the sculpting be done at Edison's Florida compound, Adams sent Longman a bound volume of photographs Mina Edison had collected, and plans began for Longman's visit to the Edisons in Florida. "By meeting him daily for which Mrs. Edison would be of the greatest possible assistance to the sculptor, would naturally include observations when Mr. Edison is in action and short sittings for the expression of eyes and mouth," Adams wrote Longman.[9]

William S. Barstow, president of Edison Pioneers, lived nearby. Adams would stay with the Barstows at the end of February through early March so that the two could be engaged with Longman during her work there. She was given measurements of the Siemens sculpture to create the companion marble. Her payment, in installments, would be five thousand dollars (more than ninety-two thousand dollars today). She agreed to arrive in Florida around the first of March. She had now promised an intense schedule for herself that would stress her—physically and emotionally.

Batchelder sent her flowers on the train to Florida and had more delivered several times to her hotel, which, she reported, always buoyed her spirits. Otherwise, she was a bit gripey—if her letters are an indication. She wrote to Batchelder every day she was in Fort Meyers and often separately to Skip, signing her letters to the "boogies"; from the "middle boogie," "your devoted wife," and "your devoted Wussa."

While she loved the Royal Palm Hotel's setting, overlooking the Caloosahatchee River with "blooming red flowers and big palm trees," her room was unattractive ("no two pieces of furniture in the same style" and they, "rather ugly"). She was "freezing" as there was no heater except in the bathroom from which she wrote her first letter. She had a writing table brought in. The food was miserable (hardly any vegetables other than potatoes). The taxi service was unreliable. Lonely, she missed Batchelder and Skip. She was "provoked" by Mina Edison.

On what she expected to be her first workday, Longman received a call from an Edison staff member who told her that she wouldn't see the Edisons, as they had guests. Longman reported to Batchelder that she tried not to show her irritation "too much," though she told the staff member that this was wasting her valuable and limited time in Fort Myers. When the staff member said the Edisons didn't want to offend their guests, she laughingly suggested that she might be offended.[10]

The next day, Mina Edison escorted Longman around the Edisons' thirteen-acre compound along the river, which included their home with its extensive porches. Henry Ford's winter estate was next door. After being shown several possible sites for her workspace, including one of Edison's laboratories (though not the "Holy of Holies"), Longman chose his private office. She described it in a letter to Batchelder:

> a little building with apparently only one room, a little porch, and in the back a lovely little garden with high walls of massive foliage and lovely flowers and vines, a rectangular pool in the center and a couple of seats. All lovely and simple and restful.
>
> Two very large table-desks are in the middle of the room, back-to-back, one Mr. Edison's and one Mrs. Edison's, his piled high with unread mail. There are bookcases at one end, a fireplace in one side and the two other sides are lined with a continuous bench, a small sink with running water set into it and the walls lined with shelves over it, and on the latter, rows of bottles filled and empty, and all sorts of test tubes, etc. As soon as you open the doors you smell the chemicals but it is not at all disagreeable. It seems that he does a little . . . experimenting here also, all alone when he feels like it.[11]

After settling on her work area, she found her calipers in boxes that had been sent from Connecticut and went to the Edison home, where Mina Edison introduced Longman to her husband. With calipers in hand, Longman carefully took measurements of Edison's face. She did not send details to Batchelder describing what the moment was for her as the legendary genius sat still while she measured his countenance. Perhaps it was these times exploring his features and looking deeply at him that created within her what turned into an unrelenting desire to make a bigger head than the Deutsches Museum's parameters. All Longman wrote in her letter to Batchelder that evening was: "Mrs. Edison was at first not very cordial but loosened up after a while. He is a dear!"[12]

By her second day on the job, she could see the reality of the situation—both Edison's physical weakness and how carefully he was being guarded, "like royalty." She wrote Batchelder: "Seven hours work today. This is going to be a terrible job! I think that it will practically have to be done from the photos you saw. Mr. E. looks so old and I doubt whether he will really pose at all. He was in twice today looking over his mail but I got very little from him. Of course the measurements help. I wish you were here, dear one, to give me your fine helpful criticism."[13]

Longman established a schedule of working three hours in Edison's office in the morning, taking a long break at lunchtime, and working another three hours in the afternoon; no more than six hours, to preserve her own health. Mina Edison invited Longman to stay for lunch on the fourth day and again the following Sunday, but Longman refused both. "I did it graciously; but as I feel just now, I don't want to see her any more than I have to; I did not like her lack of common courtesy in the beginning! I'll 'learn her!'"[14]

That evening, photographs arrived that were taken by a photographer she had hired, but they were "awful." Not the photographer's fault, she wrote Batchelder, but due to poor lighting. "At present, I am very fearful of results." She sent greetings through Batchelder to Connecticut friends who were dealing with health issues, mentioned her loneliness and how much Batchelder's letters helped, and described the taxi situation.

She had taken a taxi from her hotel to the Edisons', but it failed to arrive to pick her up at the end of the day. One time she walked back, but the second day, as she started to walk, she noticed a woman sitting on her doorstep near the Edisons' and asked if she could use her phone. Having no phone, the woman instead drove Longman herself. "Rather cheering after Mrs. Edison's treatment," Longman wrote. "She hasn't concerned herself." Closing her letter, she wrote, "Now to supper—if I can get my hands clean enough to appear. I must get a brush and some gold dust."[15]

The next day Longman reported that the situation was improving. Mina Edison was "warming"; had offered a place for Longman to rest (after Longman inquired about where a toilet was). She refused, preferring her long break midday at her hotel. "The work is so trying that I find I need all the rest of the time, except when I write to the Boogies, for rest and I have been taking it right along. Yesterday I worked a little too long—three hours at a clip seems just what I can stand well."[16]

Mina Edison told Longman that Adams and Barstow would be arriving the next day. Longman protested that she wasn't yet ready for them to see her model, and Mina Edison said she would wire them not to come. They showed up while Mina Edison was out, and the two men asked for Longman, who told them she had only had three days of work, no posing, and that she wasn't ready for them to see the plastiline model. She wrote to Batchelder: "but they were so nice about it and did not insist—so of course I relented after all and let them in! . . . I was glad I did show it to them for they were very encouraging and said I had a fine 'start.'"[17] Barstow returned to his home; Adams stayed at the same hotel as Longman and planned to be there until she finished.

Conflicted about her relationship with Mina Edison—wanting nothing from her, and yet piqued at her for not meeting her needs—she began warming to her, though, as she put it to Batchelder, it was Mina Edison who was softening: "Mrs. E is becoming almost human. Really, I pity her. She takes her job of looking after him so hard that she is hardly conscious of anyone else, I believe. But I think she now thoroughly grasps the idea that I ask no favors of any sort and desire nothing socially of her. I mentioned the poor taxi service and that I had been obliged to walk home because none came; and she offered to have her chauffeur take me any time; but I thanked her and said I'd stick to the taxis because her man might not always be available when I wished."[18]

On March 9, she had "a real sitting" with Edison, for about half an hour, and took more measurements. It was "quite a successful morning."[19]

Adams's presence proved significant. He and Longman dined together at the hotel, and she accepted his car rides from the Edison compound. It was probably his doing that Longman began accepting Mina Edison's social invitations. She was in the Edison group excursion to Puerto Gorda for lunch with Adams, Harvey Firestone and his son, plus three other men and "Miss Bogue," a guest of Mina Edison's from Chicago. They lunched at a "charming hotel with lovely grounds" and "the biggest swimming pool I have ever seen." The Firestones left to return to Miami, but Longman joined Mina Edison, Adams, and Miss Bogue for tea, while Mr. Edison stayed in his car and drank milk—perhaps confirming rumors at the time that milk was pretty much his complete diet. Longman returned with the Edisons to Fort Myers. "Mrs. Edison gets better and better," she wrote Batchelder.[20]

Some days Longman had both lunch and dinner with Adams, enduring evening conversations that continued until 9 p.m., into her letter-writing time. On March 10, she reported that the bust was progressing, though slowly. On March 11, in her last letter from Florida (the last because she figured it took four days to get a letter to Batchelder), Longman recounted three hours in the evening with Adams at a carnival and water pageant, where Mina Edison, her sister, and Miss Bogue were dressed in Dutch costumes and served hot dogs in a stand in the shape of a windmill. She sat through more extended conversations with Adams, whose long career as financier and colleague of Edison must have afforded him many stories to share. It was wearying for Longman.

"Poor, lonesome old Mr. Adams (by-the-way he is nearly blind, which I did not suspect until I came down here) is playing havoc with my rest time—through my ridiculous pity-full heart. He is here all alone with his 60-year-old chauffeur and is to drive back all alone."[21]

Without more posing from Edison, she felt the urgency of the deadline, hoping for sittings every day before her departure on the 15th. In fact, she did finish the Edison model before she left Fort Myers. Batchelder met her in Florida, and they took a boat to New Orleans, where they picked up their car (shipped from home again), and they began to travel north, with a long-planned stop at the Tuskegee Institute, to visit the Howes.

Three weeks later, she sent Adams the invoice for the first payment, due upon the completion and approval of the Edison bust. On April 11, he sent her a check. The Piccirilli brothers were waiting to receive a block of marble they expected to be right for carving Longman's model.

Her marble bust of Edison is of a younger man "in his full physical vigor," though he was eighty at the time she met him.[22] Working on the commission, with the constraints of family and museum requirements, she modeled him frontal, clear-eyed; head and shoulders, in suit and bow tie. His face is full and barely lined; his hair is receding and smoothed; there is a slight smile.

Longman finished the marble, and it was delivered to the Deutsches Museum in Munich in December 1930. She received a letter from museum staff, extending their "sincerest regards and admiration. This exceedingly successful and characteristic work of art portrays Edison's personality in a manner true to life. We greatly value having in our possession such a remarkable likeness of the eminent pioneer in the science of electricity. This work of art will be viewed by many thousands of visitors who come to this museum from all over the world every year."[23]

At the unveiling on May 7, 1931, a letter from Edison was read aloud, expressing his hope that "international friendship might be promoted by electrical science."

American sponsors of Longman's bust of Edison, including the American Institute of Electrical Engineers, as well as Edison's personal friends and associates, gifted bronze replicas to the Edison family, the headquarters of the American Institute of Electrical Engineers, the Edison Pioneers, the Association of Edison Illuminating Companies, and the Engineers Club of New York.

Thomas Edison died on October 18, 1931, at his estate in Menlo Park, New Jersey, with Mina at his side. The nation grieved together: A moment of darkness was cast as communities across the country turned off the lights on the evening of his burial, in gratitude to Edison for his work, including the incandescent light bulb.

Longman wasn't finished with Edison. She had in mind to create his head less formally, more as an ideal figure of creative genius—in colossal size—as soon as she had time.

Early in 1931, Longman had replied to an acquaintance who wrote inquiring of her well-being, "I am very well and enjoying life to the full."[24] Batchelder's father, Henry Morrill Batchelder, died that very week. His body was laid in the parlor, and the people of Salem lined up, down, and around the block to pay their respects.[25]

Longman had assimilated completely into the Batchelder family, walking along the table at dinners to greet and tease family members (and take teases from Osgood); she referred to Batchelder's parents as "mother" and "father." She had created sculptures of Henry, a niece, a large memorial marker for the Batchelder family in the Salem cemetery, and a golden bowl for her in-laws' fiftieth wedding anniversary. For her own family of origin, she had created no cemetery memorials and only one bas-relief—of Claude's wife, Mertie, an Olivet College graduate and singer of some renown. It remains at the University of Olivet in Michigan.

Figure 24.1 Longman was said to be the only sculptor for whom Thomas Edison posed. Her first portrait of him was a marble for the Deutsches Museum in Munich, Germany. Source/Credit: Photograph from the collection of the Loomis Chaffee Archives, Loomis Chaffee School, Windsor, Connecticut USA.

Forever living far apart, the Longman siblings' primal longing for togetherness, a remnant from their childhood, survived. In May 1906, not too many years after Longman moved to New York City, she received this letter from her brother Edwin, "Ed/Edd," who was farming near where he had grown up, in Dawn Mills, Ontario, Canada.

> Sometimes I think too much of my brothers and sisters and want to see them so bad it makes me discontented and dissatisfied with my home because I cannot get away to go and see them. Well, Evelyn, you dear girl, I would like to have you in my arms to give you a good hug and kiss.[26]

Years later, Ed indicated his yearning had not diminished. "I think as years roll on and we get older we get to love each other more and more."[27]

Though far-flung with few opportunities to visit one another, the Longman siblings stayed in touch mostly through correspondence, with Evelyn traveling to see them now and then. Claude visited her often in New York City; sometimes they traveled together, and she, along with Henry Bacon, visited Claude and his wife, Mertie, annually at their cabin in Lakeside, Michigan. Visits from her siblings to her new home in Windsor were rare.

During her early days in New York City, with scant financial resources, she had sent money to her sisters and brothers and later, to their children. Even while limiting her diet mostly to Triscuits, Longman had helped support Louise and her young family. Louise's troubled marriage changed for the better over time, but not until Longman announced her engagement in 1920 did Louise ask her to stop sending money. Whether or not she stopped sending it to Louise, Longman loaned a sizable amount to her namesake, Louise's daughter Evelyn, for music school.

Once when she sent money to Vally, her note said, "Here is your piss money."[28] Another message one Christmas: "Dearest Vally: Here is a little [missing word] to buy your usual 'cigarettes and whiskey' for Christmas! Lovingly, Evelyn."[29]

She would continue to send money (and fashionable clothing—the Longmans were a dapper bunch) to her family until they died, including monthly checks to Cecil, who suffered a long illness. The second-to-youngest, she outlived them all.

She was closest to Claude, who was on hand at significant moments, including her wedding at Chesterwood. While recovering from surgery, Claude wrote to Longman soon after she (and, separately, Bacon) had visited him:

> The thing that endears you to me and to many others is that the greater your success the more human and loving and approachable you become as though the perfection of your work had been reflected in your own life. I have always maintained that real success and greatness only made the one who attained it the more simple and truly humanitarian, and my knowledge of those who are doing things, yearly convinces me of the truth of it. It is this quality in yourself, Banny, Hal Bacon, Mr. French and others that arouses my respect and love and admiration.[30]

Longman wrote that her youngest brother, Cecil, was more like her than any other member of her family. Only a brother could get away with this "portrait," as Longman put it, after they had a "spat":

> A very attractive, loving, generous, strong-minded, persevering, ambitious, talented and successful young lady who has been so accustomed to seeing the opposite sex with dusty knees and be-draggled senses standing humbly before her anxious to perform any act of servitude and endure all sorts of subtle joshing that she almost understands how a man (even a brother) can have the audacity to attempt to 'hold his own' in repartee and who has still to learn that such a person may exist, although she may never have met him.[31]

Vally, the oldest, was a fiesty woman who had ten children. Bonnie French, her great-granddaughter, said Vally smoked, told dirty jokes to her uncles, and warned her daughters of the dangers of getting pregnant when a man hangs his pants on a bedpost.[32] As unencumbered by cultural restraints as Vally seemed to be, nevertheless, she was offended by Longman's nude male statue, *Spirit of Communication*. She was particularly outraged when Longman used the image on her Christmas card in 1938, the year it had been reproduced in smaller scale to top AT&T's building for the World's Fair in Brooklyn. Longman wrote:

> Dearest Vally,
>
> . . . I'm sorry you do not like its nudity; but you see, it represents a perfectly elemental, natural force, namely electricity, and I cannot imagine any kind of drapery or clothing which would not detract from its force and simplicity.[33]

Vally's third child, Mildred Valley Stinson, also was an artist, a painter. As her aunts and uncles did, she attended Olivet College, and then the Art Institute of Chicago, ten years after Longman graduated. She was among some European and Canadian artists at the time who were interested in preserving aboriginal cultures with "paint and brush." She painted three hundred portraits of native people in Saskatchewan and British Columbia.[34]

By 1931, Longman had completed two more public works: a seated workman, *Industry*, installed at Hartford's Trade School, and *Service to Mankind*, at Boston's English High School, the first public high school in the United States. *Industry* is a boxy, hefty-looking monument, with a man, dressed in work clothes, seated in a chair atop a large pedestal. One hand resting on the side of his face, intensely concentrating, he reads a schematic, which he holds in his lap with his other hand. Commissioned by the Connecticut Manufacturers Association, the pedestal's inscription honors Hartford's "industrial pioneers," while Longman's model of the working man honors those who were employed by the industrial pioneers.

About her *Service to Mankind*, which French had encouraged her to submit, Batchelder liked to say that Longman and French only turned their backs to each other once—in their companion pieces: *Service*, and French's *Alma Mater and the Student*—which were installed at either end of a hall in the high school. In Longman's group, a soldier helps an exhausted youth who is leaning against him.

On Batchelder's fifty-first birthday, in June of 1931, Longman wrote to him:

> it is only eleven years (nearly) since our marriage—and real living began for me then.
>
> Dearest, I wish the group "Service," upon which I am now working, might be dedicated to you publicly—as it is dedicated in my heart. Nothing which I have done so well symbolizes your life and work—the dominant strength—the indignation against wrong—the tenderness toward the unfortunate—especially in relation to youth.[35]

What's more, Longman revealed the impact Batchelder and their marriage had on her work:

> It seems impossible that I could have done these later works had we not known and loved each other. Those who speak loosely of the bondage of marriage know nothing of a beautiful union. My work in general has been freer in spirit ever since I knew you.

And she admitted a sense of her own lack:

> I wish I could think that I had helped you equally. Perhaps, if commissions do not come so fast in the future, I can do better. My love, whole-hearted and devoted, is yours always.
>
> Your too-busy wife,
> Evelyn Beatrice[36]

In June, Dan French wrote his last letter to Longman. It ended: "Nothing doing in the studio for the first time in its history, but Andromeda is expected presently, in marble. Do come over! Affectionately, Daniel."[37]

Longman wrote at the bottom of his letter, "We did go over—about the middle of Sept.—The last time I saw my beloved friend." He had suffered a heart attack that fall, refused hospitalization, and was too weak to work, leaving his clay model of Daniel Webster and *Andromeda* unfinished.

Daniel Chester French died in his sleep on the morning of October 7, with Mary at his side. Accolades poured in, as did friends, to Chesterwood, where Margaret had arranged the funeral service in his studio, surrounded by his work, including a plaster *Lincoln*—and, as now, a plaster of ideal *Longman* on the corner of a high shelf. Interestingly, while all other pieces of sculpture on that shelf face outward, Longman's portrait faces to the side, toward the plaster *Lincoln.*

The place was packed. Longman and Batchelder sat in the French family group. He was later cremated, his ashes spread at Concord, that little bastion of exceptional minds where his life luckily had begun.

Gone was Longman's teacher, her beloved friend, her closest colleague. From French's first take of Longman—hat feather accentuating her "dangerous" eyes—to his prophetic advice—"Write it large on the wall."—the influence of French on Longman was met by Longman's influence on French: "Pleeeease come . . ." Dana Pilson, curatorial researcher at Chesterwood, has studied and written about the French-Longman motif-sharing.[38] As with other artists, who commonly exchange motifs and ideas (though less common between artists of opposite gender), so it was with these two colleagues. Indeed, their corresponding works are a lasting tribute to that rare relationship.

Even with the ups and downs of a decades-long era that began for her in 1930, Longman always considered herself a happy person. And so she was, at the age of fifty-seven, sculpting in suburban Connecticut, living at a boys' prep school; mother of a teenager and wife of a headmaster, sailing around Cape Cod. Never one to avoid trouble, she was about to face, and create, challenges that would bring her nose-to-nose with her legacy.

NOTES

1. DCF to John Quincy Adams Ward, July 6, 1904, Chesterwood Archives; Chapin Library, Williams College, Gift of the National Trust for Historic Preservation/Chesterwood, a National Trust Historic Site, Stockbridge, Massachusetts.
2. EBL to William J. Drake, March 8, 1939, Loomis Chaffee. "I am the only sculptor who ever worked from life on Mr. Edison."
3. Rabetz, 8. Authors say Edison called her his "little girl."
4. Before he and Longman met, Henry Bacon was working for the McKim, Mead and White architectural firm when they designed Adams's power stations.
5. *Elizabeth*, ca. 1927, Richmond Art Center, Loomis Chaffee.
6. EBL to Edward Dean Adams, November 30, 1928, Loomis Chaffee.
7. EDA to EBL, December 14, 1929, Loomis Chaffee.
8. Mina M. Edison to George F. Morris, December 4, 1929, Loomis Chaffee.
9. EDA to EBL, December 14, 1929, Loomis Chaffee.

10. EBL to NHB, March 3, 1930, Loomis Chaffee.
11. EBL to NHB, March 4, 1920, Loomis Chaffee.
12. Ibid.
13. EBL to NHB, second letter on March 4, 1930, Loomis Chaffee.
14. Ibid.
15. Ibid.
16. EBL to NHB, March 6, 1930, Loomis Chaffee.
17. EBL to NHB, March 7, 1930, Loomis Chaffee.
18. Ibid.
19. EBL to NHB, March 10, 1930, Loomis Chaffee.
20. Ibid.
21. Ibid.
22. NHB to Edwin Barrie, January 11, 1932, Loomis Chaffee.
23. "J.C.B., Deutsches Museum" to EBL, undated, Loomis Chaffee.
24. EBL to Newcom Carlton, January 3, 1931, Loomis Chaffee.
25. Skip's unpublished memoir, Loomis Chaffee.
26. Ed Longman to EBL, May 13, 1906, Loomis Chaffee.
27. Ibid.
28. EBL to Vally Stinson, March 12, 1947, Bonnie French.
29. EBL to VS, Christmas 1936, Bonnie French.
30. Claude Longman to EBL, undated, "Dear Little Sis . . . ," Loomis Chaffee.
31. Cecil Longman to EBL, February 8, 1907, Loomis Chaffee.
32. Telephone interview with Bonnie French, August 13, 2018.
33. EBL to Vally Stinson, December 18, 1938, Loomis Chaffee.
34. For information about Mildred Stinson Thornton, see https://web.archive.org/web/20090207111453/ and http://westbridge-fineart.com/thornton.htm.
35. EBL to NHB, June 13, 1931, Loomis Chaffee.
36. Ibid.
37. DCF to EBL, June 25, 1931, Loomis Chaffee.
38. Dana Pilson, "Writing Large on the Wall," *Fine Art Connoisseur* Volume 18 Issue 3, May/June 2021. Also, see online exhibition at https://www.chesterwood.org/Longman-beatrice-longman.

Chapter 25

Trouble

Mrs. Batchelder is not totally without a sense of importance of money, but she cares even more about her professional reputation, to which a successful placing of this bust may contribute substantially.

—Nathaniel Horton Batchelder

Longman hung her second one-woman show at the Grand Central Art Galleries, in January 1932. Welcoming guests from the cover of the exhibition brochure would be *Song of the Pines*—as with *Victory* and *Electricity*, another young man on tiptoes, with outstretched arms, this one holding a lyre, singing his heart out. The portraits she chose to exhibit included those of wealthy New York connections; selling art during the Great Depression would depend on these folks more than usual. So, here were a portrait relief of George Foster Peabody; the marble bas-relief of the de Forests; the young *John D. Rockefeller III*; and several portraits of Loomis alums.

But also, strikingly, here was a group of African Americans: *Robert Moton*, *John Wainwright*, and *St. Helena Island Girl*. In an interesting placement, *Ideal Head* was positioned against the opposite wall: a hollow mask of a woman's scarf-wrapped, raised head; her eyes lowered; the sculpture was cut in dark, poly-chromed marble. Also called *Fragment*, a cast of it had been exhibited at one of French's Stockbridge Art Association exhibitions, where it had sold to a Loomis alum who hadn't realized that Evelyn Beatrice Longman was "Mrs. B." Longman had worked on *Ideal Head* as a study when she was an assistant in French's studio and recently had it cut. French called it "One of your best."[1]

Ideal figures—*Consecration*, *Nature*, and *Aenigma*—were placed together in one room. Longman also exhibited a small model of *Industry* installed at the A.I. Prince Technical High School in Hartford, and a smaller version of her Munich *Thomas Edison*—an 8 1/2-inch bronze, priced at $750. (A twelve-inch cast could be had for nine hundred dollars.)[2]

For the opening reception, Longman envisioned the feel of an informal Loomis get-together, with school alumni, friends, and patrons who lived in the New York City area. Roberta Thomas, wife of architect Fredric C. Thomas, class of 1921, of Coldspring Harbor, Long Island, would pour tea.

Once again, gallery director Edwin Barrie told Longman her latest exhibition at the Grand Central Art Galleries was "very greatly admired indeed and I have heard no unfavorable comments. I, personally, think it is one of the finest and most important one-man exhibitions we have ever had in our Galleries."[3]

A *New York Times* art critic disagreed. In a scathing review, her kindest words, a backhanded compliment, were for Longman's portraits: "Miss Longman is a competent portraitist, as her busts of George Foster Peabody and Thomas Alva Edison bear witness," and *Aenigma*, she wrote, has a "certain undeniable, if obviously derivative, charm."

It got worse: "When Miss Longman essays symbolism, however, the reviewer is torn between tears and laughter. The oversize youth who reads a newspaper, quite oblivious of the mechanical gadgets at his feet, is labeled 'Industry.'" The critic evidently mistook the schematics Longman had the man poring over, for a newspaper.

"An armed warrior with gritted teeth and clenched fist supports on his chest a lad suffering from fatigue; this is called 'Service to Mankind.' An incredibly ungraceful female, inspired, but how remotely, by the Victory of Samothrace, is 'Columbia Victorious,' and an uncomfortable, open-mouthed youth with a lute is the 'Song of the Pines.'"

Finally, the insult that must have stung most: "Miss Longman's masterpiece of bathos, however, is her 'Consecration.'"[4]

Daniel Chester French was not around to console.

Barrie, in a letter addressed to Batchelder, wrote from the Galleries: "Unfortunately, there are a certain number of young people writing for art pages and associated with museums that are trying to be smart and ultramodern but I find that most of the substantial people of the world appraise their efforts about as you have the article in the Times."[5]

If public criticism—new to Longman—was more evidence that the tide was turning away from classical, allegorical, figurative art, she was undeterred in tenaciously creating beauty her way. At this point, her greatest ambition was to create beauty in two monumental ideal statues. As with her smaller ideal works, she would proceed without commissions or an idea of where the sculpture would be installed. Storing smaller ideal statues was not a problem. But a huge space had to be found for monumental works, so

Longman was setting herself—and Batchelder—up for significant challenges, especially considering the Great Depression and the eventual World War II years.

Her plan for *The Good Samaritan*, (or "the angel"), with Batchelder's face, ministering to a sick man, was to find placement and then begin the two-year process of enlarging the group. Ever attuned and ever dedicated to Longman's efforts, Batchelder already had approached a former Harvard classmate about the possibility of Harvard commissioning a monumental "angel." While Longman considered it an ideal of compassion and service, a more pragmatic Batchelder saw the possibility of placing it as the World War I Memorial that Harvard was considering. He wrote to Colonel Arthur Woods, who had visited the studio and admired the smaller study: "It represents the purpose with which many of us went into the war, and is free from the conventional and hackneyed symbols of many war monuments."[6]

Instead, Harvard eventually rebuilt a chapel as their War Memorial and installed in its Memorial Room *The Sacrifice*, Malvina Hoffman's marble sculpture of a mother praying to heaven at the head of a fallen soldier.[7]

Others who saw Longman's angel when visiting Chiselhurst praised it. Batchelder replied to one admirer:

> Many have loved it, but none have yet been able to arrange for its erection. Mrs. Batchelder's hope has always been to have this done in heroic size, with a somewhat splendid setting. She likes it better than almost anything she has ever done, and she would like the execution and placing of it to be not pretentious, but at least quite handsome. Unfortunately, all these things cost money, and I am afraid that in these days money is hard to raise.[8]

While others may have loved the work, Howard Bement was rhapsodic in a letter he wrote to Longman: "I don't believe you have the slightest idea of what my visit to your studio did to me. It was a great spiritual experience. . . . I have seen most of the great art of the European galleries, and have responded to it with what I am sure is a keen sense of appreciation, but seldom has even great sculpture stirred my feelings. . . . Here in your work was combined, as I had never seen them combined before, beauty, sentiment, and eloquence."[9]

So much for bathos, in his view.

Bement had visited Longman to enlist her to create a medal of appreciation for Philip Clarke, a banker and generous trustee for the Asheville School, in Asheville, North Carolina, where Bement was headmaster. Having experienced *The Good Samaritan*, he decided he wanted to give it to Clarke instead of a medal. Longman agreed to have a reduction cast for him, lowering her normal price and with the caveat that she could make a bigger one at some point. "I am almost as anxious for you to have 'The Good Samaritan' as you are to have it yourself. An artist thrives on appreciation of her work, and your evident joy is a continuing source of pleasure for me."[10]

"Mrs. Batchelder is almost as happy as you are over the outcome," Batchelder wrote to Bement. "She is quite the most generous person I ever knew, and will do anything she can for appreciative people."[11] The recipient, Clarke, wrote: "I'm hopeful the extent to which I shall always cherish it will ultimately justify my undeserved possession of so lovely a thing."[12]

There would be another war before Batchelder would find a place for a colossal angel. As he cast about to memorial committees from Boston to Los Angeles, Longman looked for other creative opportunities, competing to create a façade for the new neoclassical federal building in Hartford that would house the post office. It would be one of the first public works projects of the Great Depression. As she had years before in her first commission, she won this one—her last—once more, as she had all of them, against men. Her sketch depicted two mail carriers meeting on horseback to hand off the mail. The work of art on the front of the building would be fifty-five feet above the sidewalk.

As she had with the doors of the Naval Academy chapel, she committed to something she'd never done before. Unlike those doors, however, and unlike her many other bas-reliefs, at which she was exceptionally accomplished at this point, this thirty-four-foot-tall relief would be one-dimensional, requiring a shallow cut into limestone. She would take on portraying animals for the first time (other than small renderings of storybook characters). Most notably, she would give a nod to a contemporary style; the large horses would have Art Deco flourishes.

To create a work that was more than a simple line drawing in stone, Longman visited The Metropolitan Museum of Art to study Greek and Egyptian incising. She worked out her own method, using a v-shaped cut, at varying depths and widths, designing the image around the seams of twenty-four limestone slabs so that the joints wouldn't cross the riders' heads.

Again, the project became a family effort; she included her Loomis family and her Batchelder family. Osgood Batchelder, Batchelder's brother, filmed a Loomis alum riding a horse in a meadow. The captain of the Loomis football team posed for one of the riders, as did a swim instructor and Skip's sailing teacher. It was no doubt Loomis carpenters who built a black box three feet square and twelve feet long with a projector at one end and a screen at the other to show the film in Longman's light-flooded studio. She also spent many hours drawing trotting horses at a nearby farm on Cape Cod.

When post office officials couldn't come up with a fitting inscription, Longman and Batchelder conferred with Loomis Latin teacher John Edmund Barss. Government officials approved his inscription. A Loomis alum earning money for college had prepared the plastiline surface—six inches deep and eighteen feet long—and marked the surface where the stone seams would be, as well as the letters on either side of Longman's horses. Batchelder, donning a blue apron as Longman's "first assistant," incised the plastiline model alongside his wife.[13]

Using the v-shaped tool, she etched into the plastilene, making deeper and wider cuts to create a sense of depth, on the flat surface. Longman worked on the model in her studio from September to December of 1932. After a plaster mold of the plastilene was made, studio assistants used it to enlarge the image on the stone façade. It would take four or five cutters standing on scaffolding above Hartford's High Street, behind sheets of canvas to protect them from winter weather, another eight weeks to chisel the work.

The building was dedicated in 1933. Though it no longer houses the post office (rather, the IRS), Longman's relief—the closest she came to making abstract art—remains.

During Christmas break of 1935, as the Great Depression had slowed commissions, Longman took a step that would guarantee an even greater challenge for her supportive manager of a husband. She got out her measurements and her photos of Thomas Edison and began work on a monumental-sized model of the famous inventor. For Longman, it would be an ideal figure—her biggest; her last—a "masterpiece," of "creative genius."

> Batchelder, still trying to place the gargantuan angel, evidently saw the writing on the wall and repeatedly asked, "But what are you going to do with it?"
>
> Longman's reply was: "I don't know. I only know that I have wanted to do it for years—that I must do it, and that I have the needful time now."[14]

Since her "memorable sojourn in Florida years ago" to model the portrait of Edison, she wrote to Barstow, "I have been filled with a strong urge to do another one just as soon as commissions permitted. . . . That time never came until this winter . . . and immediately after Christmas I began work on a new Edison, and have been at it enthusiastically—madly—ever since."[15]

She told Barstow she had worked the past several weeks "as I have seldom worked before to create what I believe will be truly a masterpiece of portraiture. . . . This work is large—the head three and a half feet high on a base over two feet tall, intended to thoroughly dominate, as a smaller head could never do, any place, outside or in, where it might go. This is the very Spirit of Invention—Edison, the driving force, with the indomitable mouth and the far-seeing light of genius in his eye. The head alone is shown; such a Spirit is timeless and should not be 'dated' by clothes. The base is formed by conventionalized clouds, one shaft of lightning flashing across them. The idea is 'Genius rising from the Eternal Elements.'"[16]

Perhaps Barstow would help find a setting for it. "Of course, next to the joy of creating a thing, the artist's greatest concern is a permanent place for it," she wrote him. "I see this head placed high, perhaps against the rear wall opposite the entrance of a spacious and high interior, where a splendid light from above could be arranged for both day and night, impressive far beyond the power of a mere portrait, however good, and dominating not only by forcefulness of personality and intensity of expression, but also by size, everything in that interior—as Edison dominated in his lifetime."[17]

Another person who might help with placement was Henry Ford, she wrote to Barstow. "Mr. Ford is the individual who could do this in a big way if he felt so inspired." And there was the upcoming Tricentennial World's Fair; perhaps electrical associations might use such a portrait as the nucleus of their display. If so, her head might be enlarged further for outdoor viewing. Better yet, she suggested to Barstow, perhaps her larger Edison could be installed at a proposed Edison Memorial in Menlo Park, New Jersey, in the room where Edison's inventions would be displayed; there she could see the head as "a pervading spirit and crowning glory."[18]

Figure 25.1 Longman's colossal Edison, which she considered a masterpiece, is her ideal portrayal of creative genius. Source/Credit: Photograph from the collection of the Loomis Chaffee Archives, Loomis Chaffee School, Windsor, Connecticut USA.

She suggested that an architect be employed at the outset to work with her in creating a setting, and she encouraged Barstow to come see her new *Edison* himself, even in its unfinished form, promising to meet him at the train and provide food and lodging at the Head's House.

A month later, near the beginning of Loomis's spring break, heavy rains began to fall, and Batchelder announced an early start to school vacation. At 4 p.m., as dams along the Connecticut River gave way, students were quickly delivered to the train station, just as the campus, surrounded by water, became a real island. The 6:08 train never came, so the boys hid themselves in case school staff came to take them back to campus. Finally, a train, rerouted around the flood, arrived, and the boys arrived in New York at 1:30 a.m.

Students in the infirmary who could walk were wrapped in blankets and transported the next morning by boat; three others were carried out on stretchers and set in the outboard motorboat. School buildings had two to four feet of water in their basements; faculty were without electricity and heat for days. The first night, remaining faculty, staff, and families were treated to a community meal of steaks—on hand to serve 270 people at an athletic banquet that evening—now canceled without notice. Chef Albenge cooked the steaks on a kerosene stove and open fire in the fireplace of the dining room; the steaks were the primary nourishment for those remaining at Loomis for days to come.

The gymnasium and Longman's studio were most damaged in the flood. As the waters began to rise, pieces of sculpture were moved to higher ground in her studio. But by 10 p.m., Batchelder realized they hadn't been moved high enough. He and the man who served as butler took flashlights and rowed in a boat into Longman's studio; they managed to rescue Henry Bacon's first sketch of the Lincoln Memorial and a plastiline bust of Horace Taft "stripped of shoulders to save weight and brought out unharmed, smiling the characteristic Taft smile," Batchelder later reported in the *Loomis Alumni Bulletin*.

Skip was at Harvard by then, but he and his childhood friend Don Smith, perhaps home during their spring break, each wrote of their experiences during the flood. "Mrs. B was concerned over the damage to the studio," Smith wrote. "What would happen to the incomplete Edison's bust . . . in the middle of the studio? The flood water was then up to his nose."[19]

Skip and Smith paddled the rowboat into the studio. "We found it rather exciting to be actually afloat in the studio that was normally on dry land," Skip wrote. "We rowed about to retrieve things like floating wooden step ladders, one of which was bashing into the bottom of Mr. Edison, then done in plasteline. . . . I am proud to say that Don and I rescued Mr. Edison from the bashing of that floating stepladder."[20]

The campus, with an ample supply of firewood, remained without electricity and heat on the sixth day. The water was still high, but it had receded to the point that it was just below the front porch of Longman's studio. "When the waters receded," Don Smith wrote, "Edison's face had dropped over three feet—rested there in gloom."

There had been five feet of water in the studio; the floor had to be replaced, the walls had to dry, which took a while as the moisture had collected in the bricks. Longman couldn't work in her studio for months.

The Loomis gardener's home was ruined in the flood. Longman was instrumental in getting the family moved to a home on higher ground and refurnishing it. She was on hand the day the family moved in. The grateful gardener's wife and Longman exchanged a warm embrace and kisses.[21]

In 1938, Batchelder enlisted William Conklin, a New York City lawyer, to help find a patron for the *Edison*. Conklin, under the direction of John D. Rockefeller Jr., had set up a bank in Harlem for African Americans (with African American employees and white executives). Batchelder wrote Conklin that the colossal *Edison* had been cast in plaster, and Longman was altering it to a greater height and tipping it slightly forward to look down on the beholder. He encouraged Conklin to bring people to Windsor to see the bust in its new manifestation. Longman "has put her heart into this work, and she wants to see it executed."[22]

People came, eventually. In 1940, George J. Giger, who was on the Edison Park Commission, visited Windsor to view the colossal *Edison* and planned to bring other members of the Commission. Importantly, he brought John Coakley, advertising manager of Thomas A. Edison, Inc. Giger expressed his hope that Coakley would help secure an "active interest in your fine work" and that he might "bring about a greater interest from the Edison family to help us carry on the plan of having the bust cast in bronze and suitably erected."[23] Nothing came of Coakley's visit—until 1945, when he planned to include Longman's colossal *Edison* in his agenda for the Edison centennial birthday celebration coming up in two years.

Longman wrote to Coakley, evidently to make sure he understood the value of her work:

> This is not a mere portrait bust. It is a monument to a great personality which must be seen to be appreciated, to which creation I gave the greater part of four years of hard work, and everything I have of artistic ability, coupled with admiration and affection which I learned to feel for Mr. Edison during the two weeks spent in his private laboratory in Fort Myers, Fla., while I was working on the bust commissioned for the Deutsches Museum in Munich.[24]

The work had grown another six inches.

> I call this monument "Genius rising from the elements," it being just the head and neck emerging from a base of rocks. I felt it should be timeless and not

"dated" by clothes. The height over-all is about six feet, the head itself somewhat over four feet—really colossal. It is suitable for erection out of doors, or indoors if the place has sufficient size and height. If it is to be used, I should wish to see possible sites, and to advise about pedestal, lighting, and so on.[25]

While the potential opportunity to show the Edison at the Centennial Celebration might have led to permanent placement, there was certainly no guarantee. Meanwhile, Longman and Batchelder continued to pursue every possible connection. Coakley, whose son, John, was a student at Loomis at the time, raised the possibility of placing the huge figure in Milan, Ohio, Edison's birthplace. Longman agreed that "the simple, little house in which the genius was born and this powerful presentation of his mature personality would make a fine combination."[26] But if it were to go there, other copies should be placed elsewhere. Impelled by her work with Peabody, she now suggested a wholesale lot of colossal Edisons to Coakley:

> I think it would be a pity if the bust were not somewhere also, too, certainly somewhere in the East—at Menlo Park or, as you had suggested, in Central Park, or some other place where it might be readily seen by people in the metropolitan area. It has inevitably occurred to me, also, that Mr. Ford might be interested to have a copy of the bust at Dearborn.
>
> I don't want to suggest wholesaling the bust, but, really, it is a pity, when a great work of art has been created, to have a unique copy at large cost, when successive copies could be made for much less than the original and the work seen by many more people. Sculpture in this respect is quite different from painting, because there is a faithful process of reproduction, and one copy is as authentic as another.[27]

She had earlier estimated that her cost for the colossal Edison in bronze would be thirty-five thousand dollars. An updated cost for the bronze casting was more favorable and she offered to have it delivered to a selected site for twenty-five thousand dollars. Included would be her consultation for the setting and the cost of placing the bust. "If it can be arranged that there are two busts, I will provide them, delivered to the sites . . . for a total of $37,500."[28] Three busts would be forty-five thousand dollars. And she offered to stick to those prices for the foreseeable future unless the casting costs increased drastically.

Coakley reported in the fall of 1946 that a vice president of the Edison Foundation was "very much interested" but urged, we "keep it in the back of our heads for the future. It is very easy to insist that something be done about it, yet very hard to find someone who has the wherewithal to do the something."[29]

He suggested placement more locally, in Hartford, "which would at least accomplish the first step of our objectives—to see the bust cast in bronze.

"I have had other acknowledgments . . . which are highly commendatory, but all feel that there are too many steps which must be first accomplished before we can progress to the stage of preparing plans for monuments. I knew that this would be the case, so I am not impatient with the situation. It is a matter that must be pursued with both caution and patience."[30]

Of another Coakley idea, and Longman's happy assent, that the colossal *Edison* be placed in New York City's Central Park, Robert Moses, the commissioner of parks in New York City, wrote that while he considered the idea of a bust of Edison in Central Park or some other city park an "excellent one," he reported that it was "absolutely futile" that the City would appropriate funds for it. He suggested Edison associates foot the bill, which he estimated would be fifty thousand dollars, for casting the bust in bronze and installing it.[31]

While the search for placement of Longman's angel and her colossal *Edison* continued, as resources for commissions dwindled, Longman sculpted portraits of friends. Using sandblasting, she created a delicately lovely pine tree and ocean waves in a Deco style on a memorial in Beechwood Cemetery, Barnstable, Massachusetts, for the Hinkle family. Around the same time, she modeled a life-sized, colored plaster portrait in high relief mounted on wood of her friend Jean Hinkle, of Osterville.

In honor of another Cape Cod neighbor, she modeled a bust of Harvard economics professor F. W. Taussig. Taussig's children paid for the bronze casting; Longman donated her time. When Harvard accepted the bust, she then offered to make a companion piece, of Harvard president Lawrence Lowell, another Cape neighbor. Harvard said it had no funds for purchasing art, but they would find a place for a donated sculpture of "the most brilliant and successful teacher of government that we have ever had."[32]

Thomas Sovereign Gates, president of the University of Pennsylvania, wanted to gift the bust of Lowell to the Cambridge university, as a gift from his university. Harvard accepted.

In return, Lowell asked Longman to make a bust of Gates, which presented her with a quandary. She had been paid five thousand dollars for the Munich *Edison*. Her "standard" price for a bust was four thousand dollars. When artists lowered their fees during the Depression, she had lowered hers by 25 percent. She had charged three thousand dollars for a recent bronze bust of Batchelder's colleague, Taft School founder, Horace Taft. At this point, in 1941, artists were reducing their prices again; Longman would charge someone she didn't know $2,500 for a bust. But this was someone she did know—plus, she felt a debt to the subject, Thomas Gates, because he had given Skip a trip to California to sail with his stepson in the International Star Class races. She considered one thousand dollars. . . .

All three educators' busts were placed and dedicated later that year. And then matters got worse.

As the United States entered World War II, the Office of Production Management prohibited the use of copper, one of two main substances in bronze, for making statues, beginning January 1, 1942. Copper, already in short supply, would be needed for making shells. Paul Manship, president of the National Sculpture Society, requested an exemption for the small number of sculptors in the country, suggesting they wouldn't have to use "virgin bronze . . . but rather that the use of scrap metal will suffice."[33]

Longman sent a letter as well: "I should be the last to want to impede the program of our defense efforts, but I wonder if it is not possible to permit the use of scrap metal for art casting instead of eliminating the process altogether."[34]

Gargani Foundry, where Longman had many pieces cast, stopped all castings, writing to Longman that they had received notice from the Office of Production Management that the use of copper and copper-based alloys had been prohibited for statuary castings.[35]

The Medallic Art Company, another foundry that created castings for Longman, got so much government work that they couldn't do castings even when Batchelder rounded up some used copper. All their castings went to the government. They offered Longman a silver replica or a plastic cast painted in bronze. Longman considered those possibilities and determined the plastic cast details were too "soft." She did, however, turn to the Galvano "electrolytic method" for creating three silver reliefs. "It is somewhat more expensive than bronze, but, properly toned and lacquered, it is serviceable indoors and quite handsome."[36]

Gargani, whose two sons were in the service, didn't get government contracts, and he closed his business in October 1942. Batchelder offered to send some copper from half-tone plates and a fourteen-pound bronze head from Europe.[37] He did send the bronze head and fifteen pounds of copper so that Gargani could have another foundry cast a small bowl with a nude figure Longman had modeled.[38]

A few small commissions were delayed indefinitely. Not one to sit and wait, Longman met with a professor in charge of the ceramics department at MIT to consider a gold-leafed, non-shrinking terra cotta, but the professor's kiln was too small for her model.[39] And she worked on small projects that could be put in plaster and placed on hold until bronze was available, including a bas-relief portrait of Skip; his wife, Elizabeth ("Betty"); and their first child, Hope.[40]

There were, naturally, immense changes at Loomis during World War II. Some faculty and students served in the war, and some were killed. Facing labor and many other shortages, students pitched in around campus in new ways. There were only intramural sports; no traveling. The school's gardens and farming operations provided a diet primarily of milk, eggs, and a variety of vegetables. Batchelder and Longman shut up parts of the large Headmaster's House and did much of their own cooking. For a few months in 1943–1944, a Japanese author and teacher, Kanjitsu Lijima; his American-born wife, Kyoko; and their two children were released from an internment camp to do domestic work and live on the third floor of the Head's House.[41] Inspired to work for world peace, an idea supported by Batchelder, who was president of the Connecticut Peace Conference in 1942–1943, Kanjitsu left employment at Loomis to attend seminary. Batchelder and Longman were on their own again.

Finally, more than fifteen years from conception and with ongoing efforts to have her giant genius installed publicly, Longman's heroic bust of *Edison* at least would get a brief public showing—for the centennial celebration of the inventor's birth, on February 11, 1947. Held under the sponsorship of the Naval Research Lab, which Edison had established for government research outside of Washington, D.C., the exhibit of Longman's colossal bust would no doubt grab attention while ensconced on the landing of a broad flight of stairs leading to the Museum of Science and Industry in Rockefeller Center, New York City. Among the thousands who would pass by it, perhaps finally someone would instigate its purchase.

Longman and Batchelder had, of course, considered the logistical challenges of moving the giant. She created a removable section of the plaster model at the top of the head. Inside the opening, she attached two crossed pipes so that a hook could get a firm grip to lift it.

In copious communication with the Edison Centennial Committee, the Museum, Rockefeller Center, a Hartford trucking firm, a New York rigging company, and Longman's onetime assistant, sculptor George Lober, plans for installation were set. Batchelder sent out a mimeographed minute-by-minute schedule of the installation.

It began one night, a week before the celebration, during what turned out to be another dramatic weather event, a winter storm. Longman and Batchelder left that afternoon for New York City to be at the museum by 7:30 the next morning. The city was jammed that evening, and they ended up in an unfamiliar hotel. When they called back to Loomis, they learned that the Hartford trucking firm hadn't brought a big enough truck. After business hours, Batchelder's secretary and the school business manager had to find another trucking company. Loomis students helped load the crated bust onto the last-minute truck, which carried its precious cargo over slick roads for eight hours. Longman and Batchelder spent an anxious night wondering if *Edison* would arrive safely.

It did, and the rigging company was on time the next morning so that the enormous head could be moved indoors before office workers reported for duty at 8 a.m. However, the door clearance measurements the Rockefeller Center employees had given Batchelder didn't take into account the large brass hinges. The crate sat on the sidewalk in stormy wind, as the door and its hinges were removed.

The pedestal was wrangled through the doorway, but getting the head through was more challenging, and finally the base had to be shaved. The process of lifting the pedestal and head up the stairs to the landing was a challenge, too: It required different lengths of legs on the hoisting apparatus, and there were no places to tighten ropes along the way. Getting the head safely in place and favorably lit took all day, but at 5 p.m., Longman and Batchelder headed for home, "well-nigh exhausted."

It was especially nerve-racking for Longman, as the plaster cast was fragile. Already rebuilt in the plastilene from flood damage, there were reports of damage to the plaster—the left cheek—and later to the hair on one side, in the hauling of the huge piece to and from its placement in the museum.

In the two weeks while on exhibit, the ideal genius head did get attention, favorably. Coakley hired a film crew to create a newsreel before the piece was moved from the Windsor studio, and it was shown at the museum. Reporters covered a luncheon at the museum in which many luminaries were in attendance, including Longman, Batchelder, Mina Edison, and Charles Edison.

Longman reported the favorable reaction in yet another letter seeking permanent placement of the Edison head, this time to the president of the Fort Myers Chamber of Commerce: "Among those who saw it were the members of the Edison family and members of the Edison Centennial Committee. All of these people were very complimentary in their expressions of opinion as to the validity of the likeness and the grandeur of the sculpture as a whole."[42]

In spite of all the attention, there were no takers to purchase the mammoth head, and at the end of the two-week exhibition, Longman and Batchelder had it moved from the museum to the Modern Art Foundry on Long Island. The price of casting had increased, due to it being a little larger than the foundry had expected and due to employees' current demands for raises. However, concerned about damage to the vulnerable plaster, they decided to have it cast, at their own expense, for $2,250.

As the search for placement continued, Batchelder wrote to Winthrop Rockefeller, who had visited the museum and signed the guestbook. His ask was masterful:

> I presume the Rockefellers, officially or individually, can hardly escape solicitation for contributions to the Edison memorial projects. If you like the bust, it would be a great satisfaction to Mrs. B and me if the Edison Foundation were told that the portrait project had a certain priority in the collective Rockefeller mind. We would not think of asking you, because of friendship, to give the bust; nor would we think of asking you to increase the contribution that might otherwise be made to the Edison Memorial projects, merely suggest that whatever contribution would be made anyway might be applied to this particular memorial and not to some other.[43]

Carrying the cost of the casting, Batchelder upped the intensity of finding a buyer, and he and Longman hired Coakley in October 1947 as an exclusive agent, agreeing to his 25 percent fee. Longman was willing to take a cut in any payment to her, should he sell it for less; he would still get the 25 percent fee of the original price.

A year later, in a letter to Coakley, Batchelder put his finger on the fear at the root of this dilemma: "Mrs. Batchelder is not totally without a sense of importance of money, but she cares even more about her professional reputation, to which a successful placing of this bust may contribute substantially."[44]

The difficulty placing the colossal *Edison* and the angel had become a threat to Longman's legacy.

Following receipt of that letter, late in November, Coakley wrote optimistically, "at long last" he had a "strong nibble" for the purchase of the bust and its placement on the Village Green in Milan, Ohio, Edison's birthplace. Longman arranged for the bronze to be patinaed before the prospective clients viewed the bronze at the foundry.

But that nibble did not result in a sale. The relationship with Coakley grew more contentious. At one point, Coakley wrote to Batchelder, "You are the toughest sales manager I ever worked for."[45]

This was in response to a letter Batchelder had sent to him in which he had told Coakley, "I can't say we're desperate."[46]

Longman's legendary drive and determination to create beauty in her very big way had come up against a cultural shift in artistic preference, the Great Depression, and World War II.

NOTES

1. DCF to EBL, October 20, 1929, Loomis Chaffee.
2. NHB to William J. Drake, March 25, 1932, Loomis Chaffee.
3. Erwin S. Barrie to N.H.B., January 27, 1932.
4. K.G.B., "Sculpture by Evelyn Longman," *New York Times*, January 22, 1932.
5. Erwin S. Barrie to NHB, January 27, 1932, Loomis Chaffee.

6. NHB to Colonel Arthur Woods, February 29, 1924, Loomis Chaffee.
7. In 1922, Martha Bacon had donated it to Harvard to honor her husband, Robert, a Harvard alumnus who served as ambassador to France and on General Pershing's staff.
8. NHB to Mrs. James M. Grainger, February 12, 1932, Loomis Chaffee.
9. Howard Bement to EBL, February 15, 1934, Loomis Chaffee.
10. EBL to Bement, March 8, 1934, Loomis Chaffee.
11. NHB to Bement, March 19, 1934, Loomis Chaffee.
12. Philip R. Clarke to EBL, June 22, 1934, Loomis Chaffee.
13. Mary H. Dole, "Spirit of the Mails Immortalized in Stone," *Hartford Daily Courant*, January 1, 1933, 51.
14. EBL to William Barstow, February 17, 1936, Loomis Chaffee.
15. Ibid.
16. Ibid.
17. Ibid.
18. Ibid.
19. Don Smith, "Draft: Another Vignette of Loomis in the Days of Mr. and Mrs. Batchelder," Loomis Chaffee.
20. Skip's unpublished memoir, Loomis Chaffee.
21. J. Edgar Park, Longman's Memorial Bulletin, Loomis Chaffee.
22. NHB to William Conklin, August 17, 1938, Loomis Chaffee.
23. George J. Giger to EBL [no date], Loomis Chaffee.
24. EBL to John Coakley, September 17, 1945, Loomis Chaffee.
25. Ibid.
26. EBL to Coakley, June 15, 1946, Loomis Chaffee.
27. Ibid.
28. Ibid.
29. Coakley to EBL, October 28, 1946, Loomis Chaffee.
30. Ibid.
31. Robert Moses to Coakley [no date], Loomis Chaffee.
32. Jerome D. Greene to EBL, November 28, 1939, Loomis collection.
33. Paul Manship to Clarence Hewitt, November 6, 1941, Loomis Chaffee.
34. EBL to Hewitt, November 11, 1941, Loomis Chaffee.
35. Guido Gargani to EBL, December 10, 1941, Loomis Chaffee.
36. EBL to Pauline E. Epps, February 25, 1944, Loomis Chaffee.
37. NHB Gargani, October 13, 1942, Loomis Chaffee.
38. Batchelder to Gargani, October 30, 1942, Loomis Chaffee.
39. Batchelder letter to Georg Lober, April 3, 1942, Loomis Chaffee.
40. Nathaniel Batchelder "Skip" Batchelder graduated from Harvard in 1939 and married Betty Burnquist, a Wellesley College alumnus, in 1940.
41. Karen Parsons, "From Internment Camp to Headmaster's House," *Loomis Chaffee Magazine*. https://www.loomischaffee.org/archives/post/~board/archives/post/from-internment-camp-to-headmasters-house.
42. EBL to president, Chamber of Commerce, October 16, 1947, Loomis Chaffee.
43. NHB to Winthrop Rockefeller, February 21, 1947, Loomis Chaffee.

44. NHB to Coakley, November 26, 1948, Loomis Chaffee.
45. Coakley to NHB, January 28, 1949, Loomis Chaffee.
46. NHB to Coakley, January 27, 1949, Loomis Chaffee.

Chapter 26

Longman Sleeps

She smiled at the world until it had to smile back.

—Daniel Chester French[1]

At the close of Loomis chapel on the morning of February 26, 1949, students were told there would be a special assembly at 12:20 that day. They were not given a reason, but for the fifth period to be cut short, they knew there had to be a hefty purpose. Four students had been apprehended the night before during an illegal outing into Windsor; perhaps the headmaster had it in mind to use that misdeed to extol one more time the wisdom of following the rules.

As they gathered back in the chapel ten minutes before lunch break, they were on the lookout for Batchelder's menacing eyebrows. Eyebrows at ease, they were relieved to see the head did not look angry. Suspecting they were curious, Batchelder teased them that they might be expecting the announcement of a worst-case scenario. But he said, no, it wasn't about the students so much; rather it was about "Mrs. B" and himself—how at the end of every summer, they were less and less inclined to leave their home on Cape Cod just as the prettiest season was coming into its full splendor. This fall would be the fall they would stay. This was Horton Batchelder's way of announcing he and Longman would retire in June.

The Loomis congregation was experiencing the momentous end of a remarkable era. From its start, Batchelder, and now, after twenty-seven years, Evelyn Beatrice Longman Batchelder, seemed synonymous with Loomis School.

Batchelder cast his reassurance that a new headmaster as well as the faculty were extremely competent, that the school would be in good hands. This plan had been in the works for five years, Batchelder told them. Two things had to be accomplished before his retirement: establishing an endowment for the school, and Longman building the angel in monumental size—as a memorial to students who died in World Wars I and II. Both had been accomplished.

When Batchelder finished talking and nodded—the usual signal that students were dismissed—he turned to Longman, who stood to walk out with him. Spontaneously, the crowd rose to their feet, applauding. Thunderous and heartfelt, this benediction continued as Batchelder and Longman—smiling at the boys, faculty members—made their way down the center aisle and out of the chapel. They could still hear the ovation as they strolled the senior path toward the dining hall.[2]

Batchelder had seen to it that a one-million-dollar endowment goal was within reach. And Longman's five-ton bronze angel had been installed outside her studio and dedicated during graduation the previous June. It wasn't a highly visible location, nor, truth be known, Longman's first choice. But with some additional context, it was fitting that the Loomis trustees had accepted Longman's gift of her beloved angel-grown-huge, into a memorial for those of the school who had died in either war. Her small angel, the *Good Samaritan*, re-envisioned, resized, and renamed—*Victory of Mercy*—still symbolized compassion and service.

With help to build the giant armature and cover the plastilene, she had begun enlarging her angel and fallen man in October 1945.[3] In February 1946, Batchelder wrote in a letter that "In some ways it is one of the most complicated things she has ever done, but I think one of the most glorious.[4]

"Her monument for the boys lost in the war is an arduous task . . ." he wrote. "Curiously enough, in spite of her experience, this presents problems that Mrs. B didn't altogether anticipate."[5] It might be noted that, while there was no doubt of her ability, she had no French or Bacon or Bancroft to advise her during the building of her last two monumental, three-dimensional works.

Batchelder explained the symbolism in the group to a reporter for the *Hartford Courant*, something Longman probably wouldn't have done: "The prostrate figure might represent a fallen soldier or a prostrate nation. . . . The kneeling figure could be either the individual assistance offered by organizations of mercy . . . or . . . international assistance."[6]

In her new rendering, Longman placed the barrel of a cannon-sized gun under the head of the wounded man. "The gun barrel was selected as an instrument of war common to all the services, and it could represent any of them or war itself," Batchelder explained.[7]

Longman "happily" worked on the big figure, he said, and often called it "a labor of love."[8]

Following the war, Longman also inscripted another memorial for Loomis. It is a large tablet with the names of thirty-nine students, alumni, and faculty members who died in World War II. It remains on a wall outside the chapel.

During its development in her studio, onlookers and visitors praised the angel group at various times: "I am still carrying about in my soul, or 'inward eye,' or whatever you call it, the memory of your group—the cup of cold water and the restful poise of an angel's wing."[9]

"I have been haunted by the beauty of your 'Victory of Mercy.' Only three times in my life have I been so deeply moved."[10] This adoring visitor included a poem he wrote about the statue.

By the spring of 1947, the plaster was finished, and Batchelder negotiated shipment to the Modern Art Foundry on Long Island. Then, a delay: Former first lady Eleanor Roosevelt, chair of the United Nation's Commission on Human Rights, was expected at Longman's studio to see the huge angel. In early June, she had written that she actually couldn't come, that she was too busy at Lake Success, the New York village where the United Nations was meeting-based while their New York City headquarters was being built. Longman thought her angel would fit right in at the UN building, so one "no" wouldn't suffice. She wrote back to Eleanor Roosevelt with a detailed suggestion about traveling the sixty minutes to a meeting place where she and Batchelder would pick her up and drive her the rest of the way to Chiselhurst.

"Please don't think that I am over-insistent," Longman wrote. "I have just had so many people say to me that this work carries too great a message to be limited to the Loomis School that I feel I have to make some effort to have people in influential positions see it."[11]

Eleanor Roosevelt did not come. She referred the matter to Wallace K. Harrison, director of planning for the building of the UN headquarters. He wrote that upon Roosevelt's request, he would see that *Victory of Mercy* was given "every consideration" for installing in the new building.[12] But Longman's angel was not accepted, and plans for its installation at Loomis proceeded.

Batchelder arranged for the model to be delivered to the Long Island foundry by mid-August. The cast was expected to be installed for a June dedication during Graduation Week of 1948. By May, Longman hadn't seen the finished bronze. The installation site was prepared; the concrete and granite pedestal were installed. A nervous Batchelder inquired about its progress: The angel wings were being cast. Finally, the week before graduation, the monumental angel arrived. Delivery was complicated; Batchelder would be dealing with contested transport payments for months.

The huge memorial was finally installed the day before graduation. On the afternoon of June 11, following commencement and a Glee Club concert in the quadrangle, the Loomis community walked to Longman's studio, where

Figure 26.1 The hard-to-place monumental "Good Samaritan" became *Victory of Mercy* following World War II, and was given a fitting home outside Longman's studio at Loomis the year before the Batchelders retired to Cape Cod. Source/Credit: Photograph from the collection of the Loomis Chaffee Archives, Loomis Chaffee School, Windsor, Connecticut USA.

every year Batchelder and Longman hosted a farewell reception for graduates and their families. The crowd gathered outside in front of the draped monument. Student leaders pulled the cords on either side, slowly removing the cloth, which they then bundled up in their arms as they stood gazing at the giant angel and the fallen man. The audience was stone-silent.

Standing off to one side, Batchelder kissed Longman, and they walked into the studio to receive guests. So long in coming, Longman's colossal desire to create a colossal angel, and the colossal job of finding a home for it, was finally achieved.

Three months later, the board of trustees, in an official act of gratitude, gave Longman an illuminated copy of a resolution that declared, in part: "All the labor of the artist in its composition and completion is her lasting contribution to the memory of those who died, and to those who for unnumbered generations hence will, by its quiet eloquence, be nobler men and women. There is no measured value to that which lifts the spirit. Her works are cornerstones of the buildings that endure."[13]

Longman had already declared her retirement. But, characteristically, she continued to create small works people requested, including an emblem for Chaffee School and a fiftieth-anniversary medallion for Robert de Forest II.

The following year, again at graduation, the Loomis School celebrated Batchelder and Longman at the end of their reign. The alumni association gave them a new Buick. They completed their move to Cape Cod, where their house on Oyster Harbors featured a studio for Longman. She encouraged her grandchildren to dig into a wooden box and play with the plastiline amid *Destiny*, *Victory*, *Girl from St. Helena Island*, *Aenigma*, the plaster bust of their grandfather, and other sculptures in the studio, including French's marble portrait of her.

Placed thoughtfully, as if for one of her gallery exhibitions, *Song of the Pines* was set in the center of a circular driveway; *Peggy* stood on a wooden pedestal at the end of the driveway; the *Youth Eternal* fountain was in the yard outside the kitchen; the head of a laughing girl, reminiscent of *Bacchante/Peggy*, was a newel post on the staircase; and *Consecration* proclaimed a symbolic presence from a table in the front hall.

In 1950, Longman had a heart attack, and her health continued to deteriorate. The early years of poverty, the Triscuit years, the years and years and years of pushing her body . . . it was as if when she stopped working, her health finally did, too.[14]

Neither Batchelder nor Longman were on hand at the Naval Research Lab in Anacostia, Washington, D.C., in December 1952, when Charles Edison pulled a cord and the drapery tumbled off his father's colossal head, unveiling Longman's "masterpiece." Though it had taken more than fifteen years, the Edison Foundation had come through with funding, as John Coakley had hoped it would.

Coakley attended the dedication, and an hour later, waiting for a train at Union Station, he pulled out his legal pad and wrote a three-page letter relaying the celebration to Batchelder, who had given his representative detailed instructions about the installation. Coakley reported that there were two cases in which Batchelder's (or really, Longman's) instructions were not followed: Her signature was inscribed on the tall plinth rather than on the head's base; and, "despite the text of all the advance stuff I filed, Longman was referred to as the sculptress rather than sculptor."[15]

The *Evening Star*, which covered the event, also referenced Longman as a "sculptress."

Nevertheless, said Coakley, the moment Longman's *Edison* was unveiled was "wonderful! Somehow the whole thing was completely right."

Longman had explained her views about the monumental Edison much earlier to Henry Ford in a letter in which she tried to guilt and otherwise convince him to come to her studio to view her new rendition of Edison:

> It is colossal in size made so for two reasons: first, because the size itself helps to express the greatness of the man; and second, in order that it could never be placed anywhere perfunctorily.
>
> The head is the monument, and it is as much greater than the Munich bust in spirit as it is in size.[16]

She reminded Ford that Jacob Schmidlapp had brought him to her studio and that the auto manufacturer had invited her to Detroit, where he would give her a tour of his factory. In the letter, she told him she had been to Detroit, but hadn't wanted to inconvenience him. Now he could return the favor by coming to Windsor to see her mammoth statue of his friend.

Ford never came.

The setting at the Naval Research Lab, "the birthplace of radar," is simple but dramatic. Longman's huge—five-times-life-sized—head of Edison sits atop a fifteen-foot-tall granite plinth at the entrance of a "mall" leading west toward the Potomac River.[17] Nondescript (except for equipment on roofs), secretive, and formidable-appearing buildings line quiet streets of the campus.

His back to the mall, *Edison* faces the lab entrance's tall iron gate, opening, if you have clearance, to the high-security facility. (Without clearance, visitors can see *Edison* by looking between the gate's iron bars.)

Rather than the elegance of the white, bow-tied, marble, nearly-smiling *Edison* for the Deutsches Museum, this *Edison*, the "genius," still smiles slightly, yet it has the furrowed brow of someone looking unswervingly into a perplexing dilemma. Longman created the base to represent, in an abstract way, clouds with a break in them, as if lightning had struck.

"His face as you showed it was entirely satisfying to me as typifying his expression when he was somewhat worried over a problem, which was of course very frequently the case," wrote Thomas Robins, who had been secretary of the Naval Consulting Board (Edison had been president) when they sought two million dollars from Congress to construct the Naval Research Lab in the early 1920s. Edison had envisioned it as a "laboratory staffed by civilian scientists under Navy management, devoted to the scientific interests of the Navy."[18]

Robins also wrote: "My only desire is to express my complete satisfaction and pleasure in seeing such a beautiful piece of work as you have done in modeling this reproduction of my old friend who, as you know from your contact with him, was not only a great genius but a very sweet person."

Some of those on the committee to oversee the *Edison* bust for Munich, after seeing the larger piece, said they thought the "genius *Edison*" was greater.[19]

Charles Edison, former secretary of the navy and former New Jersey governor, wrote to Longman and Batchelder, as well:

> I want to tell you how awe-inspiring is the marvelous bust . . .
>
> I am truly sorry that it was impossible for either of you to be present. . . . I know that you too would have been thrilled by the occasion.
>
> It is a marvelous piece of art and Mrs. Batchelder can feel proud of having been the sculptress.[20]

Batchelder no doubt read Coakley's report, as well as the congratulatory messages to Longman. They had read to each other, to Skip, to Loomis students, and their grandchildren all their life together. Batchelder did all the reading now—not only news, but passages from their favorite authors. Every morning, they had breakfast in a sun-drenched window, watching light enliven the colors of the bay, the black duck family swimming about, the trees, the variety of birds at the feeders. Batchelder took Longman for drives to see friends, to explore the Cape, which sometimes turned into adventures, including one to a beach during the winter when he thought the sand would be frozen. It wasn't. Longman sat in the stuck Buick with the heater on while Batchelder trudged two miles for help.[21]

It was a trying time, especially the last year, when Longman could only say a few words. She had a new job, Batchelder reported: to let him, friends, a nurse, and a cook take care of her. At her memorial service, Batchelder explained that Longman had done that job with her characteristic charm. "Words were unnecessary; outstretched arms expressed welcome and an infectious laugh told of a happy spirit."[22]

During her many long naps, Batchelder wrote a history of the first fifty years of the Headmasters Association.[23] It was in her sleep that Longman died, at home, on March 10, 1954. Her funeral was held at the lovely old Barnstable Meeting House that she and Batchelder had been instrumental in restoring. *Song of the Pines*, the young man happily singing, greeted guests in the vestibule. A baritone, Job Negeim, was on hand to sing Handel's "Where'er You Walk"—"blushing flowers shall rise, and all things flourish where'er you turn your eyes."[24]

The woman who had created so many elegant cemetery memorials did not create one for herself, or her husband. Her ashes, as well as those of Batchelder, who died two years later, were spread at Chesterwood—in the glade where they had married.

In his eulogy to Longman, neighbor J. Edgar Park spoke of her character and the character of her sculpture, saying at last, "For she saw beauty in truth."

Painter Charles Vezin had written to her, "I know of no man or woman, ancient or modern, that makes the marble or the bronze breathe as do you."[25]

Marjorie Waite Peabody told Longman that in the portrait she did of her adopted father, "The nostril almost quivers with the breath of life, and the eye sees a vision."[26]

Daniel Chester French had told Batchelder that their Beatrice "smiled at the world until it had to smile back."

Longman, with Batchelder's incomparable help, had accomplished her most challenging ventures: her monumental ideal pieces still stand. Not at the

United Nations, but just outside her old studio, now a student residence, Longman Hall, *Victory of Mercy* speaks to young people, of compassion and service.

The colossal genius, *Edison*, looms not in New York City's Central Park, but in the very place scientists face every day outside of Washington, D.C., reminding them of the required wisdom and the gravitas of their work.

And so, after all, it is Longman who has the last word, speaking her truth in beauty. Her sculptures survive. More than fifty can be seen by the public, and

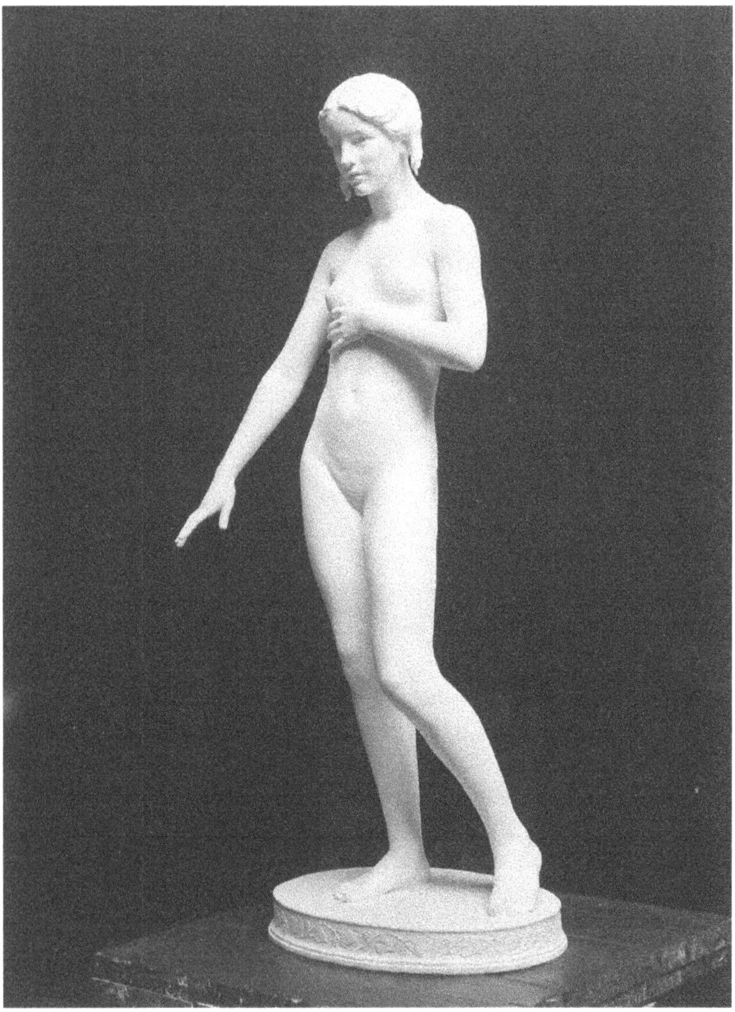

Figure 26.2 Longman's *The Future*. Source/Credit: Photograph by A.B. Bogart. From the collection of the Loomis Chaffee Archives, Loomis Chaffee School, Windsor, Connecticut USA.

at least seventy-five are in private collections. Three of her ideal sculptures remain—a fourth, unlocated, but, presumably, somewhere—still speaking for her, expressing her values, and, very likely, her hope for the world.

Consecration: a woman and man embracing
Nature: a woman contemplating the egg she holds
Destiny: a woman resting her head on her arm
The Future: a young woman, offering her hand

NOTES

1. NHB, unpublished memoir, Loomis Chaffee.
2. Frank O. Grubbs, *The Loomis Alumni Bulletin*, Volume XVII, Number 2, Winter 1949, 2–3.
3. EBL to Alexander Mascetti, October 3, 1945, Loomis Chaffee.
4. NHB to Mrs. S. Burton Buck, February 6, 1946, Loomis Chaffee.
5. NHB to "Jeannette," October 28, 1946, Loomis Chaffee.
6. "Headmaster's Wife Giving War Statue," *Hartford Courant*, November 10, 1945.
7. Ibid.
8. NHB to Mascetti, December 11, 1945, Loomis Chaffee.
9. Richard M. [indecipherable name], no date, Loomis Chaffee.
10. Lyman Bunnell to EBL, November 9, 1946, Loomis Chaffee.
11. EBL to Eleanor Roosevelt, June 17, 1947, Loomis Chaffee.
12. Wallace E. Harrison to EBL, June 12, 1947, Loomis Chaffee.
13. "Resolution of Appreciation," Loomis Chaffee.
14. This phenomenon has been observed in wheat farmers in Oklahoma. When the harvest and planting are done, farmers have their heart attacks.
15. Coakley to NHB, December 3, 1952, Loomis Chaffee.
16. EBL to Henry Ford, January 30, 1939, Loomis Chaffee. Longman wrote, beseechingly: "I am impatient waiting for the enthusiasm of others to blossom into action. You loved him; you have the power to do, and I believe the vision to see how great a memorial this would be—if you will see the bust."
17. "Rites Honoring Edison Discloses Navy Study of Signals from Space," *Washington Evening Star* [no date], Loomis Chaffee.
18. Thomas Robins to EBL, December 11, 1952, Loomis Chaffee.
19. EBL to Ford.
20. Charles Edison to EBL and NHB, January 13, 1953, Loomis Chaffee.
21. Skip's unpublished memoir, Loomis Chaffee.
22. NHB, "Evelyn Beatrice Longman" funeral bulletin, Loomis Chaffee.
23. Nathaniel Horton Batchelder, *The Headmasters' Association. A Half Century of Retrospect* (Falmouth, MA: Kendall Printing Company, 1955).
24. NHB, EBL's funeral booklet, Loomis Chaffee.
25. Charles Vezin to EBL, September 25, 1930, Loomis Chaffee.
26. Marjorie Waite to EBL, June 8, 1938, Loomis Chaffee.

Appendix

List of Longman Sculpture

This list of Longman's works gives a sense of the scope and intensity of her career. It is a work in progress, as the sculpture changes hands over time.

STUDENT WORKS AT THE ART INSTITUTE OF CHICAGO

Dorothy, 1899
Plaster portrait bust
Unknown location

Margaret, 1899
Plaster portrait bust
Unknown location

Sketch of Mr. N, 1899
Plaster portrait
Unknown location

Puritan Maiden, 1900
Plaster figure
Unknown location

Oratio Virginis, 1901
Bronze sculpture
Unknown location

PUBLIC MONUMENTS AND MEMORIALS

Victory, 1904
Gilded staff (a mixture of plaster of Paris and fibrous materials)
Destroyed at end of Exposition
Louisiana Purchase Exposition, St. Louis, Missouri
Silver medal, Louisiana Purchase Exposition

Silence/Storey, 1905
Bronze bas-relief
Lowell Cemetery, Lowell, Massachusetts

Louisa Maria Wells, 1906
Marble bas-relief
Lowell Cemetery, Lowell, Massachusetts

Benson Family, 1907
Bronze figure
Woodlawn Cemetery, Titusville, Pennsylvania

Mary Ryle Memorial, 1907
Bronze bas-relief
Setting designed by Henry Bacon, architect
Danforth Library, Paterson, New Jersey

U.S. Naval Academy Chapel Doors, 1908
Bronze bas-relief
Annapolis, Maryland

Slocum, 1909
Marble bas-relief
With Daniel Chester French
Forest Hills Cemetery, Boston, Massachusetts

Timothy Murphy, 1910
Bronze bas-relief
Henry Bacon, architect
Upper Middleburgh Cemetery, Middleburgh, New York

Faith, Hope and Charity, for Foster Memorial, 1910
Granite figures
Foster Mausoleum, designed by Henry Bacon, architect
Upper Middleburgh Cemetery, Middleburgh, New York

Horsford Doors, 1911
Bronze bas-relief
Wellesley College Library, Wellesley, Massachusetts

Laura Gamble Thomson, 1914
Marble bas-relief
Spring Grove Cemetery, Cincinnati, Ohio

Bronze frontispiece, for organ, College Hill Presbyterian Church, Cincinnati, Ohio
Image sometimes referred to as "Hood"
Image also created for memorial for "Mrs. Hoyt," Chicago [No other information]

Genius of Electricity (*Golden Boy*; *Spirit of Communications*), 1914
Gilded bronze figure
Originally atop AT&T Headquarters, 195 Broadway, New York, New York; currently, 208 S. Ackard St., Discovery District Plaza, Dallas, Texas

John Pierpont Morgan Memorial, 1914
Bronze tablet with lettering
American Museum of Natural History, New York, New York

Fountain of Ceres, 1915
Staff bas-relief and figure
Court of the Four Seasons designed by Henry Bacon, architect
Panama Pacific Exposition, San Francisco, California
(Destroyed at end of Exposition)

Eagles, wreaths beneath speeches inscribed on the walls of the Lincoln Memorial, 1916
Marble
Henry Bacon, architect
Lincoln Memorial, Washington, D.C.

William Boyd Allison Memorial, 1916
Bronze, granite. Figures, bas-relief
Setting designed by Henry Bacon, architect
Iowa State Capitol grounds, Des Moines, Iowa

Illinois Centennial Memorial, 1918
Marble, granite. Bas-relief, eagle

Henry Bacon, architect
Logan Square, Chicago, Illinois
William Merchant Richardson French Gold Medal

Great War Memorial, 1920
Granite
Henry Bacon, architect
Naugatuck, Connecticut

Memorial for Mrs. Otis S. Northrop, 1922
Marble
Unknown cemetery, Waterbury, Connecticut

Pediment of Employers' Liability Assurance Building, 1923
Granite
Boston, Massachusetts

Spirit of Victory (Spanish-American War Memorial), 1927
Bronze figures
Bushnell Park, Hartford, Connecticut

Patriot's Monument, 1927
Bronze
Village Green, Windsor, Connecticut
(Longman donated the work to the town of Windsor.)

Founders of Windsor Monument, 1930
Granite, bronze
Palisado Green, Windsor, Connecticut

The Craftsman (Industry), 1931
Bronze figure
A.I. Price Technical Trade School, Hartford, Connecticut

Service to Mankind, 1932
Bronze figures
(Companion to Daniel Chester French, *Alma Mater and the Student*)
English High School, Boston, Massachusetts

Pony Express, 1938
Limestone relief
Federal Building, Hartford, Connecticut

Thomas Alva Edison (*Creative Genius*), 1935–1947
Bronze head
U.S. Naval Research Lab, Anacostia, Washington, D.C.

Hinkle Memorial, 1939
Stone
Beechwood Cemetery, Centerville, Massachusetts

Victory of Mercy, 1948
Bronze figures
Loomis Chaffee School, Windsor, Connecticut

PORTRAITS

Louise, modeled in 1903; cast in 1910
Tinted marble bust
The Metropolitan Museum of Art, New York, New York
Original colored plaster owned by George Foster Peabody, Saratoga Springs, New York; ivory-toned plaster, owned by Mrs. Louise Friendly Jones, Bangor, Maine

Margaret French, 1903
Tinted plaster bust
Chesterwood, A Site of the National Trust for Historic Preservation, Stockbridge, Massachusetts

Milton Herbert Bancroft, 1903
Bronze head
Unknown location

Aenigma, 1906
Tinted marble bust
Loomis Chaffee School, Windsor, Connecticut
Second place John Quincy Adams Ward Prize
Charles Noel Flagg Prize, Connecticut Academy of Fine Arts

Frances, 1908
Head
Tinted plaster, Wadsworth Atheneum Museum of Art, Hartford, Connecticut
Marble in private collection

Laura Bacon, 1909
Marble head
Private collection

Peggy/Margaret French as a Bacchante, 1912
Head
Plaster, cement, and bronze versions at Chesterwood, A Site of the National Trust for Historic Preservation, Stockbridge, Massachusetts
Bronze. National Museum of Women in the Arts, Washington, D.C.; Newfields, A Place for Nature and the Arts, Indianapolis, Indiana; Memorial Art Gallery, University of Rochester, Rochester, New York. Private collection.

Col. Robert Means Thompson, 1909
Bronze bust
Field House, U.S. Naval Academy, Annapolis, Maryland

Senator Henry Clark Corbin, 1911
Bronze bas-relief
Governor's Island, New York, New York

Memorial to Triangle Fire Unknowns, 1912
Evergreens Cemetery, Brooklyn, New York

Jacob Godfrey Schmidlapp, 1912
Bronze bust
Cincinnati Art Museum, Cincinnati, Ohio

John Stewart Kennedy, 1912
Bronze bust
Originally: United Charities Building, New York, New York, Hamilton Hall, Columbia University, New York, New York

Henry Bacon, 1918
Bronze head
The Metropolitan Museum of Art, New York, New York—gift of Longman
Olin Memorial Library, Wesleyan University, Middlebury, Connecticut—gift of Longman

Henry H. Peck Memorial, 1919
Bronze bas-relief
Waterbury Hospital, Waterbury, Connecticut

Gwendolen Sedgwick Batchelder Memorial, 1919
Marble bas-relief
Loomis Chaffee School, Windsor, Connecticut

Alice Freeman Palmer, 1920
Bronze bust
Hall of Fame for Great Americans, Bronx Community College, New York City, New York; Treasure Room, Wellesley College Library, Wellesley, Massachusetts

Theodore Chickering Williams Memorial, 1923
Marble bas-relief
All Souls Unitarian Church, New York City, New York
Watrous Gold Medal

David Rockefeller as a Child, ca. 1925
Marble bas-relief
Rockefeller Collection

George Parsons as a Young Boy, 1923
Marble head
Private collection

John D. Rockefeller III at 17, ca. 1925
Plaster bas-relief
Rockefeller Collection

Daniel Chester French, 1926
Bronze bas-relief
National Portrait Gallery, Washington, D.C.

Marcellus Hartley Dodge Jr., 1926
Bronze bas-relief
Princeton University Art Museum

Ivan G. Olinsky, 1926
Bronze head
Florence Griswold Museum, Old Lyme, Connecticut
Shaw Prize, National Academy of Design

Leonore Olinsky, 1927
Tinted plaster. Bas-relief portrait
Private collection

Tosca Olinsky, 1927
Tinted plaster. Bas-relief portrait
Private collection

American Galahad, 1927 (Ely Buell head/ideal figure)
Bronze bas-relief
Dartmouth College, Hanover, New Hampshire

William Jackson Palmer, 1928
Bronze bas-relief
Union Station, Denver; replicas at Union Station, Salt Lake City; Hampton University; Mexico

Judge Alden P. White, ca. 1925
Bronze bust
Originally: Essex Institute, Salem, Massachusetts

Fred Judson Kidde, 1928
Bronze bas-relief portrait
Unknown location

Henry Alvah Strong Memorial, 1928
Bronze bas-relief. Life-sized, three-quarter figure
Unknown location

John Henry Wainwright, 1928
Bronze head
Hampton University, Hampton, Virginia

Robert Russa Moton, 1928
Bronze head
Unknown location

Girl of St. Helena Island, 1929
Bronze head
Loomis Chaffee School, Windsor, Connecticut

Mr. and Mrs. Everett Sweezy, 1929
Toned marble. Bas-relief
Unknown location

Hollis Burke Frissell Memorial, 1930
Bronze bas-relief group
Hampton College. Reproductions at Penn School, St. Helena Island, South Carolina; Tuskegee Institute, Alabama

James Howard Kidde, 1930
Bronze head
Unknown location

William Gleason, 1931
Bronze bust on oak base
Originally: The lobby, Gleason Works, Rochester, New York

Thomas Edison, 1931
Marble bust
Deutsches Museum, Munich, Germany
Bronze replicas, Edison family, associates

Emma Sedgwick Barss Memorial, 1931
Granite
Unknown location

James Henry MacDonald Memorial, 1932
Bronze, granite. Bas-relief portrait
MacDonald State Park, Avon, Connecticut

Horace Hutchins Work, 1933
Bas-relief
No other information

Horace Taft, 1934
Bronze bust
The Taft School, Watertown, Connecticut

Henry Pennypacker, 1937
Bronze relief
Harvard Art Museums, Harvard University Portrait Collection, Harvard University, Cambridge, Massachusetts

William Broughton Allbright, 1938
Bronze life-sized figure
Unknown location. Originally Barnstable, Massachusetts

James Lee Loomis and Peter M. Fraser, 1938
Bronze. Double portrait relief
Original location: Connecticut Mutual Centennial, Hartford, Connecticut

Frank William Taussig, 1939
Bronze head
Harvard Art Museums, Harvard University Portrait Collection, Harvard University, Cambridge, Massachusetts

Jean G. Hinkle, 1939
Colored plaster mounted on wood. Relief
Private collection

George Foster Peabody, Lover of Mankind, 1940
Marble. Bronze. Relief portrait
Originally placed: Skidmore College, Saratoga Springs, New York; Saratoga Spa; Yaddo (gift from Longman)

Abbot Lawrence Lowell, 1940
Bronze head
Harvard Art Museums, Harvard University Portrait Collection, Harvard University, Cambridge, Massachusetts

Freddy, 1941
Bronze bas-relief portrait
Private collection

Thomas Sovereign Gates, 1941
Bronze bust
Hospital of the University of Pennsylvania, Philadelphia, Pennsylvania

William Blakeslee Hall and George Elisha Hall Jr., 1943
Bronze relief
Private collection

John Woolman Higgins, 1944
Plaster relief portrait
Unknown location

Walter Kidde, 1944
Bronze relief
Private collection

IDEAL SCULPTURES

Consecration, 1915
Marble. Bronze. Figures
Bronze, Wadsworth Atheneum, Hartford, Connecticut
Marble and bronze versions, private collections
Silver Medal, Panama Pacific International Exposition, San Francisco, California

The Future, 1917
Marble figure
The Parthenon, Nashville, Tennessee
Gold medals in New York, Philadelphia, and Chicago

Compassion and Service/The Angel/The Good Samaritan, c. 1923
Study for *Victory of Mercy*
Bronze figures
Asheville School, Asheville, North Carolina

Nature Contemplating the Source of Life, ca 1922
Marble figure
Plaster, exhibited the Second Retrospective Exhibition of the Art Institute Alumni Association, Art Institute, Chicago, Illinois
Unknown location

Destiny, 1926
Marble figure
Loomis Chaffee School

Creative Genius (see: *Thomas Alva Edison* listed under Public Monuments)

OTHER WORKS

Victory, 1903
Three-foot reductions of St. Louis Fair statue: Union League Club, Chicago; Chicago Art Institute
Thirty-five reductions to thirty inches with pedestal: Atlantic Fleet for a trophy; St. Louis Art Museum; Toledo Art Museum; Loomis Chaffee School; Metropolitan Art Museum; other collections

Torso of a Woman, 1911
Patinaed bronze
Metropolitan Museum of Art; St. Louis Art Museum

Seated Female Figure, 1911
Patinaed bronze
St. Louis Art Museum; Metropolitan Museum of Art; private collection

Head of Athena, ca. 1914
Bronze. Gift from Longman to Henry Bacon
Wesleyan University library

Silver Document Box for Jacob Schmidlapp, 1916
Unknown location

Nymph Panels, ca. 1920 (Also known as *Graces*)
Cast from base of *Ceres*
Loomis Chaffee School, Windsor, Connecticut
Private collection

Winged Head, 1923
Plaster, shellacked
Hirschl & Adler Galleries, New York City, New York

Ideal Head. Also called *Fragment*, 1929
Bronze head
One in unidentified location; one in private collection, courtesy of Conner-Rosenkranz, New York

Song of the Pines, 1929
Bronze figure
Original lost in fire at Wickham Estate, Hartford, Connecticut
Longman's now in private collection

Mater Dolorosa, 1930
Bronze figure
Private collection

Columbia Victorious, 1930
Bronze figure
Unknown location

Playful Putto on Seahorse, 1933
Bronze figure
Exhibited at Gardens on Parade, World's Fair 1939, Flushing Meadows, New York
Earlier, private home in Hartford, Connecticut
Minneapolis Institute of Art, gift of Susan Batchelder Plimpton

Madonna, 1934
Bronze figure
Grace Episcopal Church, Windsor, Connecticut

Satyr Head, 1939
Bronze with green patina
Private collection

Bowl with Baby on the Rim, ca. 1940
Bronze
Private collections

MEDALLIONS

French and British War Commission Medallion, 1917
Daniel Chester French, obverse; Longman, reverse
Bronze
Walters Museum, Baltimore, Maryland; Museum of Art, Cornell; Yale University Art Gallery, New Haven, Connecticut; Johnson Museum of Art, Ithaca, New York; American Numismatic Society, New York, New York; Metropolitan Museum of Art, New York, New York; New-York Historical Society, New York, New York; Chesterwood, A Site of the National Trust for Historic Preservation, Stockbridge, Massachusetts

Mr. and Mrs. Robert W. de Forest 50th Anniversary Medallion, 1922
Bronze. Chesterwood, A Site of the National Trust for Historic Preservation, Stockbridge, Massachusetts; The Metropolitan Museum of Art, New York, New York
Marble. The Metropolitan Museum of Art, New York, New York

George Foster Peabody Peace Medal, 1925
Penn School, St. Helena Island, South Carolina

Diabetes Medallion, 1934
No information

George Foster Peabody Medal for Broadcasting, 1939
Bronze
Grady College of Journalism and Mass Communications, University of Georgia, Athens, Georgia

Henry and Amy de Forest 50th Anniversary Medal, 1949
Gold-plated bronze bas-relief double portrait
Museum of Fine Arts Boston, Boston, Massachusetts

Camp NYDA Medal, ND
No information

Live and Let Live Medal, ND
Metal alloy

FOUNTAINS

Youth Eternal, 1920
Marble
Hecksher Museum, Huntington, New York; Loomis Chaffee School, Windsor, Connecticut

Young Pan (Boy and Fish) Fountain, 1925
Bronze
Rockefeller Collection; Loomis Chaffee School, Windsor, Connecticut

Baby Wall Fountain, 1928
Bronze with green patina
Private collection

Well Fountain, 1937
No description
EBL donated to Harvard University, Massachusetts, for the garden of Dr. and Mrs. Richard Mott Gummere, Harvard University, Cambridge, Massachusetts

BATCHELDER FAMILY

Horton, Jr, Age 5, 1922
Marble bas-relief
Private collection

Nathaniel Horton Batchelder, 1922
Bronze head
Loomis Chaffee School, Windsor, Connecticut; plaster, private collection

Mr. B with Football, 1925
Bronze figure
Private collection

Eleanor (a baby), 1927
Marble head portrait
Loomis Chaffee School, Windsor, Connecticut

Henry Morrill Batchelder, 1940
Bronze bas-relief portrait
Batchelders' gift to Merchants National Bank of Salem, Massachusetts

Skip, Betty, Hope, ca. 1942
Marble bas-relief
Private collection

Newel Post Head, 1923
Bronze
Private collection

Children's Bowl, 1927
Gold
Loomis Chaffee School

WORKS AT LOOMIS

Joseph Ezra Goodrich Memorial Plaque, 1922
Teacher of agriculture
Bronze bas-relief portrait

Clean Athletics Award (Stowe Wilder portrait), ca. 1923
Bronze relief

George Hodges Bartlett, 1925
Plaster bas-relief

Elizabeth Barss (Sometimes spelled Elisabeth), ca. 1927
Marble bust

Charles Edgar Sellers Memorial, 1934
Science teacher and baseball coach
Bronze tablet

Virginia Palmer, 1936
Bronze relief portrait

John Metcalf Taylor, 1937
Bronze bas-relief and inscription

Pine Garden Medallions, 1938

Dogwood Garden Medallions, 1938

René Chernuy, 1940
French teacher
Bronze bas-relief

John Edmund Barss, 1941
Teacher of Latin
Bronze bas-relief

Ulric Brower Mather, 1941
Math teacher
Bronze bas-relief

Howard Randlett Morse, 1942
Business manager
Bronze bas-relief

Loomis Boys who Died in WWII, 1946
Lettered on the wall. Gold leaf

Index

About the Author

Journalist **Patricia Hoerth Batchelder** was a feature and profile writer for the *Washington Star*, as well as a co-author with her father of his memoir, *The Life and Times of Henry Bellmon.* She lives in the CommonWealth Urban Farm community in the heart of Oklahoma City with her husband, peace activist Nathaniel Horton "Batch" Batchelder III.

www.ingramcontent.com/pod-product-compliance
Ingram Content Group UK Ltd.
Pitfield, Milton Keynes, MK11 3LW, UK
UKHW020813310325
5233UKWH00004B/29

9 798881 804244